RIGHTS AND WRONGS IN SOCIAL WORK

# RIGHTS AND WRONGS IN SOCIAL WORK

## ETHICAL AND PRACTICE DILEMMAS

MARK DOEL

First published 2016 by
PALGRAVE

Palgrave in the UK is an imprint of Macmillan Publishers Limited, registered in England, company number 785998, of 4 Crinan Street, London, N1 9XW.

Palgrave Macmillan in the US is a division of St Martin's Press LLC, 175 Fifth Avenue, New York, NY 10010.

Palgrave is a global imprint of the above companies and is represented throughout the world.

Palgrave® and Macmillan® are registered trademarks in the United States, the United Kingdom, Europe and other countries.

ISBN 978–1–137–44126–3 paperback

This book is printed on paper suitable for recycling and made from fully managed and sustained forest sources. Logging, pulping and manufacturing processes are expected to conform to the environmental regulations of the country of origin.

A catalogue record for this book is available from the British Library.

A catalog record for this book is available from the Library of Congress.

Printed and bound by CPI Group (UK) Ltd, Croydon, CR0 4YY

# CONTENTS

# The Road Not Taken

Robert Frost

Two roads diverged in a yellow wood,
And sorry I could not travel both
And be one traveler, long I stood
And looked down one as far as I could
To where it bent in the undergrowth;

Then took the other, as just as fair,
And having perhaps the better claim,
Because it was grassy and wanted wear;
Though as for that the passing there
Had worn them really about the same,

And both that morning equally lay
In leaves no step had trodden black.
Oh, I kept the first for another day!
Yet knowing how way leads on to way,
I doubted if I should ever come back.

I shall be telling this with a sigh
Somewhere ages and ages hence:
Two roads diverged in a wood, and I—
I took the one less traveled by,
And that has made all the difference.

# ACKNOWLEDGEMENTS

It is with sincere thanks that I acknowledge Pete Nelson for starting this journey and for his companionship along the way; and, specifically, for providing the background to the example dilemma in Chapter 6, 'Cheryl Hampton'. (All the names used for the people in the dilemmas in this book are fictional.)

I am indebted to Carol S. Cohen and Marianne Chierchio who inspired the example dilemma in Chapter 3 ('Regina and Donna'). In this same chapter, 'Humerah' first appeared in my book with Lesley Best, *Experiencing Social Work*; in revisiting Humerah's story I would like to pay my respects to Nasa Begum, who sadly died in 2011. Nasa was a great campaigner and had a firm handle on rights and wrongs.

It has been necessary, and always illuminating, to stroll into social work specialisms that are no longer my bread and butter, and it is with particular gratitude that I thank Judith Livsey and Leo Selleck (Adoption Social Worker for Barnardo's) for allowing me to use their case dilemmas, which proved ideal for the 'Decision-Making' chapter. My thanks, also, to Anne Hollows for putting her considerable networking abilities at my disposal and making valuable links to guide me into this social work specialism. Further thanks to Leo Selleck for pointing me in the direction of 'moral luck', which eventually grew into the final chapter of this book.

I am indebted to Caroline Goy for her very helpful comments and observations regarding 'Cheryl Hampton', and my thanks to Paul Stapleton for making the links.

Liz Allam has been a marvellously instructive reader of early drafts, commenting on a number of chapters, especially Chapter 10 ('Social Media'). As an active participant in social networking sites, Tarsem Singh Cooner has also leant helpful insights, for which I am grateful.

I enjoyed re-reading texts left dusty since my first degree, which included philosophy, in particular *Democracy and Disobedience*, written by my then tutor Peter Singer; though it is over 40 years old, it remains wonderfully fresh and current.

My thanks to the anonymous reviewers of the draft manuscript for their thoughtful suggestions and, of course, to the team at Palgrave – first Catherine Gray, then Peter Hooper, Louise Summerling, Cathy Tingle and Gogul Bactavatchalane, for their support, encouragement and hard work in turning my manuscript into this book.

Of course, I take full responsibility for any wrongs in the text.

Mark Doel
Sheffield 2015

# 1 INTRODUCTION

## Starting with questions

How do you know what is right? Then, if and when you know what is right, how do you *do* what is right? Is doing right *as a social worker* different? And, as a social worker, once you know what is right how do you *do* what is right? Ought we to cultivate social workers who are like the general populace, or do we want social workers who have special moral qualities and, if so, what are these qualities? How ought you to decide what to do in those situations where doing right for one person conflicts with doing right for another – is there an over-riding 'rightness'? Is it more important to do good or to avoid wrong? And how do all these questions connect to values, ethics and morals?

This book is based on the premise that good social work springs from a better understanding of rights and wrongs. Social work is not at all unique in this respect (think of the complexity of medical and legal ethics) but social workers are particularly entwined with notions of rights and wrongs, with the relationship between the individual and society, and with the struggles of power and marginality. Social work's holistic perspective on individuals in their families in their communities in their society makes the social worker's moral landscape especially interesting and challenging; and the powers that social workers can exercise give them a particular responsibility to be accountable, morally accountable, for their actions. This duty is the keener because the individuals and communities with which social workers work are often poor and marginalised, though not without their own resilience and strengths.

*'This is social work – so of course there is no right and wrong!'* is a favourite line of mine in workshops, so the title of this book, *Rights and Wrongs in Social Work*, is a bit of self-parody. However, it leads into a second premise, that an understanding of rights and wrongs is, in fact, crucially important, and is best cultivated by asking questions, then asking the further questions that arise from these first questions, and so on. That is not say that I will avoid considering responses to questions but these responses are not answers. Questioning a fact – 'What colour is that wall?' – can have an answer: 'It's white'; but an ethical question – 'Ought that wall to be white?' – does not have an answer,

1

merely an endless set of further questions ('What other colours could it be?'), observations ('Being white helps to keep the room looking light') or reflections ('Why do you ask that?'). This book is designed to help this process of asking questions and to ask increasingly *better* questions, if not necessarily the right ones; and to help in formulating further questions, observations and reflections. It is based on the belief that through this process we approach a better awareness of rights and wrongs in social work.

## Organisation of the book

There exists a considerable literature on values, ethics and dilemmas in social work, which includes Akhtar, 2012; Banks, 2004, 2010, 2012, 2014; Barsky, 2009; Barnard *et al.*, 2008; Bauman, 1993; Beckett and Maynard, 2005; Bell and Hafford-Letchfield, 2015; Carey and Green, 2013; Clark, 2000; Dickens, 2012; Dolgoff *et al.*, 2009; Gray and Webb, 2010; Hardwick and Worsley, 2011; Held, 2006; Horne, 1999; Hugman, 2012, 2013a; Hugman and Smith, 1995; Joseph and Fernandes, 2006; Lonne *et al.*, 2015; Parrott, 2006; Parsons, 2001; Porter, 1999; Pullen-Sansfaçon and Cowden, 2012; Reamer, 2006; and, more generally, Warnock, 1998. There are whole books written on topics merely touched upon in the chapters that follow, so I approach this task modestly. My hope is that another book is justified by the particular organisation of the material and the treatment of the issues in the chapters that follow.

I have centred the eight themed chapters (Chapters 3–10) around a core set of dilemmas. Each chapter clusters around a theme that is central to the everyday experiences of social workers. Of course, in any single sequence of events, a social worker might encounter ethical issues and practice problems that relate to all eight of these themes; but frequently there is a core category, for example *relationship boundaries and disclosure* (Chapter 7). Indeed, in gathering 66 different dilemmas from social workers at a conference workshop, each dilemma sat comfortably in one or more of the eight themes (see Chapter 8 for more about this). However, the organisation of themes into discrete chapters is not intended to obscure the messy reality of practice with its smudgy overlaps between all of these categories; the boundaries between the chapters are very porous. To use a topographical metaphor, each chapter maps the same mountain, but from different points of the compass.

### Singularities – significant moments in time

There are variations in the way we each learn best, but the power of example seems to be universally effective in triggering deep learning. The introduction of a concrete, specific situation onto the page is designed to pin down the questioning process. This method is well established in adult pedagogy (Freire, 1970) and reflected in research methods such as critical incident analysis (Butterfield *et al.*, 2005) and narrative inquiry (Clandinin and Huber, 2010; Gardner and Poole, 2009), where no hypothesis is to be proved and there is no single truth. However, this method is more easily supported in live workshops where interaction is possible; on the page the challenge is to have a conversation with the reader that avoids bulleted lists of trite trigger questions whilst not overloading the page with the author's soliloquy. I hope that balance is achieved in the chapters that follow.

The style of the theme-based chapters draws from **narrative** and **case-based ethics** (words in **grey** are included in the Glossary at the end of the book) in which stories and case-based reasoning are used to reveal ethical issues (Banks and Nøhr, 2012). In particular, I use the notion of a **singularity** to help with this questioning process. There are various meanings attached to 'singularity', but I am taking it to signify a moment in time when a very particular action has a significant impact on what happens next, and a different action would entail an alternative future. The film *Sliding Doors* is an entertaining example, in which entering (or not entering) a carriage on the London Underground is the difference between the lead character meeting the love of her life, or not meeting him. Being a film, she gets the chance to replay this singularity. *Groundhog Day* (1993) is another fictional example; indeed, so common is this device in cinematography that we can surmise that the idea has a strong hold on the collective imagination and it is something we draw learning from. *The Road Not Taken*, Robert Frost's poem reproduced on page vii, tells it best.

The singularities presented in the dilemmas in each chapter are points when the social worker is caught in a significant moment in time, presented with a choice which sometimes might not even be seen as a choice, so it is not necessarily recognised as a road travelled or not. The occasion might or might not be experienced as a dilemma, and the social worker might or might not be aware of ethical issues. The value of the singularity is that it pauses time in a way that is not possible off the page in the 'real' world, so it allows a rehearsal of the range of issues associated with any action. In the actual world, these issues are too often unexposed, either by the forgetfulness of routine or the push of other events pressing on available time.

Some readers might wonder whether the scenarios you will encounter are 'true'. As it happens, the vast majority of situations have been taken from 'fact', though the alternative futures suggest different trajectories for the stories. Flanagan (2015) makes the observation that 'the difference between stories perceived as factual and those viewed as fiction is not as distinct as it may appear'. The artist Lucien Freud (1922–2011) noted: 'There is a distinction between fact and truth. Truth has an element of revelation about it' (cited at a 2015 exhibition at Christchurch Mansion, Ipswich).

There are Big Events in social work, such as whether to take someone's liberty because they are judged to be a threat to themselves or others; or to remove a child from the care of its parents. These Big Events are rarely *moments*; usually they are the accumulation of many preceding singularities, everyday moments, some of which came and went without any recognition of their significance. Yet it is the singularities that add up to the Big Event; by the time the Big Event arrives, in all likelihood it is inevitable. As we will explore in more detail in the next chapter, the ethics to suit singularities, the *everyday ethics* (Banks, 2016), is not as available as the *epic ethics* of much classical theorising. My hope is that the Example Dilemmas, with their moments in time, will contribute to our understanding of an *everyday ethics* and its relationship to the Big Events; also, that these dilemmas will help your deliberations about not getting it wrong, as well as those about getting it right. Being wrong (or the fear of it) can provoke practice that is risk averse and feels oppressive to practitioners. So thinking about 'not getting it wrong' is just as significant as getting it right.

Some chapters incorporate a 'balance sheet' method, with a list of pros and cons. This approach can be helpful in steering towards a decision or a moral conclusion, but it is rarely a clincher. The length of one side of the balance sheet does not reveal the relative importance of each 'fact'. Balance sheets indicate the value of marshalling facts, but also expose the ultimate limitation, that knowing *what is* does not point in a clear direction to *what ought to be*.

## The Big Picture

It is important to place the quotidian ethical issues faced by social workers into the larger frame (see Wolff, 2011, for a philosophical enquiry into ethics and various aspects of public policy). For instance, is it possible to pursue ethical social work practices in an agency organised around profit? Is it inevitable that the imperative for profit will conflict with the imperative for professional practice and, when this happens, is it also inevitable that the profit motive will be paramount? Or is there no difference between the need to balance the books in a publicly funded or not-for-profit agency and the need to balance those same books in a private agency?

The Big Picture is also the connection between individual professionals' ethical decisions and the broader ideologies that underpin (or undermine) them. As the Swedish ethical code for social work professionals notes:

> Ethical dilemmas in social work may be related to overall ideological issues: To what degree is the public society responsible for the individual citizen? How much of the responsibility for a person's situation and future is entirely his

own? Which ethical values and norms are essential for judging the balance between the responsibility of the public society and that of the individual? (SSR, 2006: 6).

The singularities are contextualised alongside these kinds of broader ethical issues. The Big Picture sections frame the everyday ethical issues faced by social workers with contemporary news stories, in which *epic ethics* parallels the *everyday ethics* of social work encounters. In some chapters there are additional parallels with an historical event.

# Definitions and guidance

## Values, ethics, morals and codes

Colloquially, the terms *values, ethics* and *morals* are used fairly interchangeably, but Joseph and Fernandes (2006: 25) think it careless to mix them indiscriminately and make these distinctions:

> Values: moral principles and standards
> Ethics: the study or the science of morals OR principles of behaviour
> Morals: a sense of right and wrong or a standard of behaviour

Ethics are 'concerned with what people consider "right" while values are concerned with what people consider "good"' (Dubois and Miley, 1996: 122). Terms from moral philosophy are highlighted in grey (e.g. **utilitarianism**) and are explained in the Glossary on pages 183–187.

Social work values are a range of beliefs about what is worthy and valued in a social work context, and include general beliefs about the nature of a good life and a good society and how to achieve these through social work practice. Banks's (2006) research into 30 different countries' ethical codes revealed a consensus of four guiding ethical principles: respect for persons; service user self-determination; social justice (equality); and professional integrity. These are very broad principles about which it would be difficult to find disagreement and which might be open to quite disparate interpretation when put into practice (Doel *et al.*, 2010). Hence the use of singularities in Chapters 3–10 to pin down these and other values.

Other guidance about the nature of social work values comes from a *Statement of Principles* (IFSW/IASSW 2004) jointly agreed by the International Federation of Social Workers and the International Association of Schools of Social Work. This Statement focuses on two primary values: human rights and human dignity (a **duty-based, deontological** ethical approach); and social justice (a **consequentialist, teleological** approach).

We will explore these ethical approaches in more detail in Chapter 2. The Statement is explicit about social workers' ethical responsibilities:

> ➤ Social workers should foster and engage in ethical debate with their colleagues and employers and take responsibility for making ethically informed decisions.
>
> ➤ Social workers should be prepared to state the reasons for their decisions based on ethical considerations, and be accountable for their choices and actions. (IFSW/IAASW, 2004: 5.10–11)

The IFSW/IAASW Statement is one of principles and core values, not a code; it is expected that each national social work association derives its own code of ethics. In the UK, social workers in the public sector (the majority) are also expected to subscribe to a public service ethos which includes service to others and putting the needs of others first (Nolan, 1995). However, the notion of a statement of values and a code of ethics is controversial, seen by some as an example of one philosophical mindset (Western) imposing its way of thinking on other less powerful mindsets.

My own position on codes is one of some scepticism and a concern that their existence might induce ethical torpor rather than rigour – a sense that someone else has done the thinking so we don't have to. What research knowledge we have about reference to codes of ethics in everyday practice suggests that it is minimal (Doel *et al.*, 2010), perhaps because codes are conceived at such a level of generality that social workers struggle to apply them to the singularities of practice. This same research indicated that social workers are more likely to take a **case-based** approach to ethics than one based on principles.

Comparing Italian and British codes of ethics for social workers, Cavaliere (2014: 66) noted interesting differences in 'authorial attitude' – in the Italian 'we find a bare, detached definition of the code and an introduction to rules to be complied with' whilst the British code 'relies on terms which come within the "affective" sphere' to convey the social workers' emotional and emphatic commitment towards service users. Whereas the British (BASW) code chooses 'should', the Italian uses the prescriptive modal, *deve* (must). Cavaliere's study was restricted to the British and Italian codes, but an exploration of the grammar of the Indian code (a 'Declaration of Ethics') reveals the style of a personal commitment in the words, 'I pledge to ... ' (BATSW, 2002). These textual differences ('cultural grammars') between codes convey subtle cultural meanings that are not immediately evident.

Illustrative sections from codes of ethics are included towards the end of each themed chapter.

## Dilemmas, issues, problems, challenges

A dilemma is:

> A situation that often involves an apparent conflict between moral imperatives, in which to obey one would result in transgressing another.
>
> (Zerbe, 2008: 115)

> When two or more ethical imperatives are equally important but require opposite behaviours.
>
> (Hardcastle, 2011: 4)

> A purposefully disorienting experience from which transformative learning can be gained.
>
> (Mann, 2016)

Is there a difference between a difficult decision and a dilemma? Between a practice dilemma and an ethical one? Ethical problems involve difficult choices, but it is clear what is the right action to take; the difficult choices in ethical dilemmas are compounded because it is not clear what is the right course of action. Banks (2012: 20) describes an ethical dilemma as 'a choice between two equally unwelcome alternatives' and draws a distinction between ethical issues, problems and dilemmas. I will be using 'dilemma' more broadly, largely because I think the choices can be various and not necessarily undesirable (it strikes me as a moral responsibility to choose the best course of action even when both or many are considered desirable). A fine distinction between a practice problem and an ethical dilemma usually proves difficult in reality, as most of social work practice (most of life) rubs against ethical issues, sometimes recognised as posing a dilemma, other times not. Let's take this simple example:

> There is a rainstorm and I have an umbrella. No dilemma of any kind here – I take out my umbrella and use it to keep off the wet. But in this next rainstorm I have an umbrella and I am with a group of four friends, none of whom has an umbrella. Now there is a dilemma and the choices are many, not just two; some may be desirable, others not. That is part of my dilemma, because I am ignorant as yet of what I *ought* to do. What are the ethical issues? I have yet to think about them. At first sight it is a practical dilemma, whether to use the umbrella alone or to share it, and if sharing it, in what manner, as it will not cover the five of us. However, this practical dilemma is shot through with ethical ones – early on in my decision-making I will be asking "What *ought* I to do?" and reaching to moral philosophy for an answer, whether I know it or

not. And, of course, decision-making is usually time-limited: if I don't put up the umbrella whilst I am weighing up the problem, we all get wet.

Parting ethical issues from practice problems seems as difficult and unnecessary as separating the red and the blue in the colour purple. This is not to say that it isn't helpful sometimes to consider what are ethical issues and what are practice problems within a dilemma, but it is unnecessary to struggle to define the dilemma as *either* ethical *or* practical.

Banks (2012: 19) usefully reminds us that 'it is important to see the whole of social work as comprising ethical dimensions and to focus on the ethical issues in practice as much as the ethical problems and dilemmas'.

## Consulting the wise professionals

'There are value judgements on which reasonable people might differ.' (Lord Hoffmann, quoted in Ian McEwan's *The Children Act*, 2014: 13)

The last word in each of the themed chapters is given over to 'the **wise professionals**'. There are different ways to ponder these wise professionals. They could be real people whom we hold in high regard because we admire their personal and professional qualities and seek to emulate them. They might be imagined professionals, idealised versions of ourselves, the practitioner we seek to become. Perhaps the wise professionals are the voices in our own heads, if we only take the time to listen to them. The wise professionals are the embodiment of reflection and mindfulness, the 'Voice of Experience' (Thompson, 2016) that challenges received wisdom and reframes it; they perfect the improvised performance of the 'wise person' (Payne, 2007, 2009). They engage in **phronesis**; that is, they are virtuous people who are able to use practical reasoning born from experience. The wise professionals are an ethical reference group exercising **philosophic scepticism** and with whom we can engage in **Socratic dialogue** (Yassour-Borochowitz, 2004).

The wise professionals are plural because, as Hoffmann states in the header, there are indeed different value judgements that are illuminating, so we listen to them all, respect them and understand each to have its own value. Much moral philosophy takes the individual as its basis, so the *group* of wise professionals is a reminder that any dialogue with ourselves is better when we invite many voices to join.

I suspect that the wise professionals' understanding of morality is that it ought to be based on a belief in others' interests and cannot be based solely on one's own. This would be a good fit for the principles of public service (Nolan, 1995). Whilst discounting the existence or value of 'moral theorems' to be proved or disproved, the wise professionals do see a place for reason and argument in morality rather than a purely intuitive, non-rational commitment. If morality is not open to reason then we are doomed at best to live in isolation from one another and, at worst, to throw things at one another from our respective corners of the room/world. However, it is wrong to deny the force of emotions and intuitions in moral life. Above all, I think the wise professionals would want to guide us to the significance of interpersonal ethics, the relationships between ourselves and, indeed, between humans and the physical and animal environment. But perhaps I am projecting too many of my own beliefs onto these wise professionals.

There are two central qualities for ethical practice that I hope the wise professionals would counsel. The first is trust. Trust is a key component in professional integrity (BASW 2014: 10) and central to the development of relationships, which are crucial for social work practice (Ruch *et al.,* 2010). We should trust to our wise professionals, too; and we should trust to the journey they take us on. As the French saying goes, *le chemin se fait en marchant* – 'the path is made by walking it.' We should, therefore, be wary of following well-worn tracks, precisely because they are well worn. The second quality is care. Care emphasises the interpersonal and relational aspects of social work and its empathic qualities. In the next chapter we will see how an **ethics of care** has developed to address the inadequacies of classical ethics theories, and one more suited to the values of social work.

# 2    RIGHTS AND WRONGS

## Finding your inner moral philosopher

The ethical and moral issues at the heart of this book have been the subject of serious thought for many millennia. My purpose in the chapters that follow is to relate these timeless discourses to social work and to the everyday judgements that social workers must make during the course of their work. But first, before you consider your own response to the detail of a dilemma (that will come soon enough in the chapters ahead) I would like you to reflect on how deep or broad your engagement is with ethical and moral issues.

How interesting do you find these following questions?

1.  Suppose that being well-off could be bought at the price of personal excellence, would it be a reasonable bargain? Put another way, is it better to have the goods most worth having or to be the sort of person most worth being?

2.  Can someone be too virtuous for their own good?

3.  Is there such a thing as moral weakness and moral ignorance? If so, what are they and how might they show themselves?

4.  Do you think that each individual human person has an 'infinite worth'?

5.  When is it right to practise self-denial?

6.  Is the desire to do what is right sufficient in itself?

7.  How do we know that an act is 'conscientious' or not (for example, that someone who refuses to fight in a war is refusing out of conscientious pacifism rather than cowardice)?

One of the book's aims is to help you connect with your 'inner moral philosopher'. The first step is to be self-aware about how exercised you are already; to stretch the metaphor – do you take brisk moral walks regularly, or are you out of condition? This ought to be no more a moral judgement than discussing your physical fitness though, in practice, these judgements often carry unspoken moral weight.

The seven questions above are framed at a fairly high level of abstraction – apart from the last, there are no illustrative examples to pin them down. Perhaps you are a more concrete thinker and prefer your moral philosophy shaped into real, if hypothetical, situations:

1. Is a fatally ill young person better off knowing the unhappy truth or believing a reassuring lie?

2. Would it be right for the owners of a shelter to exclude their neighbours during a nuclear attack?

In responding to these questions, you might take a step back and ponder how these responses are being framed. What guides your thinking? Are they well-worn thinking tracks or are you finding yourself in new territory?

## Different approaches to ethics

Ultimately, moral discourse is about finding out what it is that is really important for us – what we value – as individuals, as communities and as a common humanity. How do we live well together? And what do we do when others want to do wrong?

Philosophers are those who have made it their main work to investigate how 'what is really important' can be understood or explained. Frequently, these investigations cluster into –isms, such as **intuitionism**, which was a dominant approach in Western philosophy in the early twentieth century (Moore, 1903). However, the inability of intuitionism to explore what it was to be 'good', other than to state that moral truths were self-evident, was found to be unsatisfactory. This pattern of 'mixed blessings' – part of the picture clearly in focus to the detriment of other parts – reoccurs throughout ethical theorising.

There is much disagreement not just 'about what is morally right or wrong but about *what it is to be* morally right or wrong. How are moral problems to be distinguished from those that are not moral?' (Warnock, 1967: 73). Do all problems contain a moral element? And can moral disagreements be resolved or lessened by the use of reason and discourse? In this book I take an approach that moral issues cannot be resolved in a prescriptive manner (injunctions about what should be done), but rather by the application of philosophic scepticism, a process that helps to arrive not at a definitive conclusion but at a point where action can be taken. This is my meaning in getting in touch with your inner moral philosopher and consulting the **wise professionals**.

## Duty-based

Duty-based ethical theories (also known as **deontological**) argue that acting morally means doing your duty regardless of consequence. An example is Judaeo-Christian ethics, beginning with the catalogue of absolute duties and restrictions listed in the Ten Commandments and, for Christians, incorporating the teachings of Christ, such as 'love thy neighbour'. Duty-based moral philosophies, theist or otherwise, are based on dos and don'ts.

It would be a mistake to characterise all religions as solely duty-based codes, but the Dalai Lama believes that 'any religion-based answer to the problem of our neglect of inner values can never be universal, and so will be inadequate. What we need today is an approach to ethics which makes no recourse to religion and can be equally acceptable to those with faith and those without: a secular ethics' (Dalai Lama, 2013: xiii-xiv, quoted in Thompson, 2016: 117).

**Kantian** ethics are duty-based, but do not rely on a belief in a god and concern themselves more with motivation and will. It is not a *moral* choice for me to become a social worker if the choice is made because I need an income, or even because I have a commitment to social justice or compassion for oppressed persons; these are all pragmatic or emotive motivations, rather than springing from a sense of duty. Even if the consequences of my becoming a social worker are tragic (I fail to protect a child's life), my actions can be considered moral if I was acting from a sense of duty – the outcome is not relevant to the moral worth of the action and intent is all (Kant, 1797).

Kant describes some duties as **categorical**, i.e. they are unconditional and must always be followed, such as the duty never to kill anyone; others are hypothetical, for instance if you want to be trusted then you ought to tell the truth. These hypothetical duties focus on achieving goals. Moral principles are ones that you would apply to everyone. These **maxims** can be made universal, such as 'do to others as you would have them do to you', where it is possible and desirable for everyone to act on this – a principle of **universalisability**. A problem with this approach is when conflicts in duties occur, as we will explore in more detail in Chapter 4.

Human rights are part of the duty-based family of ethics. Inalienable rights are those that are categorical, non-negotiable and not dependent on consequence, time or place – they are universal. The best known expression of this is the United Nations' Declaration of Human Rights in 1948:

> Human rights are rights inherent to all human beings, whatever our nationality, place of residence, sex, national or ethnic origin, colour, religion, language, or any other status. We are all equally entitled to our human rights without

discrimination. These rights are all interrelated, interdependent and indivisible. (The United Nations Office of the High Commissioner for Human Rights [OHCHR] http://www.ohchr.org)

Human rights are mentioned in 75% of national social work codes of ethics (Keeney *et al.*, 2014).

Different cultures put varying emphases on duties and rights. In India 'families and communities are important contexts for relationships, leading to more emphasis on duties than rights' (Bombay Association of Trained Social Workers (BATSW, 2002), in Joseph and Fernandes, 2006: 166).

## Ends and means

Whilst writing this book a story broke that Pret a Manger, a fast food chain, allowed a certain number of free coffees each day at the discretion of the counter staff. Receiving a free coffee becomes a different act when it is understood as a means to an end – when the beneficiaries receiving the gift are a means to increase the morale of the donors or the profits of the owners. Some counter staff were reported as deciding to give 'their' coffees to customers who seemed especially friendly; however, the result was that genuinely friendly customers now saw themselves as wanting to attract a free coffee, rather than being friendly for its own sake – a perverse and unintended outcome. This simple example illustrates the complexity of motivation and the strong sense of revulsion that people feel to being used as a means rather than being treated as an end.

Joseph and Fernandes (2006: 47) reframe the *ends and means* dilemma as, in fact, a clash between two or more values. This is a useful insight to which we will return at various points in the book (for instance, see page 64).

## Guilt and social work

Kant discounted the moral emotions, yet many people feel intuitively that emotions are inherent in ethics; for instance, that deciding to devote your life to social work because of a feeling of compassion is a moral choice, especially if you had the alternative opportunity of a highly remunerated career in investment banking.

Like compassion, guilt is one of the moral emotions. To what extent is social work bound up with notions of guilt? Guilt is one of many possible motivations for an individual to choose to become a social worker – guilty feelings about their own relative advantage, and even the possibility that their own fortune is at the expense of others' misfortune. Arthur Miller's 1940 play *The Man Who Had All The Luck* is an interesting fictional exploration of these and other related issues such as freedom and choice.

At a societal level, is state support for social work by way of tax money an expression of collective guilt? Does it matter whether social work is founded on an altruistic desire to alleviate the sufferings of those who are wronged by the workings of late capitalism, or on a collective guilty conscience that relative wealth and fortune comes on the backs of the poor and the dispossessed? Meritocratic societies perhaps manage to delude themselves that 'wealth is guiltless because poor people are the rich-in-waiting' (Gill, 2012: 138).

## Consequentialism

Kant's dismissal of consequence as irrelevant seems intuitively wrong; surely what happens as a result of our actions must be weighed in the ethical scales (sometimes referred to as **teleology**). **Utilitarianism** is one such ethical theory, based on the pursuit of pleasure and a belief that the right course of action is the one that is likely to bring the greatest sum of happiness for everyone who will experience the consequences (Mill, 1863) or, conversely, the least amount of unhappiness ('the lesser evil'). Mill believed 'higher' pleasures (largely intellectual) to be more deserving than 'lower' pleasures (largely physical), a sense of hierarchy that seems to presage Maslow's (1943) needs.

Calculating consequences is complicated and, like duty-based ethical theories, there are some aspects that seem intuitively wrong; for instance, even if the hanging of a man brings more overall happiness to the people (by way of a deterrent to violent crime) than the unhappiness of that one guilty man, does this make hanging 'right'? Consequence might be an important facet of our moral world, but it fails to wholly complete it.

## Virtue ethics

'When we ask people about their positive experiences of social work, we find that they are more likely to be concerned with the virtues of their particular social worker – their honesty, warmth, trustworthiness and intelligence – rather than whether they comply with an abstract ethical code or a set of moral standards.' (Doel and Best, 2008: xi)

**Virtue ethics** places individual practitioners firmly centre stage, in terms of their character and their ability to live 'a good life' rather than 'live up to their role' (Clark, 2006; Marquis and Jackson, 2000; Saarnio, 2000). These ideas arise from Aristotle's *The Nicomachean Ethics,* in which the Greek philosopher understands a virtue to be a way of responding to one's situation in a manner we would now likely call reflective. A social worker who had the virtues of generosity and courage might combine the two to give charitably to a service user (generosity) even though she knew it was contrary to the agency's procedure (courage). A virtuous social worker would weigh the appropriateness of her virtues, so she would not squander her generosity, nor use her courage recklessly. There is, then, a strong element of **casuism** in virtue ethics in which each case is weighed in its own right. Of course, there are difficulties with virtue theory, most notably agreeing what these virtues are and whether they reflect, or ought to reflect, different societies. We need to ask ourselves, too, is it easy (or relatively so) to be virtuous if you have the good fortune to be born into a loving family in a prosperous part of the globe?

The use of principles to guide ethical practice, **principlism**, was exemplified in social work by Biestek's (1957) seven principles for 'the casework relationship', adapted by Doel (2010: 7) for the broader scope of contemporary practice. Banks (1995: 37) identified four 'first-order' principles in social work:

➤ Respect for and promotion of individuals' rights to self-determination

➤ Promotion of welfare or well-being

➤ Equality

➤ Distributive justice

## New ethics

The moral theories propounded so far have autonomous, independent, rational beings at their core, but this is an idealised picture. The **ethics of care** (Held, 2006; Meagher and Parton, 2004; Parton, 2003) and **relationship ethics** (Banks 2012) focus on interpersonal relationships, rather than the individual's rights or virtues, or calculations of utility. One of the premises of these new ethical frameworks is that a significant experience for human beings is their dependency on the care of others, especially through childhood. Though relationship ethics are not anti-reason, they do embrace (some) emotions rather than rejecting them. Another premise is that people need to feel sufficiently connected to one another to care about values and rights (Hugman, 2013b).

The ethics of forgiveness and a belief in the possibility of change has traditionally been central to social work and probation practice. Probation officers were called on to 'advise, assist and befriend' the offenders with whom they worked in the hope and belief that this kind of relationship could bring about change sufficient to move their clients away from criminal behaviour. This form of **redemptive ethics** also included positive action in the employment of ex-offenders in these services. A greater emphasis on risk and the assessment of risk, and a less forgiving climate, has put redemptive ethics in the shade, but stories of forgiveness might change this (Cantacuzino, 2015).

Ethical frameworks are becoming inclusive of the environment, the natural world and animal life. The **land ethic** considers that '[a] thing is right when it tends to preserve the integrity, stability and beauty of the biotic community. It is wrong when it tends otherwise' (Leopold, 1949). Leopold exhorted us to consider ourselves not as conquerors but as plain members of the land and called for a new ethical relationship with animals, nature and the environment, a precursor of modern environmental ethics, and increasingly important to social work (Whiteford, 2016).

As a philosophy that seeks to describe the world as it is (**ontological**) rather than as it ought to be, **existentialism** has not been seen as providing guidance about how we should live our lives. However, existentialists believe that we are condemned to be free – we *must* choose (de Beauvoir, 1947), and Sartre (1946) argues in *Existentialism and Humanism* that there is an obligation to value your own freedom and therefore a moral value in the freedom of others. Existentialists believe we cannot escape making choices (we all have this inalienable freedom), and we arrive at our value judgements without any reliable external guidance.

> If we ... are radically free – that is, we cannot choose not to choose – then each day we are making decisions and acting upon them in ways that will not only shape our future in terms of the doors we open and the doors that we subsequently close, but also in terms of how we are, through that process, creating ourselves ... In this way, the choices we make now are projecting us into the future.' (Thompson, 2016: 94).

## Moral relativism

> Some ethical challenges and problems facing social workers are specific to particular countries; others are common (IFSW/IASSW, 2004).

Social workers frequently work with people whose values and cultures are different from their own. To what extent, then, can and ought the social worker's judgement of right and wrong sit with a service user's alternative visions of good and bad? At a broader level, if a practice is accepted as the norm in one society do other societies have the right to impose their definition of acceptable behaviour, either within their own society (such as the French criminalisation of the burqa) or in others' societies, such as female genital mutilation in some African communities; or can there be a 'global ethics' (Banks and Nøhr, 2012: 12)? As Pollard (2014: 101) notes in the British context: 'it is possible to practise forms of colonialism just down the road, across the axes of culture, class, power, and different capabilities within the diverse but global society which parts of Britain have recently become'.

Does time, as well as place, alter our moral stance? In my first UK social work job, in 1976, I used to take a two-hour lunch each Tuesday with the rest of the team in the local pub, where I would smoke, drink two pints of beer, then drive my car to see clients. The other social workers were doing the same, and colleagues and clients judged us to be 'good' social workers. In 2016 that behaviour would be illegal or disciplinary and judged bad. How can what was good in 1976 be bad in 2016, and what might this tell us about current social work? What currently good social work will have become bad by 2056?

Service users should rely on something common to all social workers, and this is the *essence* that is so difficult to define and yet it is what ultimately makes a social worker a social worker. Each social worker applying their own values to each separate situation they meet does not seem satisfactory; yet a social worker as a rule-driven clone is equally unattractive.

In **situation ethics** each situation is decided not by prescriptions or universal law, but case by case, with attention to the person in their specific situation, similar to **casuism**; general principles are used as 'illuminators' but not 'directors' (Hardwick and Worsley, 2011: 45, in the context of social work research ethics). This allows for one-off situations when a general principle might be overturned. In Fletcher's (1966) situational model, love is the central motivation that governs the morality of decisions.

## An example

How do all of these different and often dense ethical theories pan out in practice?

The literature on moral philosophy tends to use examples from extreme situations. 'Epic' ethics turns to euthanasia, abortion, wartime killings, nuclear weaponry, (de)criminalisation of sex work and the like to test out the various theories, yet most moral dilemmas are more humdrum. The social worker's average day is well stocked with ethical issues and practice dilemmas, as we shall see in the following chapters. Very occasionally they might be epic, but most of the time they are not, so we need to understand how moral philosophy helps us with the routine dilemmas and not just the life-changing ones. Since we will be considering numerous dilemmas arising from professional life in the pages ahead, let us indulge in an example that has, ostensibly, nothing to do with social work.

Returning to the Pret a Manger scenario (page 13), how might we understand this from the different ethical theoretical perspectives? The situation is that you, the counter server, have discretion to give away two free coffees each working day. How do you make a *good* decision? What is the *right* way to decide who ought to be the beneficiaries? First, and most important perhaps, you are now aware that the giving of the coffees is, in fact, a *moral* event and that the ethics of incentives can lead to perverse outcomes; without contact with moral philosophy you might not have given it a second thought and seen it as mere **pragmatism**.

The decision might be based on what the counter server believes is her duty of fairness. One server, **Shreya**, interprets this as being *representative*; in other words, over the course of a week she ought to give 50% to women and 50% to men. But now she must consider how far her duty of fair distribution extends – ought she to achieve an ethnic balance? In this **duty-based** morality, is there also a duty of *re*distribution, so that those who are less able to pay for a coffee ought to receive a free one? In that case, how might Shreya determine this? In this moral reality, influenced by an **ethic of care**, ought Shreya to be giving the free coffees to the beggar at the corner of the street or do her obligations extend only to customers of Pret a Manger?

**Finley** takes a **consequentialist** view, in which he must weigh the likely consequences of his choices and, if specifically **utilitarian**, make decisions that achieve the greatest happiness. We might reasonably assume that the gift of a coffee will always add to the sum of pleasure, but should Finley target this particular cheery soul in order to reinforce her happiness, or that man who is not looking too pleased with things, in order to try to increase his? Or might the gift actually increase the unhappy man's displeasure, as he interprets Finley's gesture as pitying or patronising? What are the consequences for the happiness of others who are not chosen for a free coffee? Might the sum of the unhappiness of six overhearing customers substantially outweigh the happiness of the chosen one? So, ought Finley to choose beneficiaries on the basis that they are the only person in the queue? However, if the beneficiary tells her friends, will they not feel even more displeasure that this has been going on 'behind their backs'? It becomes quickly clear that weighing consequences is complex. Even so, as we will see in later chapters, consequentialism is commonly employed, if usually implicitly, in decision-making.

**Elsie** considers the virtues of her customers to be paramount when she chooses. So, ought Elsie to give the free coffee to the person she feels is the most deserving, in terms of how she reads their character? For instance, the kind person who she's seen helping an old man to cross the road outside? Or the traffic warden who bravely takes a lot of stick in order to keep the pavements clear of illegally parked cars so wheelchair users are not endangered?

We might consider the counter servers themselves. In a system of **virtue ethics**, do we think Elsie has the character to be making these decisions? What about her fellow counter staff and baristas? Ought their reasoning to affect hers, and hers theirs? Much moral philosophy takes the individual as the starting point, but ought we to come to a *collective* position? How are other branches of the coffee shop arriving at their choices and how ought theirs to influence ours? We learn that one store has adopted *randomness*, throwing dice and when two sixes come up, that customer receives their coffee free – they're calling it anarcho-**existentialism**. If this causes them to exceed their allowance of coffees, they go ahead and exceed it.

Ought the counter staff to be guided by *need*? Who needs the free coffee most and how is this decided? (See Chapter 6.)

**Moral relativism** would suggest that if our coffee shop was located in a very traditional society there would be no question that the counter server should reserve their free coffees for their close family and friends and that to do otherwise would be disloyal, thus breaching the strongest code of their society. Other customers would quite understand this and not consider it to be favouritism or nepotism, as it might be described in so-called meri-tocratic societies.

In the greater picture, whose gift is this coffee anyway? Who is directing the policy of the free coffee, and where ought power to lie in modern corpo-rate relationships? And the coffee beans that make the coffee – are there ethical issues there in terms of the trading relationships between growers and buyers?

## Social workers as moral philosophers

Do you think that the baristas who have studied moral philosophy will make *better* decisions or just slower ones? Keep your response to this question in mind as you read the book, because it influences how you think about the very question of ethical issues and practice dilemmas (the **meta-ethics**), well before you consider what you ought to do about them.

Most social work education and training implicitly relies on a belief that if you reflect long and hard enough, the outcome will be *good* practice (or certainly better practice): but perhaps you share the **emotivist** beliefs of Ayer (1936) that a moral statement such as 'you ought to be honest' is just an expression of how the person making this statement feels about honesty; or perhaps you sympathise with Nietzsche's (1886) scepticism about the prospects of moral philosophy changing a person's basic prejudices. Did US social policy alter in the face of Titmuss's (1970) research that an altruistic system of blood donation, like the NHS, is more effective than a market system of blood selling? No. The power of vested interests and strongly held personal beliefs, to the point of prejudices, is hard to resist. However, this does not excuse us from an obligation to lift these moral boulders, taxing though they are and small the distance we are able to push them.

Moral philosophy is not commonly found in the social work education curriculum and 'philosophising' is not seen as sitting well alongside the hurly-burly of social work, nor with the proceduralised routines locked into large bureaucracies. In this book I hope to challenge this view, gently, and to present a case for the social worker as an applied ethicist – *a practitioner of applied moral philosophy*. To begin this journey, let us consider a pair of concepts at the core of much philosophical thought: pleasure and pain.

## Pleasure and pain

Earlier we examined the place that pleasure ('happiness') has in **utilitarian** theory. Let us look at the broader place of pleasure and pain in ethical theory (Feinberg, 1969) by first proposing three statements that we might expect to gain universal agreement and conform to the principles of **beneficence** (doing good) and **non-maleficence** (avoiding harm):

> ➤ It is right to seek pleasure and to avoid pain.

> ➤ It is right to seek pleasure that does not entail pain for others.

> ➤ It is right to give pleasure and to alleviate pain for others.

When listening to others' accounts of their own pain (physical, emotional, psychological), *ought* the listener to experience this as painful, too, albeit the pain is of a different order or nature? Is it right to experience pain from listening to accounts of others' pain? Is it wrong to experience pleasure from listening to accounts of others' pain and, if so, why is it wrong since we are agreed that seeking pleasure is good, as long as it does not cause pain in others? The person's pain could be increased by the knowledge that the listener is deriving pleasure from this pain; but if the listener could hide their pleasure completely, would it nevertheless be wrong for the listener to derive pleasure from the account of pain and if so, what does that tell us about the **a priori** (given and understood as truthful) statements in the bulleted list above?

If we intuitively feel that it is wrong for the listener to seek or experience pleasure from others' accounts of pain, what *ought* the listener to experience? Pain? Nothing?

So far this has seemed an exercise in philosophy but, in fact, it is an everyday reality for social workers. How do you feel when you hear another person's account of their pain? How *ought* you to feel? Some feelings might not seem to fit on an axis of pleasure or pain. For example, if you feel "there but for the grace of God go I" – in other words, "it makes me appreciate my own fortunate life circumstances, and I understand how easily those could have been very different and I could be suffering like this person" – is that not a kind of pleasure? If you feel overwhelmed by the person's story and don't know where to start to begin to help them, isn't this feeling of inadequacy a kind of pain? Is it 'better' if you feel anger rather than pain – anger at the injustice that the service user is experiencing?

Does it matter how the pleasure or pain arises? If I deliberately seek pleasure from accounts of others' pain is this worse than if I inexplicably and unexpectedly feel pleasure from an account of pain? If you have done your best to counter or fight off the feelings of pleasure or pain does this indicate a greater moral worth and, if so, why?

Perhaps the experience of pleasure from an account of someone's pain is an indication that the listener does not have sufficient empathy to bear the responsibility of being a professional listener? To have empathy do you have to be able to experience the other's pain? Is it right, then, to experience others' pain as your own pain? If you experience the pain to the extent that it incapacitates you and you are unable to help others (we sometimes call this burnout), is this worse or better than someone whose pleasure from others' pain means they can help many more people effectively?

Are pain and pleasure entities at either ends of an axis, or is it possible for a person to experience pleasure from their own pain? In other words, does the recounting of the pain give its own pleasure? Indeed, the catharsis of expressing one's own pain (a well-established therapeutic tool) is, surely, a form of pleasure? And doesn't the listener, or therapist, derive pleasure from being able to produce this catharsis?

Your response to this discourse on pleasure and pain will tell you much about your positioning around moral philosophy, from the agnosticism of "I don't see what this tells me about my everyday practice" to the new recognition of "this explains so much about how conflicted I often feel in the face of someone's hardship". Your thoughts on pleasure and pain might have led you to the complexities of sado-masochistic practices (SM), in which sexual pain is actively invited and given; what is your response, then, to attempts to criminalise consenting SM behaviour between adults? Whatever your response to this discussion of pleasure and pain, the dilemmas that you will encounter in the chapters ahead require responses in the form of action, or deliberate inaction, and as such we are not allowed to be agnostic. As the existentialists would remind us, we are condemned to be free, we *must* choose.

# A changing moral landscape?

> Well-being is a mutable concept. (Judge Fiona Maye in Ian McEwan's *The Children Act*, 2014: 16)

## Impact of organisational changes on values

How do changes in the way social workers are organised alter their moral landscapes? Does it matter, ethically, whether social workers are specialised or generic, whether they work in mono-professional teams or multi-professional teams, whether the directors or the agencies that employ them are, themselves, social workers?

The Probation Service in England and Wales is a chastening case example of the impact of organisational change and its relationship to professional values. There has always been a tension between the care and support functions of probation work with offenders, neatly summed up on the one hand by the professional requirement to 'advise, assist and befriend' and, on the other hand, by the political urge for retribution and restitution. Welfare-versus-justice arguments were won by the latter in the 1990s when probation training was separated from social work, then reinforced by the Criminal Justice Act 2003, 'which defined the purposes of sentencing as: the punishment of offenders; crime reduction; the reform and rehabilitation of offenders; the protection of the public; and the making of reparation by offenders to persons affected by their crimes' (Justice Committee, 2011: §28). The committee's report did add, 'Nevertheless, staff continue to emphasise the *original* values of probation, especially belief in the possibility of personal change, scepticism about the value of prison as the way to reduce crime, respect for diversity and the importance of professional relationships in enabling change' (Justice Committee, 2011: §28, my italics).

To what extent are the values that underpin the current emphasis on offender management compatible with the befriending role of former times? And do changes to the probation role, organisation and training have a reflux action on probation values, reshaping them as a consequence of the reshaped organisation of the Service?

## Social and legal changes to the landscape

Legal and political obligations are, in fact, forms of moral obligation.

(Singer, 1973: 5)

Social workers in the UK became state professionals in the years follow-ing 1945; at one point, 90% were employed in the public sector, though this percentage has reduced. As public servants, attitudes to social work-ers reflect attitudes to the state. Durkheim's (1957) belief in the state as the ultimate moral force was largely realised in social democratic societies such as post-war Britain, where the state was seen as the guarantor of eco-nomic and social security alongside personal freedom. Just a few years ear-lier, the German state had unleashed the moral tsunami of the Holocaust, yet remarkably quickly it adopted the values of post-war social democracy and rapidly relearned the value of social groupwork, for instance. The speed of social change, and of contingent dominant values, can be shock-ingly fast.

The libertarian tradition in the US has given Americans a much more equivocal view of the state, and for societies such as post-Soviet states the experience of authoritarian regimes unleashed considerable hostility to the idea of the state. In many societies, such as India, the state is associated with corrupt values.

So, the values that we imbue in the state vary according to our relation-ship with it and, of course, the state itself changes (Murphy, 2011). From the benign provider of redistributed wealth, the British state has become one that appears at best powerless and at worst collusive with locust capi-talism, in hock to the worst excesses of global capital. It is interesting to speculate how stands the moral authority of the British state currently and, therefore, its impact on the moral landscape for social work, a profession so closely allied to the values of state interventionism. Do social workers still see themselves as public service professionals who subscribe to a public service ethos – service to others and putting the needs of others first? (Nolan, 1995).

Whilst the tide of global capital has flowed contrary to the values of social work, the growth of social liberalism in Western countries has seen social work values enter the mainstream. The huge social changes that began in the 1960s – attitudes to abortion and same-sex relationships, for example – have been cemented into far-reaching legal changes in the status of sexual choice, race, gender and age, with progress on human rights that would have astonished a social worker in the 1960s (Androff, 2015). However, just as *what is* does not automatically point to *what ought to be*, so the law tells us what is possible but not what ought to be done.

## Professional values and service users

As my story on page 17 indicates, what is considered acceptable professional behaviour can swing quite markedly, but we expect underlying
professional values to change glacially. Biestek's 1957 principles are old-
fashioned only in their reflection of social work as primarily casework ori-
ented, as it was at that time; but the principles themselves and the values
that they reflect remain in place.

The value in which service users are held, the respect for the individual
and for the right to self-determination, remain central to social work and
these are embedded in professional ethical codes. The position of service
users has changed markedly over the past few decades, with much greater
service user involvement; for instance, contributing routinely in case conferences and throughout social work education in the UK. All values might
appear equal on the page of the codes of ethics, but some are perhaps more
equal than others, and some require long-term advocacy in order to be realised (Beresford and Croft, 2001; Beresford and Holden, 2000; Warren, 2007).

Ethical codes are regularly added to: 'an ongoing conversation' (Hugman,
2013b: 385), open to debate. Individual social workers have a professional
and moral duty to participate in each fresh consideration of these codes.
However, when it comes to concrete practices, the ways in which ethical
codes are interpreted varies surprisingly within the same profession (Doel
*et al.*, 2010), with quite contrary actions springing from commonly held
principles. This can often best be explained by different practitioners'
responses to *conflicting* principles and values (Joseph and Fernandes, 2006).
For instance, everybody agrees that it is right to tell the truth and that it is
wrong to kill, but what ought you to do if telling the truth will lead to a
killing? Value conflicts will be a recurring theme in the book and I will
consider them in more detail in Chapter 4.

It is reasonable to query whether there can 'be an effective, overarching
code of professional ethics if all our values are grounded in different cultures
and personal beliefs' (Hugman, 2013b: 385); moral landscapes can look as
varied as physical ones around the globe (Banks and Nøhr, 2012; Dominelli,
2004). The adoption of a single ethical code could be an example of a
powerful elite imposing its own ethical hierarchy. So, instead of an international professional code of ethics, social work has agreed a *Statement of
Ethical Principles* which aims to provide a 'moral tent' under which all social
workers can shelter, wherever they practice (IFSW/IASSW, 2004). Even so,
the difficulties when principles conflict will inevitably result in varying
interpretations of ethical practice; this lies at the heart of the dilemmas that
illustrate the subsequent chapters.

# 3 PROFESSIONALISM, POWER AND SELF-DETERMINATION

## Professionalism

The idea of professionalism is broad and open to various interpretations. Colloquially, 'unprofessional' behaviour is often associated with casual relationships or appearance, a notion that can come into conflict with some basic social work values about equality and relationship-based work (Ruch *et al.*, 2010). Professionalism and power are bound up in many ways, not least by the question of who has the power to define what is, or ought to be, professional behaviour and who determines and enforces professional standards.

## Professional ethics

Professional ethics consist of the set of values that are shared by members of the same profession, often gathered into a code to which members of a profession are expected, even required, to subscribe. Countries where social work has legal standing and where there are professional social work associations have their own national codes of ethics. An example of one of the most recent codes is that developed by the Georgian Association of Social Workers (GASW, 2005), alongside professional standards for Georgian social workers (2007). Relevant items from various national codes feature in the *Guidance* section towards the end of this chapter and Chapters 4–10.

Professional ethics take account of the position of trust conferred on individual practitioners when they exercise powers on behalf of the wider community. Professional etiquette is, therefore, of a different order than personal conduct. However, there are 'leakages' between the two and, increasingly, there is a presumption that the professional's behaviour *outside* their work role ought to be subject to greater scrutiny than someone who is not in this trusted position. So, with this thinking, my boozing and brawling in the street is not the conduct of a private individual but that of a member of the social work profession, and as such I am breaking the etiquette of that profession. This position has strong links with **virtue ethics** as it poses the implicit question: *can you be a good social worker if you are not a good citizen?*

There are ethical positions that present potential counterweights to the current dominance of virtue ethics in these matters. The first, **principlism**, draws from the notion that ethical positions should be guided by a set of principles; in this case a principle of fairness would suggest that it is inequitable that because I am a social worker I cannot booze and brawl in the street and face the same consequences as any citizen – possible prosecution if I cause nuisance, injury or damage, but not necessarily loss of employment.

Another counter-argument comes in the shape of **redemptive ethics** and reframes the question thus: *can you be a good social worker if you are not always a good citizen?* In other words, does one bad act in the street write me off forever? Can I not mend my ways and change? In recent times, recidivism has been trumping redemption: there is a widely held belief that transgressors are more likely to transgress again, rather than learn the error of their ways. Although orthodox opinion has British society becoming increasingly socially liberal (gay marriage, etc.), there are other indications that suggest a growing authoritarianism (electronic surveillance, etc.), expressed by this narrowing of belief in the possibility of redemption and a reduction in the civic appetite for forgiveness (Cantacuzino, 2015).

# Power

Social work has contributed much to our understanding of power, discrimination and emancipatory practice, in particular an analysis of power in terms of social identity and the potential for power to be both damaging and productive (Dominelli, 2002; Smith, 2010; Tew, 2002; Tew, 2006; Thompson, 2012).

## Power and powers

Professionals have the power to change people's lives; indeed, that is part of the purpose of these powers. There are many different powers and there are considerable constraints on these powers as this chapter will explore.

Individual practitioners can feel far from powerful. This can stem from a lack of authority to bring about the changes they want and the absence of resources to meet the need they have identified as a professional. The complexity of people's situations can be overwhelming and leave social workers feeling powerless. The regard in which professions are held has diminished in the face of a market ideology that has realigned clients and patients into customers: people who have learned to assert their rights and to challenge professional judgement. Customers can assert themselves without the hamstrings of accountability that tie professionals who must be more broadly accountable, and balance the rights and needs of other people and the community at large.

Even so, individual practitioners have personal, organisational and legal powers and their words 'carry weight' (Hugman, 2013b: 381). As Beckett and Maynard (2005: 114) note, knowledge of social workers' powers 'give them considerable leverage *even when they are not actually using them*'. With power and leverage come responsibility and an obligation to use them ethically.

## Ethical accountability

Power requires accountability, which means that decisions made by professionals like social workers are subject to transparent review. The Statement of Ethical Principles agreed jointly by the International Federation of Social Workers (IFSW) and the International Association of Schools of Social Work (IASSW) reveals the scope of this accountability:

> Social workers need to acknowledge that they are accountable for their actions to the users of their services, the people they work with, their colleagues, their employers, the professional association and to the law, and that these accountabilities may conflict.
>
> IFSW/IASSW (2004)

Conflicting accountabilities produce conflicting pressures based on conflicting values – dilemmas – and these dilemmas are often a complex mix of practice problems and ethical challenges in which notions of power are frequently core.

## Equality

When power is conceptualised as something to be weighed in a pair of scales, most service users seem to be highly disadvantaged and 'equality' rings hollow. Life experiences, life opportunities and life expectations are often, though by no means always, very different (Gaine, 2010). The powers deriving from the social worker's role are considerable, and social workers are frequently gatekeepers to resources. It seems hard to know where to begin to equalise the power in this relationship; even so, there are many ways in which service users hold power. It is they who have lived their own life, making them 'experts by experience' (Beresford, 2010), as long as social workers are willing to listen to this experience and welcome it. Service users are not subject to professional accountability, so they are free to focus on their own needs and wants rather than balance these against those of others. Social workers frequently have more to lose in terms of reputation and live-lihood than the people they work with. All of these factors serve to limit the power of the social worker.

However, we are mistaken if we continue to 'weigh' power on a pair of scales, the social worker on one pan and the service user on another, attempting to achieve an equality that likens a pound of apples to a pound of pears. To avoid this fallacy, we can reach to ideas from moral philosophy, especially **Kantian** notions of the moral worth of each person. In this idea we have a *qualitative* notion of equality not a quantitative one. And an *ought* for why social workers ought to strive for equality.

This equal value is not without practical difficulty. It means, for instance, treating with an equal moral worth those persons who have beliefs that would condemn large numbers of humanity to a violent death or who have committed unimaginable crimes against infants. There is a difference, then, between the person and their behaviours and beliefs. However, a **Kantian** equality can also be used to justify a very unequal economic status quo if it is not allied to notions of redistributive social justice (Rawls, 1958). We will return to this shortly.

Although equality is enshrined in law (in the UK, the Equality Act, 2010, in which it is unlawful to discriminate in nine protected characteristics), it is far from a universally accepted value. Many in India would think it right that 'the Brahmin be given greater privileges in the temple than the Dalit' (Joseph and Fernandes, 2006: 26) because of the belief that the Dalit's inequality and the power of the Brahmin is part of their very essence.

## Self-determination

It is right to do everything possible to preserve the identity of a person's self, particularly when a basic right, such as freedom, is being removed. Self-determination relies on a sense of self, yet social workers find themselves working with some people where this identity is distorted, is fading or has been assaulted by others. It is, therefore, a great challenge to make self-determination meaningful when there is an absence or confusion of self.

Promoting people's own capacity for problem-solving in their own lives is right for many different reasons. Self-direction is valued as a moral good, not least because people are generally the best judges of what is good for them, but also because the process of making these decisions for oneself is a good in itself. We value our capacity for competent self-determination and we feel we ought to help a person to maintain a sense of self, especially when there is a big transition in their life such as a move into a residential institution. Social workers have a role in helping with the possible reshaping of 'self' in the wake of any loss and grief that has caused the transition. In all walks of social work, the value of self-determination is challenged to the point of dilemma by situations where service users are working reluctantly with their social workers (Rooney, 2009).

## Social justice and self-determination

As noted earlier, the **Kantian** notion of equality emphasising moral worth and dignity can justify the status quo – respect the beggar but don't bother to feed him. Notions of social justice and redistributive economic justice are essential if we are to hold a fully ethical consideration of power and self-determination.

Self-determination is a principle based on the belief that individuals should have every opportunity to guide and direct their own lives, which means making their own decisions about what is 'good' for them. It is a belief in individuals as their own **moral agents**. Making these ideals a reality requires resources – good schooling, good health, good environment, good security and, yes, good social work – and the distribution of these resources requires social justice. Self-determination is not, then, such an individualistic activity; in fact it is entirely dependent on social benevolence and the commonwealth of society. As Tawney (1926: 264) noted almost a century ago:

> Few tricks of the unsophisticated intellect are more curious than the naive psychology of the business man, who ascribes his achievements to his unaided efforts, in blind unconsciousness of a social order without whose continuous support and vigilant protection he would be a lamb bleating in the desert.

Professionals need resources in order to fulfil their obligations to service users. 'Ethical dilemmas were created for all health and social care workers ... who found themselves in under-resourced services assessing needs that there was no money to meet' (Pollard, 2015: 92). Being unable to provide the interventions that they know are necessary leads social workers to question their own self-determination as professionals.

## Beneficence and paternalism

There are social work powers that violate the principle of self-determination, most notably the loss of liberty in a compulsory admission to mental health hospital and the removal of a child from its parents against their will (Dickens, 2012). There are other, less dramatic, acts where social workers take actions that compromise a person's self-determination. Where is the moral threshold at which point a social worker is justified in departing from the principle of self-direction, 'for the person's own good'? A libertarian might say 'nowhere' and 'never'.

The point at which unwanted intervention is generally justified is when a person's actions threaten the welfare of others. This, of course, requires a judgement in itself. What might justify intervention when a person's actions threaten only their own welfare? How do you make a judgement about whether their action is 'really' their own or whether they are not in control of their own person, no longer autonomous because of addiction, mental illness, grief or duress? Is a restoration of their autonomy feasible? If the choice is available, do you block the harm via a paternalistic intervention or restore the choice via an educative intervention?

## Self-determination, power and social identities

Power is less an individual quality than a socially ascribed attribute. The way people speak, move, dress, etc. leads others to ascribe differential power to them. Some of these attributions are made typically: in other words, by socially defined types (women, men, young people, old people, black people, white people, etc.) and some of these types have higher social status in some societies than in others. So power attaches to some socially defined groups more than others; however, socially ascribed power is very complex in practice, with individuals often occupying multiple identities, sometimes referred to as 'intersectionality', and, perhaps because of personal qualities or economic power, they break through their categorical situations (Andersen and Hill Collins, 2015).

When social worker meets service user there are differences and similarities in terms of socially defined categories (dis/ability, sexuality, social class, etc.) and these have significances, sometimes great, other times less so. Social identity is always relevant to an understanding of practice and ethical dilemmas; sometimes it plays its part on the sidelines and at other times it is centre stage.

## Professional self-determination

Professionalism, power and self-determination come together in the question of how much professional autonomy a social worker has the power to exercise. If a social worker judges that the best way to work with a service user who is withdrawn and uncommunicative is to meet them in an informal setting, a café or a pub, does that social worker have the autonomy to take that course of action? Ought the social worker to seek permission from the supervisor, or is it 'easier to seek forgiveness than permission'? Ought the social worker to seek out the agency's professional standards for guidance; and if the guidance is unhelpful what professional and moral obligation does the social worker have to challenge and change the guidance? Social workers and service users often experience parallel problems and dilemmas but, like the singularities we discussed in the introductory chapter, they are not always recognised. Ethical exercise will expose these parallels and help social workers and service users make a powerful alliance.

## Exploring dilemmas 1

In this scenario we will explore issues of professionalism and power in the relationship between a social worker and her supervisor.

> **Regina** is a supervisor in a voluntary organisation working with asylum seekers. She supervises a small team of three social workers. Over a coffee, Regina has been talking about an upcoming party with a fashion theme and sharing her frustration at not finding the right outfit. A few days later **Donna**, one of the social workers, comes into Regina's office and presents her with a box and tells her that she has found just the thing for her party and that it is in the box. Regina is taken aback and before she can say anything, her phone rings and Donna takes this as a cue to leave, popping the box down on Regina's table.
>
> Regina ends her call and opens the box to take out a very attractive dress that she likes and does just the job – just her size and style for the party. Regina feels uncomfortable but can't quite put her finger on why. Whatever the answer, Regina moves the box to a top shelf in her crowded room to think it over.

1. **Ought Regina to accept the gift or return it to Donna?**
   Regina has decided that this is a dilemma – whether to accept Donna's gift or not. What questions might Regina be asking herself?
   Perhaps make your own list before reading on.

   **1.** Did I give a wrong message by talking about the party?

   **2.** Did Donna think I was dropping hints?

▶

◀

**3.** ... In fact, was I unconsciously dropping hints?

**4.** Is Donna's gift a thoughtful gesture, an act of simple kindness?

**5.** Is Donna's act a manipulative ploy to put me in her debt?

**6.** How does Donna's gift make me feel?

**7.** Was I mistaken to answer the phone instead of talking about the gift there and then?

**8.** Do the rest of the team know about this gift?

**9.** Do I let the rest of the team know if they don't?

**10.** Does it make it too big a deal if I talk to the rest of the team?

**11.** How would the rest of the team view it? As an act of impetuous generosity or as Donna currying favour?

**12.** How much did the dress cost?

**13.** What is the agency's policy about accepting gifts?

**14.** Would it have made any difference if it had been a birthday present or a gift presented as part of a special occasion?

Behind these factual questions lie some ethical issues:

*Motivation*

**2. Ought the meaning behind the gift, and the act of giving, to have a bearing on what Regina should do?**
All social acts have meanings that include overt, stated ones and others that are covert, sometimes not even known to the person doing the deed. Cynics tend to look for underlying motives and view most behaviour as selfishly driven; naïve opinion denies the existence of this Machiavellian world, accepting meanings at face value. For some, no matter what the consequences of the gift, if Donna's intentions were good and she had no **maleficence** in the deed, then it is a good act, in accord with **virtue ethics**.

*Timing*

**3. Ought Regina to have acted one way or the other immediately, or was she right to take time to reflect?**

▶

Regina has accepted Donna's gift by default and though it has caused her angst in the following days while contemplating what to do, it might have caused a lot more unhappiness to Donna to have had the gift rejected there and then. If Regina returns it now, she can explain in measured tones that, touched though she is by the gift, she has given it some thought and, on balance, regretfully feels it is not right to accept it. On the other hand, although over the last few days Donna has experienced the pleasure that comes from giving, will the displeasure of having it returned be heightened by the sharp contrast with that pleasure? Indeed, might Donna have been wondering beforehand whether Regina would accept the gift and, once accepted, has she now told the others in the team about the gift, so that she will face the embarrassment of them knowing that it has been returned? This line of moral reasoning is largely **utilitarian**, 'balancing the relative advantages and disadvantages of a particular course of action from the standpoint of creating the greatest good for the greatest number of people' (Parrott, 2006: 51).

*Impact on others*

**4. Ought Regina to consider how others will feel about this?**
We could look at Regina's dilemma through the lens of relationship – primarily between Regina and Donna, but also the network of relationships within the team. Regina heeds her own emotional response and factors this into her decision-making. From the list of questions to herself, the most important is: *How does Donna's gift make me feel?* There could be many answers: touched; joyful; baffled; beholden; angry – possibly a confusing combination of these. Regina also reflects on the likely impact on team members' feelings: shared pleasure; jealous exclusion or a mix? In her decision to keep or refuse the dress Regina feels she ought to take the path that is most respectful of these relationships and takes greatest care of them, an **ethics of care** approach in which emotions are not the enemy of reason, unlike in some ethical frameworks.

*Scale*

**5. Ought it to make any difference what the dress cost?**
If Donna gave Regina a chocolate would these same ethical considerations apply? A home-baked muffin? A theatre ticket going spare? A prize

◀

she won at a raffle that she can't use? A dress for a party?... Are ethical considerations just about scale, then, and if so at what 'size' does a gift become ethically unacceptable: somewhere between the raffle prize and the dress or somewhere beyond the dress? Ought Regina resort to a principle of proportionalism?

Working to a rule of thumb that it is fine to accept a muffin but a theatre ticket is going too far is a form of **rule utilitarianism**, albeit one moderated by Regina's own judgement about where the line ought to be drawn.

### Rules

6. **Ought Regina to follow the agency's protocol whatever they are and whatever the consequences?**
   If Regina's first instinct is to retrieve the agency's 'gifts policy' from its folder and to follow it unthinkingly, she is subscribing to a **duty-based** system of ethics in which she interprets the right way to act as following the agency's protocol no matter what the outcome might be (see Chapter 9).

### Power

7. **How ought Regina to reflect on the impact of her own status?**
   So far, Regina's ethical approaches have largely neglected an analysis of power. There is inherent power in the act of giving and receiving – Donna has the power of gifting and Regina the power of accepting or rejecting. However, Regina is Donna's supervisor, with the power to accelerate or stymie Donna's career – it is only a month since Regina's appraisal of Donna, which was positive. She has managerial responsibility for Donna's work and, to some extent, her continuing professional development. Ought these factors to play a part in Regina's judgement?

   Regina ought to consider the impact of her status as team leader. With status comes power and the impact of words casually spoken (the musing over the fashion party at the coffee table) might be amplified in the ears of someone feels very conscious of being 'a subordinate'. Does this invest Regina's words with special moral responsibilities? (see Time box)

   Status and line management authority are two kinds of power, but what of economic power and how might this alter the ethics of Regina's dilemma? Donna is an exceptionally wealthy woman (her work in the asylum centre provides 'pocket money') whilst Regina is laden with debt from various failed enterprises. Does this change the dynamic in the gift transaction and ought it to?

▶

◀

**Time box**

'Who will rid me of this meddlesome priest!' exclaimed Henry II in fury at Archbishop Thomas Becket's refusal to bend to Henry's will. Four knights did exactly that, murdering Becket in his cathedral. Henry claimed he didn't actually mean Becket to be killed; but as the most powerful man in the kingdom his words 'carried weight'. Was Henry morally responsible for Becket's death, even though he didn't strike the blow and didn't give an order?

The day after placing the box with the dress on top of her cabinet, Regina goes to her own supervisor **Ron**, the head of the agency, to ask his advice about what she ought to do. Increasingly, she is feeling that she should not accept the gift, largely because she thinks it will set a precedent and also she does not want to feel beholden to Donna. However, Ron says that though there is general guidance in the agency's code of practice about not accepting gifts from clients, there is nothing about colleagues' gifts and he thinks it would have a bad effect on team morale if Regina were to return it, especially now that some time has elapsed. His only concern would have been if **Jackson**, the only man in Regina's team, had given it to her. But gifts woman-to-woman are fine with Ron and he tells Regina to keep the dress and enjoy the fashion party.

Regina leaves Ron's room, now aware that what she had really wanted from Ron was his approval, not his advice. She was using his power as head of the agency to back her own opinion, but this had backfired. She reflects on how unprofessional she would judge one of her team if they hid behind her authority when having to deny a service user something they wanted. There were times when it was right to conscript the power of others on behalf of service users, but it was wrong to do so because of your own lack of courage to say what had to be said.

Increasingly, as the days pass, Regina feels she has been complicit in a decision that she now judges to be wrong. She feels she was badgered by a more powerful person, Ron, and she decides she ought to return the dress to Donna.

So, a week after the gift of the dress, Regina brings the box down from the top of her shelves, places it on the coffee table and invites Donna into her room in order to return it.

## 8. What ought Regina to say?
To help to frame the discussion with Donna, Regina has made two lists – things she thinks are OK and things about which she has worries.

▶

*OKs and worries*

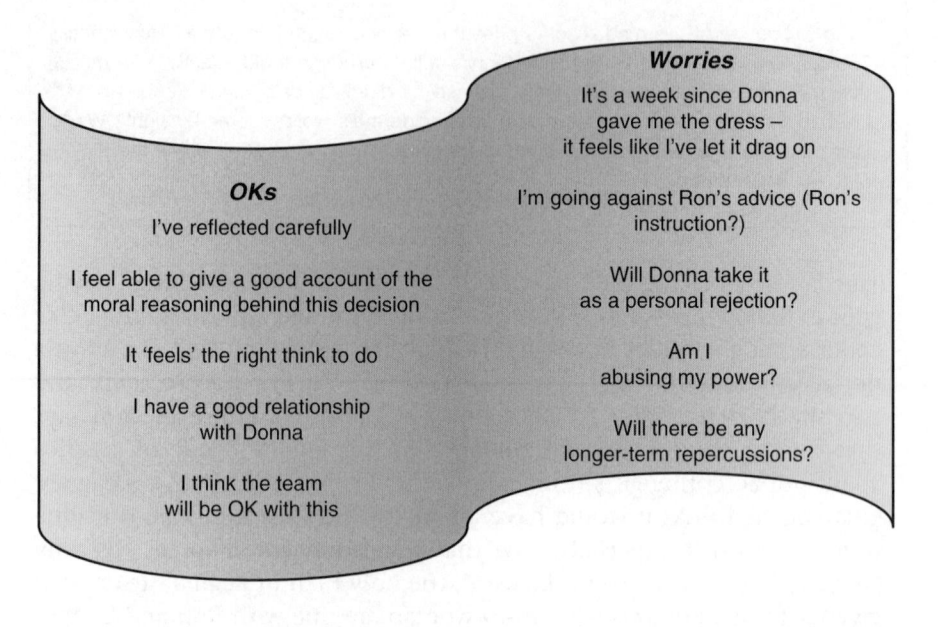

**Worries**

It's a week since Donna
gave me the dress –
it feels like I've let it drag on

I'm going against Ron's advice (Ron's
instruction?)

Will Donna take it
as a personal rejection?

Am I
abusing my power?

Will there be any
longer-term repercussions?

**OKs**

I've reflected carefully

I feel able to give a good account of the
moral reasoning behind this decision

It 'feels' the right think to do

I have a good relationship
with Donna

I think the team
will be OK with this

Consider these seven possible responses by Donna, in the light of seven alternative **singularities**. What ought Regina do and say in respect of each of them?

a. "Oh, you've got it all wrong. It's from all of us in the team, but your phone went when I handed it to you so I didn't get the chance to explain – and since then, well, you've not said a word... I was waiting for you to say something."

b. "Sure, I understand. You know, I wondered whether it was the right thing to do, but that dress was just so right for you I couldn't resist it. Would it make things better if you bought it off me?"

c. "Well, it was more by way of an offering an apology, actually. I was really embarrassed that I'd asked you for that extra day's leave the other week. I totally understand why it couldn't happen and I'm sorry I put you in an awkward position. So, the dress is not really a gift as such, more of an apology. I hope that means you can accept it – it'd make me feel a lot better actually."

d. "Why've you taken a week to say this? It's going to be so humiliating now, letting the team know you're flinging it back to me. Couldn't we just pretend you'd kept it so I can keep face?"

◀

**e.** "What does Ron think about this? I can't see he'd have any problem with it. I want to take the matter up with him."

**f.** "You know, I can't help but feel that, if it had been a white member of the team giving you this dress, that somehow that would've been alright."

**g.** "How come it was OK when you gave me that sheep ornament for my collection when you came back from holidays last summer?"

If you could go back to that moment a week ago when Donna has given Regina the dress and the phone rings, what would you have done in Regina's position?

If you would have thanked Donna and kept the dress, make a list of twists to the situation that would change your mind and persuade you that you should return it. On the other hand, if you would have thanked Donna but told her politely that unfortunately you didn't think it would be right for you to keep it, make a list of twists that would persuade you otherwise. Or are there no circumstances at all that would change your decision one way or the other?

## Exploring dilemmas 2

In this second scenario we consider the power and powers that a mental health social worker has in respect of a service user with severe and enduring mental health problems.

**Humerah** is a South Asian woman in her late thirties. She uses a wheelchair – 'everyone sees a disabled woman' – but her main contact is with mental health services. Since her late teens Humerah has had more than a dozen compulsory psychiatric admissions. She's 'lost count' of social workers and community psychiatric nurses over the years. She is a capable person who has held powerful positions in a number of companies. (There is more detail of Humerah's story in Doel and Best, 2008: 9–14.)

Humerah has stopped taking her medication.

**Nathan** became Humerah's social worker two months ago. He is a white, gay, able-bodied man so, apart from being the same age as Humerah, in many other respects they are quite different.

▶

1. **What ought to be the balance between the social worker's power to intervene to ensure Humerah takes her medication and Humerah's right to refuse it?**

Within the dilemma about what is the right thing to do lies another dilemma about what is the right way to do it. The effects of long-term medication and over-medication can be worse than the illness itself, and they can mask the person's own mechanisms for recovery. On the other hand, there are situations where the medication remains essential to maintain a person's mental health, and their belief that it is no longer needed is delusional. So, there is first a practice judgement about which of these two possibilities is the more likely in Humerah's situation.

Speaking with Humerah and reading her case notes, Nathan is alert to the fact that Humerah's medication is kept under constant review and that it is critical in maintaining her stability, and that most of the time Humerah thinks this, too; and that from time to time Humerah starts to refuse her medication, often as a precursor to a breakdown. As a result, Nathan has had a conversation with Humerah whilst she is in a willing phase about what she would like to happen when she becomes delusional about her medication.

They have discussed an 'advance directive', in which Humerah-in-sound-mind would give a directive on behalf of (future) Humerah-in-unsound-mind. Nathan has had good experiences with advance directives and he wanted Humerah to agree one, but she told him that she would not care what she had agreed when she was well – 'it would become meaningless'. Nathan accepted this and, likewise, Humerah accepted that when she approaches a certain level of dangerousness that Nathan and the professionals will take control and make these decisions for her. Humerah sums it up: 'They just need to take control – and that's not to give up control forever.' Temporariness is important, yet rules and policies often struggle to accommodate it.

Humerah tells Nathan that she knows she has been thought of as a difficult client over the years, but she reckons her previous worker was a difficult social worker. Knowing Nathan has been working in the same team with this person she asks him his opinion of the previous worker.

2. **Ought Nathan to share his views about a colleague?**

You might query where the dilemma lies because the answer is 'obviously not'. However, think about this situation more carefully. Let us accept that Nathan absolutely agrees that the previous social worker is a nightmare (indeed, she is in the midst of a disciplinary action) and, from what he gathers from the case files, her work with Humerah was poor. He is caught in the dilemma of, seemingly, telling a lie or breaking professional loyalty. The consequences of either are difficult: to tell Humerah stony-faced that he will not discuss a colleague might be Nathan's view of loyalty, but Humerah will see it as professionals closing ranks and it will distance their relationship; yet to be candid about the previous worker risks breaching confidentiality and appearing as a leaky sieve.

Although it has the appearance of a self-disclosure dilemma (see Chapters 7 and 8), in fact power and professionalism lie at its centre. Whether to come down off a fence and then which 'side' to commit to are powerful decisions. Nathan believes he ought to use his power responsibly and to deny a person's reality (Humerah's reality that she experienced a poor service) is not a responsible course of action as it implies support for the previous worker. Nathan believes an ethical answer to be a truthful one; however, it is the *difficulty* of Humerah's question that he wants to remain truthful to, so he responds:

> I know why you've asked that question and I can see why it wasn't at all easy for you working with her. I wouldn't have found it easy going either. I'd like to be more candid but I know you wouldn't want me talking with another service user about you – so, for the same reasons, I'm not going to talk more about her, only to say I understand completely.

Nathan aims to give tacit support to the truth about the previous worker, whilst conveying to Humerah the truth about his position as a professional, that he is careful with how he uses his power and discretion. He appeals to her reasoning and, at the same time, to her self-interest.

Humerah has a litigious history with her professionals and this does not stop with Nathan. She makes a complaint about him in writing to his manager, despite a verbal agreement between the two of them that if there were any disagreements or dissatisfactions they would 'have it out' face to face before turning to formal complaints. Humerah has complained about Nathan offering an opinion that there was every chance her journey might get worse before it gets better. She has asked for a South Asian social worker to replace Nathan. Nathan does not want to harm the relationship with Humerah, which he thinks is basically sound, but he does feel a bond of trust has been broken and he thinks this is central to Humerah's problems. He would like the opportunity to restore the trust and to break Humerah's disruptive pattern with her professionals.

◀

### 3. Ought Nathan to confront Humerah with his feelings?

Consult your **wise professionals** to explore the ethical issues in this dilemma and decide what values are in play.

How might it change the ethical considerations if Humerah had made this statement prior to requesting a change of social worker:

> In the future there's every chance I'll reject you. I've done this with all my previous social workers – most with good cause! But with you, I just want to let you know that you're the best social worker I've had in a long time and I want you to ignore any requests I make about getting rid of you.

Humerah and Nathan's frank discussion about their working relationship and mutual expectations has taken them forward by leaps and bounds. Humerah has withdrawn the complaint and the request for a change of social worker. Indeed, she tells Nathan that she is in a much better place and that her personal budget should be cut because she doesn't need it all and she knows the pressures on budgets (her present employment is head of the accounts section in a local business and she is very cost-conscious). Nathan is non-committal – it's the first time he's had a service user actually suggesting their personal budget ought to be reduced. He fails to act on Humerah's instruction because he knows that once cut it will be very difficult to raise it again later, and he anticipates that it will need raising at some future time.

### 4. Ought Nathan to follow Humerah's instructions?

What are the ethical issues in this dilemma? Again, consult your own **wise professionals**.

## Exploring dilemmas 3

For the last scenario we visit Oaklands, a privately run residential care home for older people, where we will consider professional power in the context of service users with impaired abilities to make decisions. **Helen** is a student social worker on placement with work-based supervisor, **Marie**. Helen is key worker for some residents, including Mr Porter (**Gordon**) and Mrs Loxley (**Joyce**) who are both in their late seventies and suffering from dementia, Gordon in the early stages and Joyce further on. Both are widowed and have known each other in the home for two years.

▶

Helen has got to know Gordon and Joyce quite well over the five weeks she has been on placement and she has come to appreciate the bond of affection between the two. Gordon is more cogent than Joyce and does most of the talking for them. His uninhibited conversation often includes sexual matters.

A double room has come vacant and Gordon says they want to move in together. Joyce agrees, but it is uncertain what kind of consent she is giving as she is frequently unclear. However, Helen has caught Joyce at some lucid times and believes it to be Joyce's wish also.

Gordon's family visit Oaklands twice-weekly; they have him to stay with them regularly. They are supportive of the proposal, especially his son, **Ashley**, who comes every Sunday. Joyce's family see her only occasionally, and they are implacably opposed. One of Joyce's daughters, **Bella**, in particular, says that her mother is in no state of mind to make that kind of choice and that it would amount to sexual exploitation. Bella says it is wrong, too, because her mother and Gordon are not married.

Helen has spoken further with Gordon and Joyce and supports the move. Her work-based supervisor, Marie, indicates support when in Helen's company, but soon backs down in the face of scepticism from **Sharon**, the manager of the home.

## 1. Ought Gordon and Joyce to be supported to move in together?

Gordon and Joyce are adults and are entitled to enjoy all the pleasures of adulthood. The question ought, then, to be how best to elucidate Joyce's 'true' feelings (Toseland, 1997). However, these feelings might be ambivalent at the best of times, even if Joyce were able to give full and articulate expression to them. Is Gordon's motivation, then, central to the moral equation? Ought we to aim to find out whether he has Joyce's best interests at heart? Or ought Joyce and Gordon to be allowed to make their own mistake, if that is what this move and intimacy proves to be? Making mistakes is easier when you have the support of your family, so ought the lack of this support in Joyce's case to have a bearing on the decision?

Joyce and Gordon have not moved into the empty double room and discussions are continuing about whether this is 'suitable'. Helen notes in her sessions with her off-site practice educator that 'suitable' and 'appropriate' seem to be the terms that are used instead of 'right' – terms that are, in fact, about values but seek to obscure the fact. She and her practice educator make up the term 'sub-ethical' for this language. Conversations with Joyce are not easy because of her dementia, but Helen gathers from one of these conversations that she and Gordon have probably already been intimate.

2. **What ought Helen to do with this knowledge?**
Consult your **wise professionals** to help Helen come to a decision, then consider who has the power, and who *ought* to have the power, to make the choice about what ought to be done with this information.

A separate and seemingly minor incident has arisen over the weekend, concerning eggs. Ashley visited on Sunday and was told by his father, Gordon, that he was no longer allowed soft-boiled eggs or, even worse, his favourite poached eggs, at breakfast. Sharon had decided that the risk of salmonella from soft yolks is too great for a "vulnerable population" such as the residents at Oaklands and that she doesn't want to be responsible for any "unnecessary deaths" just for the sake of "not eating a hard-boiled egg". She has returned from a training course in which these dangers have been highlighted, and a rumour is also going around the home that the owners of Oaklands are concerned about the risk of litigation should one of the residents fall sick. Ashley has worked himself up and is claiming a violation of his father's human rights. Gordon is meanwhile claiming that Joyce likes soft-boiled eggs, too, and wants to be allowed to eat them.

3. **Who ought to determine the eggs policy? And who ought to take responsibility if it goes wrong?**
Consider the eggs policy from these different perspectives – where do you think the major differences and similarities might lie?

Gordon; Joyce; Gordon's son, Ashley; Joyce's daughter, Bella; student social worker, Helen; Helen's supervisor, Marie; the manager, Sharon; the head cook; the owners of Oaklands; Oaklands management committee; the local press.

Consider whose voices are the most powerful and the least powerful. And what role does professional social work have in this scenario?

# The Big Picture

## Beneficence and paternalism

In the balance between persuasion and coercion how far ought a government's power be used to push its population to good health? A decade ago it was everybody's inalienable right to smoke cigarettes in public places; will sugar take its place alongside nicotine in the pantheon of bad things, swingeing taxes succeeding where the threat of bad teeth and diabetes failed? There are many roads to the good life and if one person chooses to shorten their life but live it hedonistically, is this a principle we should value? Why is there such moral opprobrium heaped on fat people, about the extra costs to the health service, when the food industry that feeds their cravings remains free to profit? Power is never far from the answer.

In my home city of Sheffield, a health promotion project gave shopping vouchers to women in poor parts of the city if they breastfed their babies (Relton *et al.*, 2014). Is this an acceptable level of persuasion or is it coercion through bribery? If the babies of these mothers lead healthier, longer lives as a result of the project, does this overrule any ethical qualms we feel about rewarding people with payments for good behaviour? Is it any different from paying men for sperm donation? Do we feel ethically squeamish because the project is a reminder that there are rich and poor parts to the city (and getting richer and poorer) and that, even through baby-feeding habits, power is reproduced across generations so that the powerful keep hold of their power (Bourdieu, 1991)?

Powerful people can harm themselves with impunity and use their wealth to buy a kind of protection from the moral force of the state to which the rest of the community is subject. Had Howard Hughes been living in relative poverty in social housing, there is little doubt he would have come to the notice of the mental health authorities and been compulsorily hospitalised. Did his extreme wealth insulate him from 'everyday ethics'?

Does the scale of the dilemma affect its moral quality, or the extent to which we feel it as a dilemma, and what is the relationship between the big issues and the small ones? For instance, in 2015 the 85 richest people in the world owned the same wealth as the 3.5 billion poorest (i.e. half the world's population). In what ways does this knowledge, and the ethical dilemmas it brings forth, compare with the dilemma of deciding whether to give the beggar in the underpass some loose change?

## Guidance from Codes, Standards and Principles

The IFSW/IASSW (revised 2014) definition of social work is:

> Social work is a practice-based profession and an academic discipline that promotes social change and development, social cohesion, and the empowerment and liberation of people. Principles of social justice, human rights, collective responsibility and respect for diversities are central to social work. Underpinned by theories of social work, social sciences, humanities and indigenous knowledge, social work engages people and structures to address life challenges and enhance well-being.
>
> The above definition may be amplified at national and/or regional levels.

The IFSW/IASSW (2004) Statement of Ethical Principles has nine principles gathered under two headings: human rights and human dignity; and social justice. One of these principles is:

> Respecting the right to self-determination – Social workers should respect and promote people's right to make their own choices and decisions, irrespective of their values and life choices, provided this does not threaten the rights and legitimate interests of others.

Before its demise, The College of Social Work (TCSW, 2012: 11) required those assessing students to:

> assess in a manner that does not stigmatise or disadvantage individuals and ensures equality of opportunity [and] show applied knowledge of the significance of poverty, racism, ill health and disability, gender, social class [and] sexual orientation in managing the assessment process.

International conventions accepted universally and of particular relevance to social work are:

➤ Universal Declaration of Human Rights

➤ The International Covenant on Civil and Political Rights

➤ The International Covenant on Economic Social and Cultural Rights

➤ The Convention on the Elimination of All Forms of Racial Discrimination

➤ The Convention on the Elimination of All Forms of Discrimination against Women

> The Convention on the Rights of the Child

> Indigenous and Tribal Peoples Convention (International Labour Organization (ILO) convention 169)

'Social workers strive to use the power and authority vested in them as professionals in responsible ways that serve the needs of clients and the promotion of social justice' (CASW 2005a: 10). This principle, expounded in the Canadian code of ethics for social workers, is typical of most national codes. It also illustrates their limitations, in terms of the 'apple pie' generality of much of their content, though the Canadian code is supplemented with a set of Guidelines for Ethical Practice which attempt to provide more detail, yet even so, beg for more. For example:

> **2.5 Avoid Physical Contact with Clients**
>
> **2.5.1** Social workers avoid engaging in physical contact with clients when there is a possibility of harm to the client as a result of the contact. Social workers who engage in appropriate physical contact with clients are responsible for setting clear, appropriate and culturally sensitive boundaries to govern such physical contact.
>
> CASW (2005b: 18)

The Singapore code of professional ethics (SASW 2004: 4) goes a little further by giving two examples of physical contact: 'Social workers do not engage in physical contact with clients where there is a possibility of psychological harm to the client as a result of the contact *such as cradling or caressing clients*' (my italics); but, again, there is no discussion of how the social worker might discern when and whether cradling or caressing *does* present a possibility of psychological harm and when and whether it might be good.

## Consulting the wise professionals

### Half victims, half accomplices

Power, at first ignored in a 'colour-blind' approach in social work, then recognised but oversimplified into convenient social identities, is – at last – becoming understood for its extraordinary complexities, bringing light to the insight from Simone de Beauvoir's epigraph from 60 years ago, referring to women, and in the wake of the Second World War: 'Half victims, half accomplices, like everyone else'. (This is the epigraph to the second volume of *The Second Sex* by Simone de Beauvoir, a quote from Sartre's play *Dirty Hands*.)

Good social work recognises and acknowledges social identities (gender, race, class, etc.) without making assumptions about what these identities might mean, either to the persons we are working with or to the society that nurtures or shuns them. Good practice understands stereotypes without stereotyping. To achieve nuanced practice might mean accepting that, at some existential level, we are all victims, all perpetrators, all accomplices. How, otherwise, could we ever justify our wealth in the face of all the poverty? What we can do, and ought to do, is construct as moral a world as possible in that part where we are **moral agents**. Social workers have more opportunities than most to construct a moral world.

# 4  VALUE CONFLICTS

The dilemmas that social workers face are often associated with conflicts in values. These stem both from *within* the profession because of the elusive, complex and contested nature of social work and its purposes; and also from the friction *between* various social systems. These seismic zones are illustrated below (Figures 4.1 and 4.2) where the overlapping edges represent the areas of regular conflicts in values.

Some conflicts play out within the individual as he or she tries to determine which of two or more values should triumph when each would lead to a different course of action; for instance whether to vote for a leader of a party with whose principles one agrees or whether to vote for a leader who seems more likely to win the next election. These conflicts can be difficult to resolve, but they need not involve other people. Other value conflicts arise between your own and those of other people – colleagues, service users, the management of the agency, the law, etc. These situations are more complex because of the number of variables involved and also because of the power dimension (see Chapter 3); some moral players in these conflicts are more powerful than others, so it is not necessarily the best (most ethical) outcome that is achieved, but the one that carries the heaviest weight.

Let us consider the different circumstances that can give rise to these conflicts in professional settings.

## Get a life

A common conflict is the struggle between meeting your own needs and meeting those of others – the value you put on your own needs and the value you place on others'. For instance, your work phone rings just as you are about to finish for the day. Do you assert your own needs by ignoring it or bend to the need of the caller by answering? The overshadowing of domestic responsibilities by professional dedication has become a TV cop cliché, but it does illustrate a real clash between the value given to domestic life and that given to work. At the far extreme of this continuum, Das and Kulkarni (2006a) describe the ultimate sacrifice of a social worker who lost her life fighting a powerful lobby of builders in India on behalf of her clients.

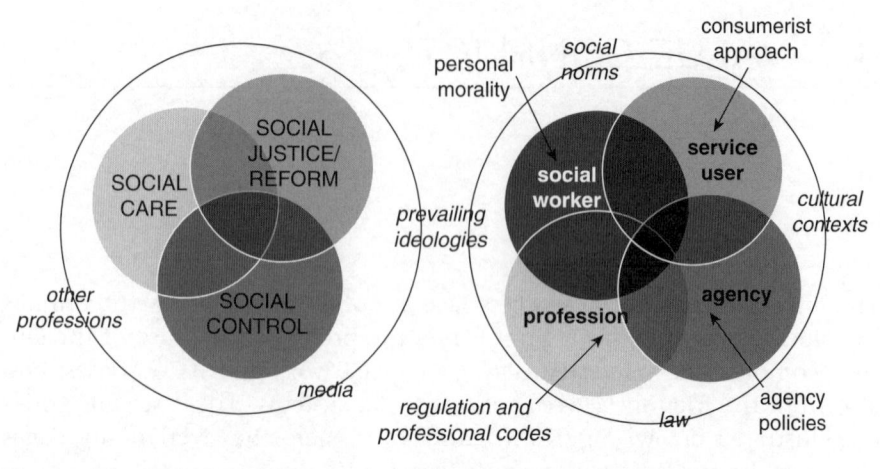

**Figure 4.1** Social work's reason for being

**Figure 4.2** Social work and social systems
(Adapted from Doel *et al.*, 2010.)

## Mind the gap

A daily conflict for many social workers arises from the distance between their own lifestyle and their services users'. Economic differences might be evident not just in daily living conditions, but in opportunities like foreign travel. This gap can feed feelings of guilt. There are parallels with the gap between the wealthy West and the rest of the world: how is it possible, ethically, to buy a plane ticket to a foreign holiday in the knowledge that the cost of that ticket would save the lives of many children in a famine-ridden foreign country? Like our current attitudes to nineteenth-century slavery, perhaps a future generation will look back to our present behaviour with moral repugnance. There is a universal cognitive dissonance that acts as a kind of self-medication against the true horror of these appalling inequalities.

The gap is not just an economic one. A social worker might wonder how her severely depressed service users would feel if they saw her partying at a club when, an hour or so earlier, she had been empathising with their trauma and distress. Is this compartmentalisation a human dilemma or an ethical dilemma and is this a salient distinction (Das and Kulkarni, 2006b)?

## Earn your crust

At the height of the radical social work movement in the 1970s there was a phrase coined, 'revolution on the rates', that poked fun at the moral ambiguity of Marxist social workers drawing their monthly pay packet from the very system they were apparently intent on overthrowing. Though we are at radical low tide for social work, there are nevertheless plenty of value conflicts for social workers working in organisations that from time to time compromise notions of good practice in social work (Dolgoff *et al.*, 2009). My first job after qualifying in social work was in an agency where I felt the practices were oppressive to the people whom it served, and the agency's systems impeded rather than facilitated good practice. However, it paid my salary and I was far from home. In the end the conflict in values, and the difficulty in making any significant changes, led me to resign.

We must ask ourselves: 'Do social workers work "at" or "for" their employing organisations?' To what extent, then, ought a social worker's priorities and the way they work be determined by the role as it is defined by their employer? How far from the individual practitioner can the power of this decision be removed before it becomes unacceptable, even unethical? For example, social workers working in the market-driven environment of much American mental health practice find that decisions about where they can put their time and resources are determined by insurance companies. The values of accounting and actuarialism are applied to judgements that were once professional and, if they wish to earn their crust, social workers must accept them.

### Time box

An extreme example of the value conflicts concerning social workers 'earning their crust' was the 1978–9 strike in various local authorities in the UK – part of the infamous 'winter of discontent'. A secret ballot of about 400 social work staff was held in my social services department to determine whether to strike for better pay and a career structure. The vote resulted in a wafer-thin majority of nine in favour of strike action. Value conflicts are not usually settled with a vote, not in professional settings, but the dominant organisational model at that time was industrial rather than the current corporate model.

All participating in the ballot had placed their trust in this democratic, majoritarian system and so the result carried moral authority even for those who had voted against. There was some compromising, with those who had voted against striking permitted to staff a rota for a team responding to severe emergencies. There was collective trust that this team would respect the terms of 'severe emergency' and not continue to work normally. Certainly, everyone was counted as 'on strike' and therefore made the collective sacrifice of loss of salary.

The conflicts were common ones about long-term and short-term value: ought the short-term suffering of service users deprived of a social work service (and the hardship for social workers and their families through loss of income) outweigh the long-term benefit of a properly rewarded profession that would then attract the best calibre of entrants?

## Square a circle

In traditional societies such as the Georgian Republic, social workers often find their 'new' adopted professional values clash with the families from which they come and with the communities where they are placed; for example, extremely stigmatising social attitudes to homosexuality and people with HIV (Doel *et al.*, 2016). In India, clients are likely to accept bribery as a way of life and as the only way some officials earn enough to live; in contrast, social workers might consider it their moral obligation to fight bribery (Das and Kulkarni, 2006a). Ought social workers refuse to bribe even if this will prevent their clients from gaining the resources they need and the clients themselves accept bribery?

The norms in social democracies are possibly in more harmony with social work than the examples from Georgia and India above; nevertheless, clashes between social attitudes and social work values, and between individual social workers and service users, can feel like trying to square a circle. How should a social worker respond when a service user uses racist language? Social workers can feel conflicted between the values of help and care, and those of challenging discrimination. They might also find it difficult to judge the balance between risk to the relationship as a result of a challenge, and risk to their integrity by colluding with racist values (more on risk in Chapter 6).

## Walk this way

Is it better to make your own worse decision or another's better one? Social workers often have a strong sense of what would be best for their service user, but offering opinions conflicts with the professional values of self-determination. Proffering solutions is a form of judgement and this can be detrimental to the service user's own decision-making capacities. On the other hand, a direction given at the right moment can prevent the service user making costly mistakes, perhaps helping them to avoid a potentially destructive relationship. Of course, there are occasions when social workers must take full control of decision-making on behalf of other people, as we explored in the previous chapter.

## Plug a hole

One of the central tenets of social work is that it is a holistic discipline in which practitioners work with the individual in the context of their family, community and broader society. Social workers are educated to understand the socio-political reasons for individuals' circumstances – the relationship between public policy and private experience and, ultimately, the links between poverty, health and social well-being. What moral obligations does this knowledge confer? At what level of intervention ought the social work to take place and how does 'good' social work take account of the charge of applying sticking plasters to one problem at a time when the problems themselves are so often related to public policy? There are constant value conflicts when the numbers who are eligible and could benefit from social work far exceed the resources available. What are the ethics of social triage?

## Meet the neighbours

For many years (up until the 1990s) British social workers worked in large public sector 'social services departments' with a director who by law was a qualified social worker. Social workers are now more commonly employed in multi-professional settings where professional values might be interpreted differently from one professional grouping to another, but close proximity means that some form of value conflicts is likely.

A classic tension is that between medical and social models of practice. For example, a medical model of obesity would consider the biological and psychological factors that lead an individual to become overweight; a social model would consider the link between poverty and obesity and the unregulated policies of the food and drinks industry, the effects of advertising, and environmental factors that inhibit walking and other activity. The medical and social models of obesity are not incompatible, but there are value conflicts about blame and responsibility.

The growth of interprofessional education means that students are likely to come into direct contact with different professional cultures and the values that support them. The hope is that with early contact will come understanding and accommodation (CAIPE, 2012).

## Four responses to value conflicts

When working with value conflicts that involve you and others, what options do you have? Let us consider a typography of response, then illustrate with example dilemmas.

### Compete

The conflicting value systems are seen as irreconcilable, the one a threat to the other. This leads to assertive, competitive behaviour in order to establish a dominant set of values.

*Compromise*

Attempts are made to settle the conflict by pragmatic moves to a convergence ('halfway between the two') or a compromise that takes something from one value and something from the other and melds them.

*Concede*

As with Competing, the values are seen as irreconcilable; one of the parties in the conflict gives way and accepts the others' values.

*Avoid*

There is an agreement, usually implicit, to pretend there is no value conflict by 'turning a blind eye' or using delaying tactics, sometimes called 'kicking into the long grass'.

## Exploring dilemmas

**Charlotte** is a social worker working with a family services agency. She has strong views about abortion, believing that it is morally wrong; indeed, she considers it to be murder. **Daniella**, one of her service users, is pregnant and wants to terminate the pregnancy.

**1. How ought Charlotte to respond to Daniella's desire to terminate her pregnancy?**

First, let us examine what choices are open to Charlotte using the compete, compromise, concede and avoid framework.

**a.** *Compete* by promoting her own principles.
Charlotte could allow herself to be led by her beliefs. This means challenging Daniella's decision, explaining why termination is wrong and advising her against it.

**b.** *Compromise* by seeking a balance.
Charlotte could disclose her own beliefs to Daniella, discuss the case against termination and suggest that she seeks advice from others who can offer the alternative case.

**c.** *Concede* by keeping quiet.
Charlotte could choose not to disclose her own beliefs and let Daniella make her decision alone.

▶

◀

**d.** *Avoid* by opting out.

Charlotte could ask her agency to provide a different social worker for Daniella on the grounds that she cannot offer balanced advice.

Let us consider the ethical dimensions involved in these choices. The main conflict, for Charlotte, lies between her desire to assert her own needs (not to inflict pain on herself by acting contrary to deeply held beliefs) and her belief in principles of self-determination that allow others to come to their own choices based on a balanced discussion of the options available. In an extreme case Charlotte might not feel that there is a dilemma, because when a human life is at stake (the foetus, as she sees it), compromise is not possible and that, though Daniella does not realise it, Daniella's moral interests are best served by keeping the baby.

However, Charlotte does face a number of difficulties if she pursues this position. First, is Charlotte working in a country that sanctions abortion through law? Charlotte might ask how the 'murder' of a foetus can be right in one part of the planet and not in another, possibly in places with common borders. An additional conflict for Charlotte is that she is a member of a profession, social work, which sanctions self-determination. In Daniella's case, this means the rights of women over the rights of the unborn.

There is also an ethical dilemma concerning self-disclosure. On the one hand, there is a good argument that Daniella has a right to know whether her social worker has a view and, if so, whether it is strongly held; on the other hand, Charlotte has rights to privacy and we would not normally find it acceptable for a social worker to be asked, for instance, to disclose their religion.

## What we learn from Charlotte and Daniella's situation

What is interesting is that the decisions about whether to compete, compromise, concede or avoid are not confined to the Charlotte/Daniella situation. Although this particular dilemma and clash of beliefs (between what is brutally over-simplified as 'pro-life' and 'pro-choice') is a common and readily accessible one, it also points the way to ethical dilemmas at a general level. Whatever the specifics of the situation, the dilemma is frequently whether to *compete* (to enter the race and assert your own beliefs and ethical position), to *compromise* (to recognise the various ethical positions that are possible and to aim for a pragmatic resolution that either takes them all on board or charts some middle or third course), to *concede* (not to assert your own beliefs, to 'park them') or *avoid* by circumventing the dilemma and finding a way of not having to face it.

▶

◀

**2. Is Charlotte's moral ground changed if she works for an agency that promotes the rights of the unborn?**

Let us consider Charlotte's wider world. She has chosen to work for *Life*, a charity in the voluntary sector that promotes the rights of the unborn. Does this affect the ethics of the options that are available to her, such as those explored in the previous section?

Certainly, by choosing to apply to work at *Life* Charlotte knew what would be expected of her as an employee of the organisation. She knows that her own ethical choice (if it is to 'compete' with Daniella's) will be supported by her employer. We might suppose that if Daniella has approached *Life* she knows what to expect, but this is not necessarily the case. Perhaps she has been referred there by a health professional who shares the same belief system (that others would describe as prejudices) as Charlotte and is hopeful that *Life* can persuade Daniella to follow what she, the health professional, considers to be the right course of action. Perhaps Daniella is feeling equivocal and wants someone to tell her to keep the baby and that is why she has chosen to go to *Life*. For instance, if you are canvassing for a political party no one would reasonably expect you to present a balanced view by also advancing the policies of other parties.

**3. Charlotte's life circumstances are very different from Daniella's. Does this have an impact on the 'moral landscape'?**

Charlotte comes from a comfortable, middle class, white British home. She has had a relatively privileged background – her parents are wealthy and have given her a stable, loving upbringing. She excelled academically and she was head-hunted for a well-paid, relatively low stress job; instead she chose to become a social worker, following a sense of duty, a desire to 'repay' her good fortune, and also to work at something she saw as ethically demanding. Being honest with herself she recognises a lot of guilt, too, arising from her awareness of her fortunate life. Charlotte has had a number of relationships and is always careful to take precautions against pregnancy, but she knows that if she became pregnant in a situation where she did not want to remain in a relationship with the father then her parents would support her, emotionally, practically and financially.

Daniella was brought up in care. Her mother has learning difficulties and she has not seen her for two years. Daniella has never known her father. Her life is described in the substantial case notes as 'chaotic' and as 'living from hand to mouth'. Nineteen years old now, she has already had one termination of pregnancy. She has few social supports and

▶

drifts on the edge of a drug-using group that commits low-scale crime to fund its drug use.

Does the contrast in the lives of Charlotte and Daniella give either of the two any 'moral authority' in their encounter? Charlotte has education and training, Daniella has lived experience. Can Charlotte advise a person whose life story and current circumstances are in such stark contrast to her own? Does it make a difference that the child that Daniella would bring into the world will have such different life chances to a child of Charlotte's? Is what is right for one not necessarily right for another? – an example of **moral relativism**?

Charlotte is aware that these two lives, hers and Daniella's, are a world apart. Except they are not.

Unknown to anybody but a few close friends, Charlotte works as a dancer in a nearby town at a nightclub, ironically also called *Life*. She has always been fiercely independent from her parents and does not accept financial help from them, and she finds that her social worker salary at a voluntary agency does not fund the lifestyle that she wants to maintain. Moreover, Charlotte gets a kick from her work as a dancer and, having recently decided that she is not bisexual but lesbian, she has found it a surprisingly good way to meet partners.

One Friday night a new woman starts work in the club. It's Daniella.

4. **What, if any, ethical dilemmas arise from Charlotte and Daniella being colleagues at the nightclub?**
Does Daniella's response to this revelation alter the moral landscape? Say she feels that it brings Charlotte closer to her own situation and, rather than seeing Charlotte as a toff, she now thinks of her as someone who shares some part of her own lifestyle. Alternatively, say Charlotte is sullied in Daniella's eyes; at least she, Daniella, has little alternative to this work, but Charlotte has the education and background to better herself.

Whatever Daniella's response to the revelation that Charlotte works in the nightclub, it doesn't change the fact that she *does* work there – so can Daniella's response affect the fundamental ethics of the situation? And are the ethics changed if, for instance, Daniella's attitude changes from one of moral repugnance to one of moral respect, once Charlotte has the opportunity to discuss her situation? In terms of **virtue ethics**, Daniella's view of Charlotte's character might be significantly altered by this encounter in *Life*, the nightclub. At another level, however, it feels that the rights or wrongs of Charlotte's behaviour are the rights and wrongs, full stop, and that they shouldn't flip-flop according to how Daniella chooses to view the situation.

5. **Does Charlotte's second employment bring her profession into disrepute?**
Ought Charlotte to have informed her employer that she is working at the other *Life*? Her employer might claim that she is bringing the agency into disrepute, alongside the social work regulator's concerns that her night work also brings the profession into disrepute. However, what is meant by 'disrepute' in these circumstances – does it just mean going against the norms – and who is doing the disreputing? Charlotte might claim to have taken reasonable precautions by taking up her second employment in another town, using an alias in the club and not talking about her day job.

Does the nature of the dancing affect the judgements – if it includes pole-dancing or lap dancing, for instance? Does her state of dress or undress have a bearing? Are Charlotte's motives material to the discussion – is it relatively more acceptable if economic circumstances forced her to find other employments, as opposed to her finding thrills from the work or, even more 'culpable', a route to make sexual contacts? Or, if there is a transgression does this stem from the failure (dishonesty?) of not informing her social work employer that she has a second job? If that is the case, ought she, then, to have informed *Life* (the club) of her employment as a social worker at the voluntary organisation, or is that different? What if Charlotte makes more money at the nightclub than from the voluntary agency – does that make social work her secondary employment, something that provides her with pocket money?

Does your view of Charlotte's employment at the nightclub change depending on which of the following two situations pertains and, if so, why?

1. **Charlotte.01** has no idea that there could be any ethical problems in working at the nightclub and just decided that's what she wanted to do.

2. **Charlotte.02** has asked herself all the questions posed above and, having weighed the possible answers, has come to a considered decision that it is ethically acceptable for her to work at the nightclub. She can explain her reasoning when asked by her supervisor at the social work agency.

There is no difference in the outcome – Charlotte.01 and Charlotte.02 end up working at *Life* the nightclub – so **consequentialist** ethical reasoning would suggest that your view ought not to be influenced by this information. However, **virtue ethics** would see good in Charlotte.02, someone who is exercising moral judgement and making a decision on the basis of it. On the other hand, a cynic might consider that she is better than Charlotte.01 at rationalising what she wants to do and dressing it up in ethical reasoning.

Charlotte and Daniella get to know one another better at *Life* the nightclub than they ever did in *Life* the voluntary agency, to the extent that Daniella confides to Charlotte that she is HIV-positive.

**6. What ought Charlotte to do with the knowledge that Daniella is HIV-positive?**

Daniella has not informed the nightclub that she is HIV-positive. The nightclub is strict that there should be no sexual contact between the dancers and the clientele, so no risk is posed to the customers or other dancers. However, Daniella confides to Charlotte that she has not informed her partner with whom she is having unprotected sex. Daniella has found stability and happiness for herself and her baby (she was convinced by *Life*'s promises of help not to pursue the abortion) and she is afraid that her partner will leave if he finds out that she is HIV-positive.

What are Charlotte's moral obligations at this point? She has discovered this information not as a social worker but as a dancer – Daniella is both service user and co-worker. Charlotte is aware that there would be no baby without the support and persuasion of the social work agency; looking back, would the knowledge that Daniella was HIV-positive have influenced her advice? Charlotte might wonder why Daniella made this recent revelation, perhaps speculating that at some level Daniella wants to be advised to inform her partner, with a hope that Charlotte can provide enough support to help Daniella to sustain the relationship. Or did it all come out after a night's work and several vodkas, with Daniella now adamant that Charlotte should just forget it? (See Chapter 8, 'Sharing Information and Confidentiality').

In the meantime, Charlotte has decided to tell her supervisor **Francis** about her work at the nightclub.

**7. What ought Charlotte's supervisor, Francis, do with the knowledge that Charlotte is working as a dancer at the nightclub?**

In Chapter 2 we looked at different models of ethical discourse and you might briefly look back to pages 11–16 before reading on.

With these in mind, we will consider four different Francises:

1. **Francis.01** subscribes to a **duty-based, Kantian** system of ethics.

2. **Francis.02** is a **utilitarian**.

3. **Francis.03** bases his judgements on **virtue ethics**.

4. **Francis.04** bases his judgements on **care ethics**.

How might the different Francises come to each of their decisions about what to do, and how might these decisions differ?

A composite, eclectic Francis, or a Francis who is just not really aware of his moral reasoning, might draw up a list of factors to consider. I've started a checklist that you can add to. What might each factor tell us about Francis's ethical stance?

*treating the situation ...*

*... lightly ...* ⟵—————————⟶ *... seriously ...*

**Cons**

Charlotte has broken the rules about second employment

She risks the reputation of the agency

**Pros**

Charlotte is a good social worker

Her service users like her

Her colleagues like her

If she goes her post will be frozen and not replaced

No harm has been done

She 'came clean' herself

Charlotte found out important information by working at the night club that she didn't get through her formal social work

I have a good relationship with Charlotte

She risks bringing the profession into disrepute

Working evenings could affect her concentration on the day job

Charlotte risks more 'dual relationships' like the one with Daniella – what if she were to meet a male service user at the club?

When the team find out it could put a strain on team relationships

Francis is a **moral agent** in this situation; in other words he is a person with values that inform his actions. The beliefs and opinions that spring from his values will influence his judgement about what to do. Let us consider these possible beliefs:

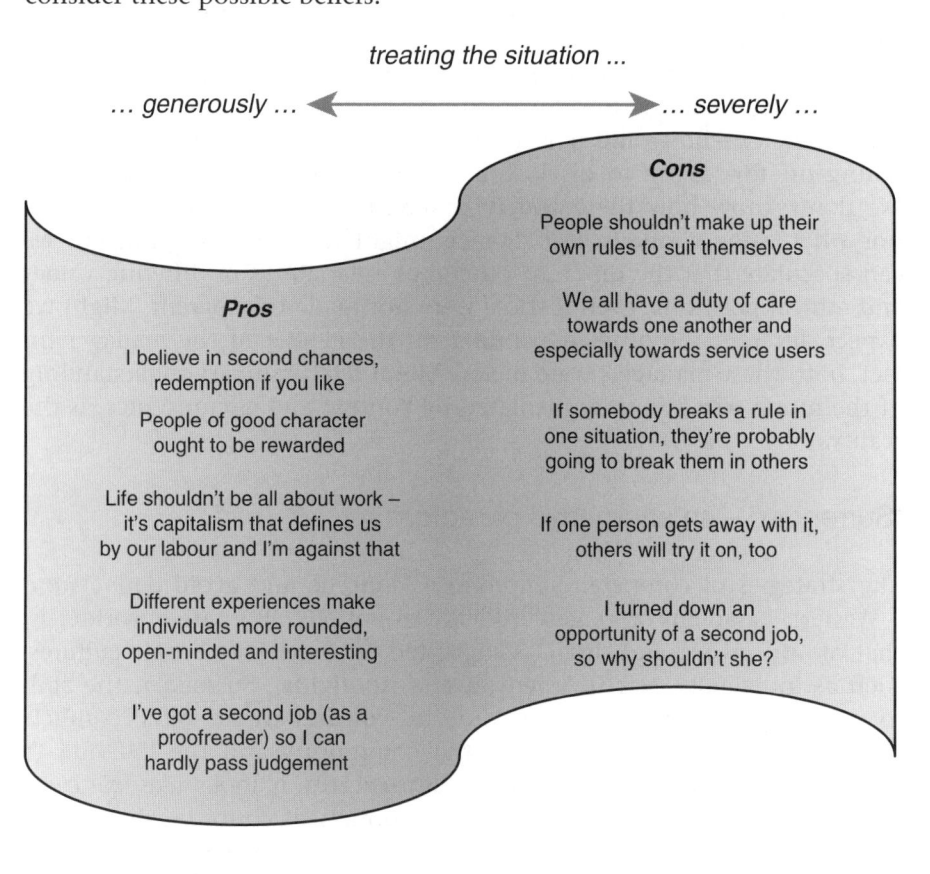

*treating the situation ...*

*... generously ...* ⟵——————————⟶ *... severely ...*

**Cons**

People shouldn't make up their own rules to suit themselves

**Pros**

We all have a duty of care towards one another and especially towards service users

I believe in second chances, redemption if you like

People of good character ought to be rewarded

If somebody breaks a rule in one situation, they're probably going to break them in others

Life shouldn't be all about work – it's capitalism that defines us by our labour and I'm against that

If one person gets away with it, others will try it on, too

Different experiences make individuals more rounded, open-minded and interesting

I turned down an opportunity of a second job, so why shouldn't she?

I've got a second job (as a proofreader) so I can hardly pass judgement

Francis is a person with certain life experiences and these, too, will influence his judgement of what he feels he ought to do with the knowledge that Charlotte has an evening job at the nightclub. For example, what bearing might these different life histories have:

Francis has recently returned from four years living and working as a social work manager on a small Pacific island where everyone knew everyone, most people had two, three or more jobs and **dual relationships** such as Charlotte and Daniella's were commonplace.

Francis is experiencing an acrimonious divorce from his partner, who left him to live with the owner of a nightclub.

◀

From an ethical point of view, *ought* these different life histories to influence the path that Francis chooses? We have evidence that, right or wrong, they do: Charlotte's situation, working as a dancer in a lap dancing club in her own time, was used as one of the scenarios in a research study of professional boundaries (Doel *et al.*, 2010: 1889). The responses ranged from a social work manager who would expect the social worker to face disciplinary action and likely be sacked to another manager in the same city who would talk it over in supervision and give her a light telling off for failing to disclose it (so, these different Francises exist). We don't know how these widely different conclusions were reasoned, nor what value conflicts each Francis might have tussled with, but we can speculate that the different outcomes emanate from differing values and ethical positions, even if these were not made transparent. Might we expect different responses depending on the gender of the manager (in fact, both these managers were male)? Moral relativism, an understanding of the moral world heavily mediated by context and circumstance, is the reality.

## 'Surrender' – an alternative paradigm

The strategies of compete, compromise, concede and avoid derive from a Western paradigm of value conflicts. An entirely alternative worldview, that of **surrender** and ritual, is suggested by some First People cultures, such as indigenous North American and Aboriginal. Surrender, the ability to let go, is fundamental to holistic cultures where value conflicts are subsumed in the solidarity of the community and the individual's will is gifted to a collective wisdom; superficially it looks like 'concede' but it stands in contrast to the Western notion of concede which is an individual choice in the face of another, often more powerful, individual. Surrender is a collective experience, often enacted through ritual in ceremonies that promote a sense of oneness at a spiritual rather than a material level (Some, 1997). This 'letting go' arises in cultures where there is a high level of empathy and interdependence, not just human but animal and natural (Rifkin, 2009). Surrender has parallels with Western notions of suspending judgement, with a similar release of creativity. Surrender is also one way of looking at the collective decision to 'let go' to the will of the majority vote in the social workers' strike described in the time box for 1978 (page 49).

However, when non-local cultures meet, surrender becomes more difficult as there is no singular authority to embrace a collective letting go. Even

▶

◀

so, empathy can enable communities with contrasting values to understand each other and to learn from one another. In practical terms, this would mean a local service placing sufficient value on the needs of a minority population that it adapts to meet these needs, rather than requiring the minority population to adapt to the service.

Viewing value conflicts through the prism of an alternative paradigm stimulates us to consider different kinds of value conflict, ones that at first seem tangential to professional life but touch on it nevertheless. For instance, in a child's early schooling what ought to be the relative value placed on playfulness and on formal learning? This conflict in values, between those that emphasise the child as a creative and inquisitive social learner and those that emphasise early years schooling as the foundation for numeracy and literacy skills, will have a direct impact on a social worker working with the children and staff in a school.

# The Big Picture

## Volunteer tourism

There is an increase in the numbers of people from advantaged countries seeking to volunteer their labour in overseas disadvantaged communities (Benson, 2011). Volunteer tourism, as it is known, has encouraged the growth of companies seeking to make a profit from this activity, as well as non-governmental organisations with relatively little experience of cross-national work joining the field. There are valid concerns about whether organisations dependent on raising funds via volunteer tourism that make profits in order to pay executive salaries are able to maintain ethical practices to the best professional standards.

What are the value conflicts in volunteer tourism and can they be reconciled? On the one hand we ought to be concerned to offer long-term solutions to global poverty and structural inequality; on the other we feel a moral obligation to give humanitarian assistance to wherever the current manifestation of global inequality has erupted. Is the volunteer's motivation one of altruistic giving of time and labour or fulfilment of a desire to visit exotic parts (volunteer tourists do not visit the 'colonies' of deprivation and poverty within their own country) or an opportunity for bragging on a blog, or a complex mix of these and other motives; and, if the time and labour 'do good' does it matter what the motivation is?

What if volunteer tourism produces 'wrongs'; for example, potential negative aspects of volunteering in orphanages and institutions? (UNCRC,

1989). Are volunteer tourists taking moral care to ensure that the organisations that they volunteer with conduct an ethical audit of the impact of the work, including its sustainability?

## Guidance from Codes, Standards and Principles

The IFSW/IASSW joint Statement of Ethical Principles (2004) recognises value conflicts in the reasons why social workers face problems:

> ➤ The fact that the loyalty of social workers is often in the middle of conflicting interests.

> ➤ The fact that social workers function as both helpers and controllers.

> ➤ The conflicts between the duty of social workers to protect the interests of the people with whom they work and societal demands for efficiency and utility.

> ➤ The fact that resources in society are limited.

Would it help if there were a clause in the professional code of practice that gave guidance about when a question of personal conscience took precedence over professional code? Would it be right to allow individual practitioners to excuse themselves from certain situations, ones that they see as morally compromising? For instance, in the example earlier, should Charlotte be allowed not to work with Daniella because she did not feel able to offer neutral advice?

In terms of clashes between the value of a personal life and the value of work, the IFSW/IASSW (2004: 5.6) Statement asserts that 'Social workers have a duty to take necessary steps to care for themselves professionally and personally in the workplace and in society, in order to ensure that they are able to provide appropriate services.'

## Consulting the wise professionals

Finally, how might the **wise professionals** respond to the discussion on value conflicts? They are likely to be clear that there is no Answer, no easy algorithm to apply. Indeed the wise professionals probably see personal beliefs, professional codes of practice and religious creeds as crude attempts to simplify situations and line them up against a slide rule of value judgements. However, they are equally unlikely to find satisfaction in an approach that is so flexible that it judges each and every situation as it stands, with no regard to any fixed points.

Perhaps the wise professionals can suggest some fixed points; not ones as specific as 'abortion is right' or 'abortion is wrong' but ones that can be applied to each and every situation to help us decide what they mean from one case to another and, therefore, what actions suggest themselves after careful interrogation of the circumstances. How about these?:

> What is fair in this situation?

> What is generous in this situation?

> What is kind in this situation?

At first glance fairness, generosity and kindness seem rather general, even slippery, concepts – but therein lies their strength. If you consider any act, personal, political or both, in history (the execution of Anne Boleyn, the defenestrations of Prague, the Holocaust) and apply the principles of fairness, generosity and kindness, we can say with reasonable certainty that they would have changed events for the better. This is not to suppose that there are not circumstances when it is right not to act with fairness, generosity and kindness: an undercover agent for the French resistance in the Second World War might regularly have to act against these principles in their personal conduct, though might reasonably argue a higher level 'fairness, generosity and kindness' that motivated their individual contrarian acts.

In Charlotte's case the wise professionals could reasonably argue that the suggestion that Charlotte be permitted to absent herself from work with Daniella because she did not feel able to offer unbiased advice would satisfy the notion of fairness, that it would be generous to Charlotte to allow her not to be in that situation and that it would be kind to Daniella to let her have access to someone with no strong moral opinions about abortion. Wisdom would suggest that we test these principles further. In the case of value conflicts these wise professionals are leaning, thus far, towards an **ethics of care.**

# 5   DECISION-MAKING

**Time box**

'A student approached the existentialist, Jean-Paul Sartre, for help with a moral quandary. The student was faced with a choice between going to England to join the Free French Forces and staying in France to care for his ageing mother. As each option held a different type of moral attraction for him, he asked Sartre for advice as to how he should resolve this practical dilemma.

'After considering the student's situation, Sartre responded with what must have seemed a very unhelpful suggestion: "You are free, so choose." At first glance, Sartre's response may seem to support an interpretation of his ethical theory as a form of subjectivism. However, Sartre's recognition that, in this type of situation, no theory of morality could help the student decide how to act does not necessarily entail that there are no objective values. It may simply be that moral values are such that they do not always point to a single course of action.' (Crowe, 2004: 29)

All the dilemmas in this book require a decision, even when the decision is to do nothing. As illustrated in 'Time box: 1940', Sartre's moral universe has us all free to choose – or condemned to choose, depending on how we see each decision-making event. The story also lends the insight that dilemmas and decision-making are by no means always about binary choices, either *this* or *that*. The limits of moral reasoning are not just that 'the scales' might fail to help us decide which of the pans is the weightier, but that the pans themselves might be inadequate or fail to provide us with the full story. Joseph and Fernandes (2006), for instance, consider that the dilemmas of difficult decisions spring not from a choice between two sides of the same coin (honesty/dishonesty) but the tension of having to choose between two *different* coins (e.g. the honesty/dishonesty coin and the causing harm/avoiding harm coin). Choosing to avoid harm might incur dishonesty, the latter not chosen as dishonesty per se but as a collateral to avoiding harm. In other words, one good (avoiding harm) has trumped another good (honesty).

One difficulty that can corrupt the decision-making process is the impact of tacit values – a failure to recognise the different 'coins'; for instance, a lack of awareness that one party is placing a high value on loyalty to the agency, whilst another has a premium on honesty, and yet another values the primacy of self-determination. These approaches may well converge to an agreed position, but they might not. Making what is valued open and transparent does not immediately resolve a disagreement but it makes it easier to consider the basis for the conflict.

It might be the choices that are creating a dilemma or perhaps it is the decision-making process itself that presents a conflict, say between **deontological** (duty-based) and **utilitarian** (outcome) approaches to decision-making (O'Sullivan, 1999).

## Value patterning

As well as the differences in the qualities that are valued, such as loyalty and honesty, participants in decision-making can have different ethical preferences. This is sometimes referred to as **value patterning** – 'current ethical decisions as linked to other ethical decisions [the social worker has] made in the past or will make in the future' (Mattison, 2000: 201). Social workers can gain a better understanding of their value patterning by considering the values or ethical principles to which they give priority from among competing alternatives.

The pattern of decision-making that reveals an individual's values might be nuanced and emerge only over a period of time and observation. A more transparent and rule-bound pattern of decision-making can be observed in *triage*. This is a classic form of decision-making based on **principlism**. It is a kind of 'extreme ethics' for situations such as the horrors of how to prioritise limited medical resources during a cataclysm like war. The primary principle is the value of life and an equality of decision-making based on the likelihood of saving life not the value of one particular life weighed against another. So, each decision is made irrespective of the value each separate life might have to the wider community. Although practical medical judgements must be made (as to how likely it is that this particular life can be saved), triage allows speedy judgements to be formed. It is an example of **rule utilitarianism**, where the rule is the saving of life. For situations of great emergency and survival it functions well by squaring pragmatism with 'quick ethics'.

Implicit values can be too comfortably shared amongst participants and the pattern hard-set, so that there is a too-easy convergence on a decision. This 'groupthink' results in a failure to achieve the best decision because of the lack of diverse values (Turner and Pratkanis, 1998). In focusing on the individual as a decision-maker we mustn't underestimate the local forces that influence his or her decision-making and the potential for implicitly coercive decision-making.

## Making decisions for others

In residential and day care facilities where individuals live in close-knit, interdependent groups it is important to emphasise the value of individualisation and empowerment (Frost *et al.*, 1999; Ward, 2007), for much decision-making has to be shared. There are special ethical responsibilities when workers have 24-hour care of people and when a person is highly restricted in their ability to communicate. As we explored in Chapter 3, there are occasions when social workers find themselves deciding a course for others because a decision that ought to be in the hands of the service user has been given to someone else as a result of a judgement about the incapacity of the person to make decisions.

When there is competition for the same resource, social workers make decisions for others who nevertheless have very full decision-making capacities. We should be mindful that this *is* decision-making on behalf of others and that it can have life-changing implications for the person who is awarded the resource and also for those who are denied it.

> You are a member of a resource group that decides on the allocation of new flats in *The Complex,* a sheltered housing complex. Some residents need assisted living such as help with personal needs, and it is the housing association's policy to have mixed occupancy of the complex, so that people of different ages and capacities are welcomed. The accommodation is highly valued and a two-bedroom apartment has come available. You have six applications. Before you read through them, make yourself a quick list of criteria you would expect to use. Put the list to one side for now and read through the applications.

*Petra Pierce and Penny*

> I am a single parent with a 22-year-old daughter with learning difficulties. Currently we are living at some distance from any day care activities for my daughter, but *The Complex* is very close to a centre that would give her valuable daytime stimulation and some respite for me.

*Mr and Mrs Quinn*

> We have recently been approved as foster parents but our current accommodation has no spare bedroom, so a move to this flat in *The Complex* would allow us to foster a child.

*Rebecca Ryan on behalf of Mrs Rose*

I am writing this statement on behalf of my mother. I have recently divorced and I am planning on moving back to be near my mother. However, because of the schooling situation for my son, for whom I have custody, I will be living across the city from her current address. The possibility of this new accommodation for my mother is ideal since it would be close to my new home and I could give her the kind of support she clearly needs. I fear that without this support she will not be able to maintain her independent living and that she would be at risk of needing residential care. Also, she tells me that she is much disturbed by her current neighbours and is unhappy about the general quality of the area and the type of people who are moving in. The spare bedroom in the flat at *The Complex* would mean her grandson could come and stay from time to time.

*Sheila and Sandra Sutter*

I am a partially sighted person, registered blind. My local shop has closed and the nearest shops are across a very busy road with no nearby crossing, so I'm dependent on the kindness of others. My sister and I live together and her sight is also deteriorating through macular degeneration. *The Complex* is ideally suited for shops and pubs for people with sight problems and a move would greatly increase independence and confidence for both of us.

*Touma family*

We came to this country from Syria six months ago, my wife, me and our two young daughters. Now we are living in one-bedroom flat, very damp with water running down walls and neighbours who abuse. Police don't stop them. In *Complex* we already know people, some from Syria, and we know flats are good and move would make our lives much better.

*Udo and Uzoma Uba*

My son is 28 and he is clinically obese. At present we are renting on the third floor of a house and he can't manage the stairs any more, so it's two months since he got out. He has become depressed and this makes him eat more, and it makes me worried for his future, not to mention mine. This ground floor flat at *The Complex* would be ideal and when I discussed it with him it was the first time I've seen him look excited about anything in a great while. I think it could be a kick-start to get him doing things again and agreeing to a stomach clamp which the doctor has recommended.

If this decision were taking place in the nineteenth century the central question would be the morality of the individual applicants, their virtues and character, linked to a strong sense of the deserving and the undeserving. Increasingly during the twentieth century the focus turned to rights and, more recently, a risk assessment approach is likely to be applied, perhaps formalised into 'a points system'. Reamer (1998) suggests that social work ethics is evolutionary. If this is so, how is social work ethics likely to adapt and develop in the future?

The need for decision-making can, itself, feel problematic and present dilemmas. Ought the resource group be campaigning for more housing rather than consigning five out of six applicants to inappropriate accommodation? Ought they be raising awareness of the impact of housing policy such as the Right To Buy council house scheme, or is this politics rather than social work?

---

Although the decision-making in these following example dilemmas is set in the context of fostering and adoption, the ethical issues are universal and transpose to other fields of social work practice and life in society.

## Exploring dilemmas 1

**Adam** is a three-year old who has been in foster care with **Mr and Mrs Brown** for a year. Adam's birth mother, **Cassie Cook**, had subjected him to unnecessary medical interventions with fictitious illnesses and there remain fears about her mental health. Adam is thriving at the Browns, who have two children of their own aged six and eight. A plan for adoption has been agreed and an adoptive family, **Mr and Mrs Dean**, has been identified for Adam. The Deans' professional backgrounds have given them much experience of talking to children about difficult issues and they have two children the same ages as the Browns'. Cassie's situation, her mental health and the possibility that she will search persistently for Adam does not faze them. They are considered to be a strong, open-minded couple.

Four months ago a match between Adam and the Deans was formally approved along with a plan to place Adam following contacts and introductions. The following month, after a series of hearings,

▶

Cassie's application to appeal the original orders was successful and the introduction plans halted as the court ruled that the adoption could not take place until the full hearing. The Deans and their children had already met Adam. Mrs Dean had resigned her position because her employer was proving unhelpful.

With court delays the appeal is not likely to be heard for another five months and the Deans wondered about the possibility of fostering Adam in the meantime, as there is a very strong likelihood that Adam will be released for adoption in due course. However, legal advice was that the court was likely to reject a change of foster parents.

**Erna**, the adoption social worker, has just learned that the Browns have telephoned the Deans to say that they, the Browns, want to adopt Adam. A visit to the Browns confirms that they have all the information they need on which to base their decision.

A meeting of professionals is called to consider the new situation and to make decisions about what to do.

**1. What ought the outcome of the meeting to be?**

Make a note now of your first 'gut' response to this question before we weigh the situation more carefully.

As we saw in Chapter 2 there is a difference between what *is* and what *ought to be*; nevertheless the first step to deciding what *ought to be* is to understand and agree on what *is*. What are the known and relevant facts of the case? Each person in the meeting should have an equal opportunity to add to the list of facts, whatever status or power they are perceived to hold within the group.

In no particular order, these facts might be considered to have a bearing on the decision:

➢ Adam's mother, Cassie, is very likely to lose the appeal in four months' time.

➢ The Browns have given good care for Adam for more than a year and he is thriving there.

➢ Adam has had stability with the Browns for well over a year, more than a third of his life.

➢ The Deans have been scrutinised by the Adoption Panel and are considered to have a high chance of success as adopters. They have made good plans for Adam.

➤ Mrs Dean has gone so far as to give up her work position in preparation for caring for Adam.

➤ Contractually, the Browns have been involved as Adam's foster carers and the Deans have been formally recognised as his would-be adopters.

➤ The Browns are legally able to apply for adoption of Adam, having cared for him for more than a year.

➤ The Browns will make an adoption application even if they do not gain the support of the local authority.

➤ Research indicates that placement moves are a factor in adoption breakdowns and disruptions.

On the basis of the information you have from the earlier passages, are there any other facts that you want to put in place; or any questions of fact that you would wish to ask those at the meeting? For example, you might want to know about the relationship between Adam and the Browns' children.

## 2. What is the dilemma?

Once the nature of the facts have been established, it is important to frame the dilemma as it is experienced by the various members of the meeting. Does each member see the same dilemma or are there different formulations of it and, if so, what gives rise to these variations? It is not uncommon at this point for dilemmas to be framed in the language of moral judgement, with swirls of interpretation. For instance: 'The dilemma is whether we ought to respect the existing agreement with the Deans or whether we should break it and keep Adam's stability at the Browns'.' Value judgements will, of course, be brought into play, but they should be held in abeyance until the meeting has agreed a non-valued statement of the dilemma. Accordingly, the meeting comes to an agreement that:

➤ The dilemma is whether to support the application of the Browns to adopt Adam or whether to support the application of the Deans.

This is both a practice dilemma and a moral one. It is a practical decision as to which of the two applications should receive the meeting's support, but the reasoning that will now inform that decision is moral. It is the professional values of the individuals convened in the meeting that will determine the value given to the one path (the Browns) or the other (the Deans). In some respects this dilemma differs from the strict definition of an ethical dilemma as a necessary choice between two unwanted courses of action (Banks, 2012) because, in this case, it is a choice between two welcome courses of action, and the dilemma is which will be the better not which would be the least worst.

**Freya**, Chair of the meeting, suggests that each person advances a principle that they think ought to be used to determine the outcome to the dilemma, assuming that the court does not uphold the birth mother's appeal.

### 3. What principles ought to come into play?

## Continuity

**Greg** starts the discussion by suggesting that surely there is a moral obligation for continuity so that the bonds of trust are not broken with the various parties. So, continuity would mean that the Browns continue to act as foster carers and the Deans continue as would-be adopters; but others in the meeting suggest that continuity could be used as a principle not just in terms of the agreed plan, but in terms of Adam's care, in which case the reverse decision would be indicated – continuity of Adam's care would suggest a decision in favour of the Browns. Although it seems right that continuity ought to be included as a principle, it seems that it will not necessarily point to one particular path.

## Fairness

**Harriet** thinks the meeting ought to use a principle of fairness. What is the fairest decision to make? When Harriet is pressed on how she would interpret fairness, she turns to a notion of an equal regard for each person in the situation including, of course, Adam's mother, Cassie. It means avoiding prejudice or bias – for instance, a possible bias towards the Deans because they are of a similar professional class to the people in the meeting. It means not advocating for a particular decision because of your own vested interest as social worker for this family or that family. Everyone agrees that an equal respect for persons is central to social work values and that it is right to be impartial, but that it still leaves the decision wide open. ▶

◀

## Least harm

Of course, whichever way the decision goes one family is going to feel enormously let down, so **Ian** wonders which family will be least harmed by the decision and whether this ought to be the principle that guides them – a **utilitarian** approach, perhaps anchored to the social justice of Harriet's fairness principle?

## Primacy of the child

Erna asks the meeting what will be best for Adam, as the decision will have the biggest and longest-lasting effect on his life. She wants to add a fact to the group's list: adoption is primarily a service for children, not the adopters. From this fact, the principle of the primacy of the child's interests follows and from that it follows that the primary principle ought to be a consideration of what is best for Adam (UNCRC, 1989).

The meeting agrees with this logic and the moral reasoning to which it is hitched. It is the fact that adoption by the Deans would mean one more move that is the tipping point leading the meeting to decide to support the Browns' application. This decision manages to combine and to satisfy all four principles – continuity, fairness, least harm and primacy of the child. Happily, it is a unanimous decision. It will be difficult for Erna, as the social worker for the Deans, to break the news to them, but the assiduous ethical process in the meeting will help her with the explanation, as well as her good relationship with the family.

As the Chair of the meeting, Freya's approach was successful because she gave equal standing to all the participants' contributions regardless of formal status or power. Moreover, she provided a framework in which the *is* of the known facts could be both separated from the *ought*, then linked the two together via the various principles that the participants wanted the meeting to consider. Freya clarified the nature of the dilemma that confronted them and she was able to rely on the professionals present to have a virtuous quality of character, often referred to as *professional integrity* (Appleton and Adamson, 2016).

Turning back to the gut decision you made immediately following Question 1, has the subsequent process confirmed or challenged it? What factors could you add to Adam's scenario that might tip the balance of decision in favour of the Deans?

In groups of people who meet regularly it is likely that Erna's principle of the primacy of the child might have been implicitly understood

▶

from the start and Freya's careful process subject to a shortcut. There are understandable reasons why meetings cut to the quick but this increases the danger of groupthink (see earlier). An early consensus in decision-making can arrive at a pre-ordained conclusion, thereby shutting out creative thinking and alternatives. Moreover, the careful unpicking of principles and processes in Freya's decision-making meeting is a useful rehearsal for Erna when it comes to sharing a convincing explanation with the Deans and meeting their likely questions. Of course, the power lies with the courts, so the meeting's decision is not final and could be steamrolled by a court's decision to uphold Cassie's appeal.

## Exploring dilemmas 2

Let us re-cast Adam's situation. He is still in foster care with the Browns, but they no longer wish to move to adoption. Nor is Cassie contesting the plans for adoption. However, in this new situation the approved adopters are not Mr and Mrs Dean but **Ed Evans** and **Fabius Fosco**.

Ed and Fabius are both in their mid-thirties and both were born and raised in Wales. Ed is Welsh–Irish and Fabius is Welsh–Portuguese. They have been partners for eight years, marrying two years ago. They came out to their parents when they decided to marry; Ed's parents already 'knew' and were very supportive, but Fabius's were upset and unaccepting at first. His mother was disappointed that she would not be a grandmother as Fabius is their only child. She is a devout Catholic, but has nevertheless grown to accept Fabius's sexuality and she has met and gets on well with Ed. However, his father remains distant and hides Fabius's sexuality from his side of the family in Portugal 'because of the shame'.

Out of respect for his father's sensibilities, Fabius has not come out to his father's sister who lives in a neighbouring Welsh town, nor the rest of his father's family in Portugal, all of whom would regard his sexuality as a sin. For the same reasons he has not revealed his plans to adopt to the Portuguese extended family, whom he has seen only occasionally since adulthood.

1. **Ought Fabius to disclose his decision to adopt to his father's family?** Can the value of psychological openness be reconciled with family secrets?

**Erna**, the adoption social worker for Fabius and Ed, works for an organisation whose mission is to promote the welfare of children and to meet their best interests. Determining 'best interests' takes skill and judgement and self-knowledge, especially about values. In this situation, as in the previous one, she draws up a list of known facts. She knows that she cannot move automatically from the *is* of facts to the *ought* of ethical decision-making, but she also knows that the one helps the other. These are some givens that she thinks are salient:

> ➢ Lesbian and gay adopters can be cut off from close and extended family because of their sexuality (Mallon and Betts, 2005).

> ➢ Family support is important to successful adoption (Adams, 2012).

> ➢ Adopted children thrive when there is 'psychological openness' about the fact that they are adopted (Cairns, 2008).

> ➢ Consequences of decisions taken now may not show themselves for many years (Selwyn *et al.*, 2014).

Some speculation:

> ➢ If Adam grows up learning that he has been kept secret from one branch of his adoptive family, he might feel inhibited from talking about his own birth family and discovering more about them.

> ➢ If Fabius's family are told about the prospect of Adam's adoption, this might cause a lasting rift between Fabius and his parents, with detrimental effects on the whole family, including Adam.

If Erna takes a **consequentialist** and **utilitarian** approach, weighing the greatest good (or harm) for the greatest number of people, she will need to consider the long-term effects of 'to disclose or not to disclose' on the success of Adam's adoption. As with most utilitarian reckonings this is exceptionally challenging.

The long-term needs of Adam point Erna to a tentative conclusion that Fabius ought to tell his extended family about the prospective adoption. There is no ethical dilemma for Erna about whose decision this should be (she believes it to be Fabius's to make), but her practice dilemma is how she might help him move towards this conclusion.

When Erna discusses what is known about the importance of psychological openness for the likely success of adoption she meets strong

➤

resistance from Fabius who becomes increasingly adamant that he will not consider telling his father's family because of the risks of rupture and the shame his father would feel. He feels sure that Adam will grow up understanding this and that there are plenty of 'normal' families where one branch doesn't speak to the other. At first Ed nods in quiet agreement with Erna's suggestions that adoptive children have their own particular needs and that it could be an added burden for Adam to see himself as a source of potential shame, but he soon closes ranks with Fabius. The two of them make the decision to keep Adam a secret from the Portuguese side of the family and shun Erna's points.

In the light of what she sees as their intransigence, Erna becomes less tentative and firmer in her judgement that Fabius's father's family ought to know the truth of what is happening, even at the risk of a rift. It would, at least, be one born from honesty, rather than a potentially lifelong lie in which Adam is hidden from half of his family. The fact that this is more easily done because they live in Portugal does not alter the psychological rights and wrongs as Erna sees them.

2. **Ought Fabius's unwillingness to disclose his adoption decision to be a 'deal-breaker'?**

Erna feels she has a new insight into Fabius and Ed's family situation and it is one that concerns her. She understands Fabius's fear of adding to the shame his father already feels about his son's sexuality and she reminds herself that her own family and social circumstances contrast sharply with his, but she is surprised that both Fabius and then Ed are so unwilling even to engage with the arguments.

What ought she do with her doubts? Take the story on yourself using the **singularity method** with which you are now familiar, so that you stop at various significant decision points and consider the *oughts* at these points.

# The Big Picture

## 'Public opinion'

There is a bigger picture to most decision-making in social work. In the example dilemmas we have used in this chapter around fostering and adoption, decisions at Erna's level are affected by the policy direction of both the government and the courts, each of which is likely to be influenced by 'public opinion', nebulous though this is. The emphasis in one arena might be the rights of families (for instance in the English courts) and in another there might be pressure for more adoption (from the UK government). Professional opinion might have a more **casuist** approach, taking each case on its particular merits without any particular push from one side or the other. The locus of power to make decisions is an expression of how much value is placed on localism. The values of localism have been losing to those of centralisation despite political rhetoric to the contrary.

## Guidance from Codes, Standards and Principles

BASW's (2014: 10) Code of Ethics states that 'Social workers should work in a way that is honest, reliable and open, clearly explaining their roles, interventions and *decisions* and not seeking to deceive or manipulate people who use their services, their colleagues or employers' (my italics). Freya's conduct of the decision-making meeting in Example 1 (page 71) will have helped Erna to live up to BASW's principle in her explanations to the Deans about the decision to support the Browns' adoption application.

The Australian code of ethics (AASW 2010: 14) recognises the complexity of ethical decision making: 'It requires time for critical reflection and should involve all those with an interest in the outcome of the decision.' However, this is a catch-22 for Erna in Example 2 (page 73) because Fabius's Portuguese family can only be involved in decision-making if they become aware of the decision (to adopt by Fabius and his husband) and, once they are aware of the adoption process, the decision about whether to involve them in Fabius and Ed's secret has been made.

## Consulting the wise professionals

### Time box

How have right and wrong been decided in the past, and how this has changed? Historic methods of decision-making have included trial by ordeal in which what is right and just shows itself through the outcome of the ordeal, such as the seventeenth-century Salem trials in Massachusetts. Beliefs in trial by ordeal were sincerely held, so how do we explain them – 'They didn't know any better'? If so, what is it that future generations will say that we 'didn't know better'? In fact, trial by ordeal had a very credible rationale when understood in its historical context – it was a way of judging right from wrong that was publicly seen as independent, free 'from the prejudices of the judge or the particular relationship between defendant and judge' (Aubert, 1980: 94).

The **wise professionals** might caution us to understand contemporary decision-making models as evolutionary. We tend to view the way we do things now as the end of the evolutionary process, but that would be a delusion. It is common to look back and discern the values that underpinned decision-making in the past as incomprehensible; it is more difficult to predict how they could change. The science fiction author, Isaac Asimov, imagined a future society in which a computer decides what the results of a presidential election would be by selecting just one representative individual and asking them various questions, avoiding the vast expense of conventional electioneering (Asimov, 1955); but 'the Voter of the Year' finds they bear the weight of moral responsibility for the success or failure of the resulting presidency. Perhaps we find this method of decision-making laughable, but would we accept it if we had the technological know-how, or would we feel that the whole population *ought* to participate in an election, even if we could accurately forecast the result?

## Leaving a trail

'One bit of advice we would give to decision makers is to leave a clear record of what they knew and the uncertainties surrounding their actions' (Slovic and Fischhoff, 1980: 127). Much of what happens after a decision has been taken can rely on moral luck – good or bad (see Chapter 11 for more discussion). It is often difficult even for the protagonists to remember the train of events and the moral reasoning that drove them, so it is important that there is a contemporaneous record – not just of the decisions, not just of the moral reasoning for the decisions, but also for the doubts and uncertainties that attended each decision point. Once a decision is made there is a tendency to consider it 'closed' and to look back at the decision-making process as though the conclusion were inevitable. If events prove unhappy, the future will be more forgiving if the doubts have been honestly recorded and the moral agency of the decision-makers is transparent for future judgements to weigh.

# 6    NEED AND RISK

One of the most famous **maxims**, popularised by Marx (1875), centres on the idea of need: 'From each according to his ability, to each according to his needs'. However, the emphasis over time on needs has rather obscured abilities; are there moral obligations to make use of our abilities, both in terms of an obligation to self-actualise (not waste our talents) and for the benefit of the community at large?

## Needs, wants and desires

There are needs that we recognise in common, such as food, love and sleep, and others that are particular, such as the way a blind person might need a guide dog and a sighted person would not. A sighted person might *want* a dog, which might fulfil a *desire* for companionship, but it is hard to think of circumstances in which we would assert that he *needs* a dog.

'I need eight hours' sleep' is different from 'I want eight hours' sleep'. If I only need six hours' sleep, yet I sleep for eight hours because I want to, I might be accused of laziness. 'I need sleep', 'I want to sleep', and 'I desire sleep' all place different moral obligations on the sleepers and those around them. We all need sleep, so deliberate sleep deprivation is wrong. Insomniacs might desire sleep as something difficult to achieve and we might agree that there is a moral obligation to alleviate the pain of sleeplessness and satisfy their desire; but is the obligation not to cause harm (by deliberate sleep deprivation) greater than the obligation to alleviate suffering (by facilitating sleep)? Acts of commission generally attract more moral opprobrium than acts of omission. Is our obligation to avoid doing harm stronger than our obligation to do good?

Need is a slippery term and this is reflected linguistically: we speak of somebody needing to pull their socks up, needing a good talking to. This is not something they want, nor is it something they recognise as a need. In fact it is my want for them: I want him to pull his socks up; I want her to have a good talking to. This leakage from need to want can cause many false dilemmas, ones that when more closely examined are created by the misuse of 'need' for 'want'.

## Competing needs

Some needs are now considered so universal that they are enshrined as rights, such as health and education. Other, 'newer' needs are still finding their place in society, such as the needs of students with dyslexia, not least because the needs vary from one person to another. It is when needs are seen as competing that dilemmas frequently arise, similar to the competing values we explore in Chapter 4. For instance, if we have one trained guide dog available and there are four people who are eligible how should we decide whose need is greatest? Indeed, ought it to be based on need at all, or should the person who has been waiting the longest automatically take precedence (the 'taxi rank' method)? Let us sketch four potential candidates, all of whom have guide dogs retiring in the next month and will need a replacement dog, except Mohmmad for whom this will be the first guide dog.

- > **Perpetua** has been blind since birth. She is 42 years old and is reliant on a dog to get to work. Since her guide dog retired four months ago her employers are paying for taxis, but they are a small independent trader and say this can only be a short-term measure.

- > **Anita** is 55 years old and was blinded in an industrial accident ten years ago. She received compensation which has maintained a good standard of living, but she has mental health problems and has been clinically depressed since her last dog retired three months ago. She relies on a dog for social contact and outings.

- > **Alan** is 72 years old and, like the other applicants, he lives alone. His only family is a daughter who has multiple sclerosis and he relies on a dog to visit her regularly. A volunteer service is currently helping Alan visit his daughter, since his last dog retired two months ago, but not with the frequency she and he are used to, and the service is only a temporary stop-gap. Alan has recently been diagnosed with bowel cancer.

- > **Mohmmad** is a 28-year-old Syrian refugee who has successfully achieved asylum and arrived in his present home a month ago. He was blinded in appalling atrocities in Homs and this would be his first dog. He is doing his best to get settled into his new community and he receives post-trauma therapy sessions and guide dog training. Others in the Syrian community offer help with his mobility, but he is a proud man and wants the independence a dog would give him.

What principles have you used to decide your priorities? Has 'need' or 'risk' been part of this process and, if so, how have you factored need and risk in each case?

Competing needs commonly encountered by social workers are those between the individual and the group: e.g. a person wishes to remain in the community but their neighbours consider his mental health is a threat; or a member of a group wants to talk about a taboo topic but the rest of the group is resistant and holds back. Another common area of competing needs is that between parents and children, such as the child of separated parents who wants to stay with her father who has previous offences. We will explore some specific dilemmas later in the chapter.

## Risk and fear

There are many good texts on need and risk in social work (for instance, Hothersall and Maas-Lowitt, 2010; Kemshall, 2002; Lonne *et al.*, 2015; Reamer, 2004; Smith, 2010; Webb, 2006), and in the space of one chapter a comprehensive survey is unrealistic; my intent is to explore the relationship between need, risk and the idea of right and wrong. Risk, in particular, has become totemic and in danger of losing its connection with values. Indeed, it is possible that the ethical issues in risk assessment make it unsuitable for social work (Parsloe, 1999; Walker, 1996). I hope the chapter will encourage readers to scrutinise risk and to highlight what it is we *value* that might be 'at risk'.

Every profession has developed its notion of risk and 'risk factors'. For structural engineers risk concerns the likelihood of stresses, for instance those that could lead to failure in a structure like a dam; for social workers the focus is personal and interpersonal, as well as attending to risks to themselves. An example of 'risk factors' for a social worker with older people is 'low, moderate or high risk of falls'. However, this does not tell us how much *value* a person places on falling compared to other facets of their life. For instance, a meteorologist forecasts a 'risk of rain'; I have a parched garden so the risk is actually one of 'not rain'. The weather forecaster has made a value judgement on my behalf and, in this case, a wrong one. Of course, falling is never welcome in the way that rain in a drought is, but **Mr Stonehaven**, an 85 year old assessed as at a 'high risk' of falling might feel that the value of his way of life at home is greater than his risk of a fall.

Risk assessments which aim to predict the likelihood of an event happening too frequently ignore the question of *value*. They can also lead to a false sense of security, as though it is the assessment that is important, not the risk: the social worker acknowledges the concerns of **Iain**, Mr Stonehaven's son, about his father's return home from hospital 'and assures him that a risk assessment has taken place' (Sieminski, 2013: 269). Additionally, the most powerful players in the scenario ought not to be accorded the privileged values. Iain values not feeling anxious and guilty and he knows he will feel both these emotions if his father returns home from hospital and has a serious fall. Mr Stonehaven, however, values a return to his life as he lived it. This situation is as much about competing and conflicting values as it is about risks, and there is every danger that the most assertive and powerful voice sets the terms of the debate (Ray *et al.*, 2009).

## The default setting

As we know from technology, a default setting is the taken-for-granted state which requires a positive act ('flicking the switch') if it is to be changed. Default settings are powerful as they maintain themselves without any effort and they can be exceptionally difficult to alter. For example, in an agency where the default setting is one-to-one work, a social worker wishing to prac-tise groupwork is likely to have to make a special case to 'flick the switch'. Moreover, the groupwork will be considered 'risky' and subject to greater scrutiny than the general default casework. Mr Stonehaven's son and possibly some of the health professionals have re-set his 'default setting' from living in his own home to institutional care and it could prove very difficult for him or his supporters to flick this switch. The dominant values have determined risk in terms of physical safety and this default position is reinforced by Mr Stonehaven's new persona as 'vulnerable person' (Bourdieu, 1991).

Without fear is there any risk? Iain's father might have no fear about going home and, therefore, for him there is no risk. The fear is Iain's; in that sense, the risk is his. Often, risk (like need) is something that one person assesses for another and, not infrequently, it is based on fear for oneself as well as for the other person.

Whilst acknowledging the value of risk assessment, especially when clinical (individualised), actuarial (aggregated) and ethical valuations are combined (Kemshall, 2013), the crucial question is *what is it that is of value that is at risk?*

## Risk and reason

Acts have an expressive value as well as a rational one. For instance, the chance that your vote will sway the result of a general election is tiny beyond measure, but voters vote because the act has expressive value. I would swap a five-pound note for a one-pound coin, a seemingly irrational act, if I needed a pound coin for a meter and I didn't want to risk a fine. There is, therefore, a difference between a *subjective* utility (the value of the one-pound coin to me at this moment) and an *objective* value (the economic value of the five-pound note). Social workers must, therefore, discover the subjective utility that a service user places on their own and other actions if they are to understand how need and risk are to be weighed in any one situation.

If you feel you can influence a decision you are more likely to take a risk. For instance, Bem's (1980: 9) research indicated that if a person is asked to place a bet *after* the dice have been rolled (and they haven't seen the outcome) they are more conservative in their betting than if placing the bet *before* the dice are rolled, even though it makes no logical difference when the bet is placed. It seems that the motivation to achieve and risk-taking behaviour are closely linked.

Judgements about risk are often subject to the reasoning of group decision-making, for example in case conferences. Do groups put the brakes on risk taking and end up making over-safe decisions, or does the relative anonymity of a group encourage much bolder action than an individual would contemplate, for instance, in very large groups such as mobs? There are some indications that groups are likely to take greater risks than individuals and, certainly, once a group is set on a course of action it can be difficult to avoid 'groupthink', when it becomes intimidating to challenge dominant opinion in the group (Turner and Pratkanis, 1998).

One of the most dramatised group decision-making situations is a jury's deliberations, when 12 people must decide between one of two risks: convicting the innocent and acquitting the guilty. When the evidence is even-handed between the likely innocence and the likely guilt of the defendant, ought the nature of the crime and the nature of the punishment affect the jury's risk taking?

## Ignorance and uncertainty

Contradictions, paradoxes, chaos and multiple realities are enemies to be conquered in much Western thought; yet perfect knowledge is impossible. How, then, do we deal with ignorance and the probabilities of uncertain events in social work? It helps to understand the common ways in which events are *actually* viewed, rather than the ways we would like to think we perceive them. For instance, events are thought more likely to happen if they are easy to recall or imagine, sometimes termed the *availability bias* (Slovic and Fischhoff, 1980). So, if a social worker has recently been involved in a situation where a risk was taken and the outcome was unfortunate, it is likely that this experience will influence decisions about a similar kind of risk in a similar circumstance the next time, even if the unfortunate outcome was due to an exceptionally rare happening. We perceive systematic patterns even when there is randomness because we have a yearning for meaning.

The desire for certainty and a wish to reduce the anxiety generated by uncertainty leads to denial of the uncertainty; overconfidence is quite common when making judgements of likelihood of risk, compounded by an unawareness of the scale of overconfidence (e.g. when respondents are asked to guess how confident they are that their estimation of a certain risk is correct they are more likely to give greater odds of their likely correctness than is the case). Beliefs frequently persist in the face of contrary new evidence, which is likely to be dismissed as unreliable or unrepresentative and initial impressions structure the way subsequent evidence is interpreted (Slovic and Fischhoff, 1980).

Even when the risk is precisely known, it is far from obvious what conclusion ought to be drawn. For instance, actuarial science might tell us that 1 in 300 dams fail when first filled, but what ought we to do with this knowledge? What benefits do dams bring that might outweigh the costs of the 1:300? If you knew with absolute precision that the odds of placing this child in that foster home were 80% chance of success (or, to put it the other way, 20% chance of failure) would this be an acceptable risk? How might you set these odds against the risk associated with the child staying in her family – if this gave odds, for instance, of a 40% chance of success in her own home and a 60% chance of failure? And how do these two sets of risk, staying in her own family and moving into foster care, relate to each other?

Of course, 'success' and 'failure' in terms of a child's life is immensely complex to determine, unlike a dam which either holds or does not. In this realm of great uncertainty values play a particularly important part in determining decisions about risk.

## Hindsight

One facet of the illusion of control is the way patterns are constructed post hoc to make sense of what we now know to be the case. Soon after Mr Stonehaven moves into residential care he becomes confused, so the social worker attributes the confusion to the disruption of his move. This might be right, but the level of confidence about hindsight is likely to be greater than justified. Moreover, the social worker might be mistaken about what *aspect* of the move has led to the confusion – hindsight suggests that it is the physical and psychological dislocation; in fact, Mr Stonehaven's doctor visits and treats him for severe constipation, after which he returns to his lucid self. The doctor tells herself, with the confidence of hindsight, that Mr Stonehaven should have been given laxatives as a prophylactic. The social worker still believes that Mr Stonehaven's retention was caused by the stress of the move, even if the laxatives removed the symptom. The run of events confirm both professionals in their beliefs, cemented by hindsight.

Professionals ought to be open about their uncertainties and to document them as the situation unfolds. Once a risk has been assessed and a decision taken, there is a tendency to close around it as though it were the obvious one, with subsequent events filtered to confirm it. **Wise professionals** continue to express doubt and to see each decision as tentative, made in the midst of uncertainty and met with the best quality reasoning and judgement available at the time.

## Exploring dilemmas

## Personal and practical assistance in social work

As we discovered earlier in connection with the example of the guide dog, need and risk are frequently at the heart of discussions about how resources ought to be distributed, and resources are frequently material ones. The relationship between personal and practical assistance has always been present, though contentious, in social work. Mayer and Timms' (1970) research unearthed the distance between the social workers' and the clients' understandings of their transactions: the former emphasising therapy, with the disbursing of money as an 'add-on'; the latter putting up with the talking in order to get the cash.

Social workers are not usually directly responsible for income support (though they have more involvement in some countries, like Norway); however, many countries' legislation makes provision for social workers to give practical help in the form of cash payments if there is *need*, especially a child in need. The lofty language of legislation and the messy reality of practice are perhaps no better illustrated than in the interpretations of need and risk in practice. A '[c]hild is "in need" if s/he is unlikely to achieve or maintain, or have opportunity to so do, a reasonable standard of health or development without provision of services'. In England and Wales this is embodied in The Children Act 1989, s.17.

1. **Ought making a payment to be an ethical issue for a social worker?**
   For some social workers, making payments is an ethical issue but not a dilemma because they either always do or always don't, based on their own value system. For others it does present a dilemma, or certainly a choice.

*I always*

> "Any parent who comes to a social work office with her three children and is prepared to use them as a barter – care or cash – is in a desperate situation

▶

by very definition. These are poor people in poor situations and even if there is the odd person who's 'trying it on', the time taken to differentiate them from the 99% who are desperate isn't worth it. Besides, the amount wasted on the odd con is paltry compared to the billions uncollected in tax from the wealthy and the multi-nationals."

*I never*

"Once you start to give money out on a Friday afternoon it's like cat-nip to all and sundry to come and get your free booze money from 'the social'. You get to be known as a soft touch and chances are it's going to go to pay for drugs anyway – even food vouchers get sold on and the cash used for drugs. I never give to beggars, I give to charities that help homeless people, and if no one ever gave to anyone on the street, there'd soon be no one bothering with the street and they would then go to the proper services. It's the same with service users on a Friday afternoon. It builds a culture of dependency."

*I sometimes*

"We've got a duty to assess each case on its own merits, as to whether there really is need that can be met by an out-of-hours payment. I oughtn't to make my decision about this case because of the possible consequences on other cases. It's important for me to be able to use my professional discretion and also for me to be able to decide between cash and vouchers. You might conclude that there is a need, but have a concern that giving cash would meet the parent's need (for drugs, for instance) rather than the child's need; with food vouchers you can target the help, but it does give the message that you don't trust the parent to prioritise the child's needs."

Ought social workers have discretion in this way? Proceduralisation can be a response to a feeling of arbitrariness in the nature of the service. Three service users, each of whom saw a different social worker – one from each of the 'camps' above – and compared notes might justly feel that a decision ought not to depend on which social worker's prejudices you happen to encounter. On the other hand, reducing need to a checklist of tick boxes with a decision overseen by a manager seems unsatisfactory and unprofessional – why bother employing a trained social worker?

Ought the manager to have to authorise the social worker's decision? What if three different managers also take the *always, never, sometimes* paths?

If a team of three social workers – *always, never and sometimes* – seems too arbitrary, would a team of three *always* social workers or three *never*

◀

social workers be any less arbitrary? Indeed, would three *sometimes* social workers be any less random?

Interestingly, the *always* and *never* workers both follow the same **rule utilitarianism** though with diametrically opposing outcomes. The *sometimes* worker is working from **Kantian** ethics, treating each person as an individual, employing the **categorical imperative**. (See Chapter 9 for more on the rights and wrongs of rules.)

> **Cheryl** and **Ryan Hampton** have three children, **Brad** aged 6, **Amy** aged 4 and **Angel** aged 2. Cheryl comes to the office late on Friday afternoon saying that she has no money to feed the children. **Anna** is the duty social worker. As an advanced practitioner she is authorised to make a payment of up to £20. She is a *sometimes* person and on this occasion, having talked with Cheryl, she decides to allow a payment.

2. **Ought Anna to accompany Cheryl to the shop to buy the food?**
   In some respects the issue of accompanying a service user to make the food purchase presents a practice dilemma, but there are ethical issues, too, concerning trust. Anna must use her judgement not just about how likely Cheryl is to spend the money on the food for which it is intended (and, therefore, the risk that it will be spent instead on drugs or alcohol), but how important the issue of trust is. Additionally, Anna has a social engagement that she is already late for; ought that to make any difference to her judgement call?

   Cheryl Hampton starts to come to the social work office regularly. The *never* social worker has his cynicism confirmed, except that each time Cheryl visits, each social worker is convinced that there *is* a need and recommends a cash payment, upheld by the manager. Cheryl is flamboyant and engaging and two of the social workers openly admit finding her sexually attractive. Everyone agrees that she is personable and amusing – 'plausible', says the *never*. There is growing concern, though, that the situation is moving beyond ad hoc payments. However, the team is very stretched.

3. **Ought the team allocate a social worker to work with the family?**
   Balancing the Hamptons' needs, as assessed by the team, and the accumulated time the team has spent patching things on Friday afternoons, it is decided that Anna will work with Cheryl and Ryan, with budgeting as a priority. When she visits their home, Anna finds the family living in abject poverty, with recent government changes to income support further worsening their situation. Anna helps Cheryl with a budget

▶

plan but Ryan, who is unemployed, makes himself scarce and several appointments that Anna makes to meet him are unsuccessful, one when she herself was not well. Cheryl does her best to excuse him.

A few weeks into the new plan with Cheryl, the children's school phones to report that one of the children has an injury that looks suspicious.

Following some initial investigations, a meeting is called and it is agreed that there are sufficient concerns and inconsistencies in the accounts of the injury to progress to a formal investigation. (In England and Wales this would be conducted under The Children Act 1989, s.47). During this time it comes out quite by chance that one of the library assistants in the building that is shared with the social work team has seen Cheryl on more than one occasion in the library toilets drinking a bottle of sherry. A case conference is arranged to consider options.

A few days before the conference Anna's symptoms worsen. She has been getting headaches and sweats and when she uses her home blood pressure monitor the readings are high, though not dangerously so. She suspects it is the pressure of work. Is she a risk to herself? Is there a risk to the quality of her decision-making at this time? On the other hand, she feels it is crucial that she attends the case conference as she now feels that she knows the family well and she wants to press the case that extra help in the Hampton home would reduce the risk of injury and maintain the family as a whole. She knows that there are some attending who tend to play things safe (i.e., to her mind, they give most weight to the risk to their reputations from the possible commission of an injury, rather than the less visible and more long-term risk to the children from removal from the home). Anna does not want to risk the progress of the case and her own part in it by going on sick leave, but she also wants to take good care of herself.

### 4. Ought Anna to sign off sick?

Anna's emergency doctor's appointment shows her blood pressure is raised but not critical and she is prescribed blood pressure medication. She decides that she will not take sick leave. However, she is uncertain whether to mention her condition to her team leader.

### 5. Ought Anna to tell her team leader about her high blood pressure?

Anna's responsibilities lie to her service users, to herself, to her profession and to her employer. She decides that it is right to tell her team leader, but also to offer her own solution – continuing work but with a review of her workload to see if there are any cases she could close or move. She admits to herself that there is some utility in her decision as she is confident that her good relationship with the team manager will lead to the decision she wants (and she is correct), so she wonders whether she would have decided on a different course if she thought she would have been given a different response. She knows it *ought* not to make any difference, but she reflects how it is easier to act virtuously when you know the outcome will serve your purposes.

The case conference meets to consider the results of the investigation and to decide what action to take in respect of the Hampton family. Representatives from education, health, police and social work are present, as well as the parents and a supporter, and a minute taker:

- **Jackie** (Independent Chair on behalf of the Safeguarding Children's Board)
- **Cheryl** and **Ryan** Hampton and their supporter **Jonny** (Ryan's brother)
- **Anna** Tomlinson – the family social worker
- **Karin** Olsen – school nurse at Brad's school
- **Carly** Seuss – assistant at Amy's nursery
- **Glynis** Jones – health visitor
- **Gary** Mbara – designated safeguarding officer at Brad's school
- DC **Sean** O'Leary – police officer in the Public Protection Unit

As is her practice, Anna meets with Cheryl, Ryan and Jonny 20 minutes before the meeting is due to begin. She draws a picture of the room in which the case conference will be held and who will be there, as she has found this helps to prepare them for what is likely to feel very intimidating. If there are obvious social differences between the parents and the professionals (for instance, if Cheryl and Ryan are black and all the professionals are white) there is even more cause for careful preparation. If the Chair allows, Anna brings the parents into the room before the professionals arrive, so it is professionals who join the parents and not vice versa.

## Ethical positions and values in the case conference

Is it possible to get from an *is* to an *ought*? In other words, do the facts of the case point to what ought to be done? If you made a list of the facts as known in the Hampton family case (plus those that you would want to know and could find out), would this predict what you *ought* to do? The **emotivist** philosophers believed that it is impossible to move from *is* to *ought* and that stating something ought to happen is no different from stating 'this room ought to be painted red', a matter of personal preference or belief. Yet this feels unsatisfactory, not to say wrong. Although a set of facts do not automatically point to what ought to be done, we must search for a moral discourse if only to find ways of deciding between the tensions that arise from the conflicting values that lead people to different conclusions about what ought to happen, even when they are all agreed on the 'facts'.

To illustrate, let us pose a range of values held by the different people involved in the Hampton case conference. These values are usually implicit, below the surface, but we have asked each person to describe in a nutshell what they hold dear and what will guide them in appraising the facts before them. A little background biography is given.

*Local context*

Last year in the neighbouring district there was a much-publicised case where evidence of child abuse was discredited by further medical investigation.

**Jackie**, the Independent Chair, has been involved in a case where the children were returned to their family and one of the children subsequently died. She has only recently been promoted to her present position.

"Children ought to grow up in an environment free from violence. We can't afford to take any risks with this top priority."

**Cheryl**, the children's mother, no longer seeks to charm, and she appears brittle and defensive. She does most of the talking for the couple. When Anna met her before the conference, she thought she smelled alcohol on her breath.

"Kids belong with their parents and when they're poor and struggling, the parents need a helping hand, not a punishment."

**Ryan**, the children's father, takes a back seat, just as he has since Anna has known the family. He is quietly spoken and generally confines himself to nodding in agreement with Cheryl.

" Yeah, kids belong with their parents. We need your help, not to be punished."

**Jonny**, Ryan's brother and the couple's supporter in the meeting, works in the plumbing trade. He has a smart, respectful appearance, but he is wary and chooses his few words carefully.

"You shouldn't persecute parents for being poor. Most do their best and they slip up every now and again. Kids need their parents."

**Anna**, the social worker, feels the birth family is the natural and foremost environment for children to grow up in, and that not enough resources are put into families to help them support themselves. She has witnessed a number of destructive adoption breakdowns.

"Families ought to be supported so that their children can grow up in the family home."

**Karin**, the school nurse, has returned highly enthused and focused from a training course on safeguarding which highlighted all the different kinds of abuse that children can be subjected to. She talks with certainty.

"Often things are going on that we just don't know about. Brothers and sisters need one another, so whatever happens, the children must be kept together."

**Carly**, the nursery assistant, was herself in residential care and is still in touch with staff there whom she found loving and supportive. She tends to mumble and is not very forcible.

"Children need a warm, supportive environment to grow up in and if this can only be found outside their birth families, we ought to move them."

**Glynis**, the health visitor, is very experienced and is beyond retirement age. She has worked in this particular community for decades and knows several generations of families. She doesn't mince her words.

"People can be very devious and they often don't even really know what their own needs are, never mind their children's. Communities are getting all broken up, so we are the only protection for these children."

◀

**Gary**, the teacher with school safeguarding responsibilities, first studied law before retraining as a teacher. He stresses the right to family life enshrined in the Human Rights Act and what he sees as the state's moral authority to intervene in the lives of children.

> "We have a duty to search for other family members who can care for the children if needed."

**Sean**, the police officer, has recently separated from his wife whose alcoholism he could no longer cope with. He speaks authoritatively.

> "Above all, children need stability so if they are taken out of their family's care they ought to be considered for adoption to look after their long-term needs."

Each member of the case conference has a value position, some similar and some contrasting, and about which they have varying degrees of self-awareness. Each position leads its holder to weigh a different value against different kinds of risk – some risks weighed more heavily than others. What is it that each person in the case conference values that might be 'at risk' as far as they are each concerned?

There is inevitable subjectivity in each person's judgements, but their different responses to uncertainty shape the way in which they make their views and beliefs known or not. Since it is reasonable to assume that everybody in the room has the best interests of the children at heart and, in this case, the facts are agreed (though perhaps not by the parents), it can only be the values that are leading to different perceptions of need and risk and, therefore, outcome.

The way each person presents themselves can affect the way that decisions about need and risk are made. This is known as presentation bias. Who are perceived to be powerful persons in the conference and what impact might this have – do strength of feeling and conviction carry weight as well as the power ascribed to different roles? Ought imbalances in power to be addressed and, if so, how?

A colleague of DC Sean O'Leary enters the conference to slip a note to him, excusing the interruption by saying that it is urgent. On reading the note Sean indicates that he has relevant information which he cannot divulge to the full meeting and he requests a 'closed section' which would necessitate the Hamptons and their supporter leaving the room. Jackie, the Chair, is unhappy about allowing this, so the note is passed

▶

to her. It reveals that Ryan was involved in an incident of domestic abuse seven years ago. In the end no charges were brought but the incident remains on file.

### 6. Ought a closed section of the case conference to be permitted?

Jackie considers the information is relevant, but her dilemma is whether she is justified in breaking the principle of openness and transparency which has guided the conference in order to protect Ryan's privacy, given that there is every likelihood that Cheryl does not know about this prior incident. If the case eventually comes to court, the information is likely to come to light then, but Ryan might like the opportunity to talk to Cheryl himself about it. On the other hand, asking the parents and Jonny to leave risks them thinking the information is even more serious than it is and risks breaking the trust that will be necessary if the meeting's decision is to keep the children at home and work with the family.

On balance Jackie decides that the privacy principle outweighs the transparency principle and she allows a closed section.

On hearing the information about Ryan, Carly (the nursery assistant) says she already knew all about this but that she hadn't known whether she could say anything. She's known Ryan since they were little – they were at school together and she got on well with him. There were rumours at the time, says Carly, that Ryan was more victim than perpetrator and that it was his then partner, **Nicole**, who was 'dishing it out'.

### 7. Ought Carly to continue to play a role in the case conference?

Jackie had read out the usual disclaimer at the beginning of the conference about participants declaring any interests, but Carly had not thought this had applied to her. The words are mouthed at the beginning of each conference, so that they have lost their meaning or force. Carly's feelings of relative powerlessness also meant that she did not feel assertive enough to ask questions ("Ought I to continue in this conference with the knowledge that I have?" "Ought I to disclose the knowledge I have about Ryan's history?"). This illustrates the dangers involved when the less powerful voices are not heard or do not feel they can make themselves heard.

---

Let us pose a version of this case conference in which Anna finds her values are different from the rest of the people there and that hers is a lone voice for supporting the children in the family home.

### 8. How ought 'lone voices' to be valued?

We saw in Carly's case the impact of power on the way in which risks might be weighed and information valued (see Chapter 3 for more on power). How ought we to respond when the conflicting values are very one-sided, with all the professional voices urging one course of action and just one lone voice counselling another, perhaps one that is based on her understanding of the impact of 'risk assessment' on the broader community and the connections between poverty and notions of need and risk (Lonne *et al.*, 2015; Smith, 2005)? In Chapter 4 we considered four different strategies for conflicting values – compete, compromise, concede, avoid. In this scenario, with the values irreconcilable, it is likely to be a question of competing, then conceding to the dominant view, with the safeguard that any decisions that point to the children's removal from the home will be further tested through the courts.

Jackie, as Chair of the conference, has a responsibility to enable all voices to be heard respectfully, to look for any points of possible convergence, and to help participants in the meeting to understand the value differences, rather than personalise the conflict or generalise to differences between professions overall.

———————

In another alternative scenario, Cheryl Hampton nods off intermittently in the conference. Anna notices that something is not right and she asks Cheryl if is she is OK. Cheryl becomes defensive, then verbally abusive, and it is seems that she is under the influence of alcohol.

### 9. Once Anna suspected alcohol on Cheryl's breath ought she to have queried Cheryl's suitability to attend the conference?

In fact Anna had noticed that Cheryl looked a little unsteady before the conference and asked her if she had been drinking; Cheryl told her that she had been so anxious in the build-up to the conference that she had been to the doctor who had prescribed a sedative and it was making her a bit woozy. Ryan confirmed that this was so. When asked by Cheryl if she felt clear-headed enough to attend the conference, Cheryl had said she did.

*Four months later …*

Investigations with the Hamptons uncover domestic abuse, but it is Cheryl who is abusing her husband, Ryan. In fact he has been doing the childcare and covering for his wife's chronic alcoholism. It comes

◀

to light that Cheryl has two older children by a different father in a different part of the country and that they were taken from her care and placed for adoption. Cheryl was diagnosed with a profound personality disorder.

Brad, Amy and Angel were placed with foster parents, but have now returned to the care of their father.

*An aside, eight months earlier ...*

It transpires that neighbours of the Hamptons had reported neglect and ill-treatment of the family's dog to the animal welfare society and the animal had been removed several months before Anna started to work with the family. In fact, the dog was taken from the care of the family before the children were, and no calls were received at any time from the neighbours in respect of the children. The dog escaped from its new owners and made its way back to the family home, a full eight miles across an urban landscape. The dog was reunited with the father and children.

## The Big Picture

### Terrorist attacks and the media

42 people die every day (on average) from terrorist attacks and this number is increasing. If we knew that publicity for terrorist events in the media increased the risk of further similar incidents, ought knowledge of these incidents to be censored? A study analysing more than 60,000 attacks between 1970 and 2012 suggested a link between the number of newspaper articles devoted to an initial terrorist incident and the number of follow-up attacks over the next few weeks (Jetter, 2014). The research calculated that on average an additional article in the *New York Times* results in between one and two casualties from another terrorist attack within the next week. The study was confined to newspaper reports, but we can surmise that exposure from internet videos in recent years might further increase this risk.

The dilemma lies between balancing the public's right to know and limiting the public's exposure to increased risk. Is there a justified *need* to know about these incidents? Ought other factors to be taken into account such as secondary trauma to people reading about these atrocities? Ought the motivation of the news media to influence our judgement; for example, if the reason for giving free publicity to terrorists is to increase sales, and therefore profits for the news moguls and their shareholders? Or ought people to be treated as autonomous individuals who can make an informed choice as to whether they read about these kinds of news story and, if they find them distressing, avoid them?

How ought social work to work with communities 'rendered suspicious' by notions of radicalisation and terrorism (Heath-Kelly 2012: 394)? Ought social work to play a role in providing support to people 'at risk' of radicalisation, the 'vulnerable people' identified in the Prevent strategy or are these strategies disproportionate, discriminatory and too restrictive of free speech? How ought social work to respond to the idea that 'there should be no "ungoverned spaces" in which extremism is allowed to flourish without firm challenge and, where appropriate, by legal intervention' (UK Government, 2011: 9)? If social workers were asked to fill these 'ungoverned spaces' what ought our response to be? Indeed, social workers are amongst those groups who are charged by the Prevent strategy with identifying 'vulnerable people'. In the Hampton example used in this chapter, what ought social worker Anna to do if she hears Cheryl Hampton making comments that are supportive of the violence committed in the Paris killings in 2015?

What of the *bigger* Bigger Picture? The 42 people who die every day from terrorist attacks pale in comparison to the 7,000 children who die each day from hunger-related causes. Their deaths are relentless and largely unwitnessed. Which story ought to make it to the front page?

## Guidance from Codes, Standards and Principles

The Swedish code of ethics has a section devoted to ethical dilemmas and risks, giving 11 example dilemmas, one of which is 'the right of the child to advantageous living conditions versus the right of the parents to exert their parentage and live their family lives on their own terms' (SSR 2006: 6). Interestingly, one of the general risks that the Swedish code poses is the risk of social workers' increasing insensitivity, even plain cynicism, arising from the stresses of the job and disappointment over service users' behaviour (SSR 2006: 6). 'Risk to self' is often interpreted in a physical sense, but this Swedish code reminds us of the risks that lie between the necessary toughening to cope with the pressures of the work against the threats to the ethics of care that first brought you into social work.

Reference to interprofessional working is common in codes of ethics, such as the exhortation to 'recognise and respect the roles and expertise of workers from other agencies and work in partnership with them' (Northern Ireland Social Care Council, NISCC, 2002; 6.8) and the seventh principle in the Irish code: '[I]n seeking to respond to the needs of individuals, groups and communities social workers will seek to involve other professionals and agencies as appropriate.' (IASW 2007: 4)

## Consulting the wise professionals

The **wise professionals** are you at your best practice and what you aspire to in all of your practice. What reflections have these wise professionals to make in respect of the rights and wrongs of need and risk?

One reflection is that ethical practice requires an acknowledgement of the limits of your knowledge and a willingness to temper passionate beliefs with the understanding that they might be wrong. The studies reported earlier in the chapter about people's tendency to overconfidence about their estimates of risk are a warning in this respect. Ethical practice is being aware that there are others who are likely to question your own beliefs and wanting to find out why.

Wise practice recognises that judgements about need and risk are themselves judged severely if there is a belief that mistakes could have been foreseen at the time. It is important, then, to document uncertainties along the way, and to include acts of omission as well as commission. Acts of commission generally attract more moral opprobrium than acts of omission because the latter are less visible, but omissions can be harder to pinpoint. If reputational risk (to self, profession, agency) has figured in the calculations, this too should be registered.

The social context of need and risk is often taken for granted but good risk-taking requires scrutiny of the social 'default settings'. Consider this statement by a parent who transports their child to school each day in the family 4-by-4 vehicle:

> "It's to avoid the risk. The fear of something happening to **Olivia** on her way to school is just too much to bear and if anything did happen to her I would feel so guilty that I'd not been there and I could've prevented it by taking her in the car. I'd be seen as a bad parent."

The social default setting in Olivia's parent's world is an individualistic one in which their responsibilities are almost solely for Olivia. The risk of damage to other children (by collision with their vehicle or pollutants from the exhaust) are not part of the calculation, nor is the idea that Olivia might receive social protection in her walk to school. Olivia's parent's assessment of risk is driven by anxiety, not just of the fear of what might happen to Olivia but by their own guilt and the blame they perceive others would pile on them. The fear (and therefore the calculation of risk) is as much self-serving as it is about Olivia. In fact, an actuarial assessment might reveal that Olivia is at risk of more harm long-term from the lack of exercise because of the omission of a walk to school; this is unlikely to alter Olivia's parent's assessment of risk because it does not take into account the self-serving elements of their own calculations.

Our wise professionals counsel us to search for the 'default setting' and to question it in the light of a broader social ethic and the marginalisation and poverty of many of the families who are considered 'at risk'. At risk from poverty? It is this broader social ethic that is such a distinguishing feature of social work practice.

# 7 RELATIONSHIP BOUNDARIES AND DISCLOSURE

Social workers are licensed to get close to people. Indeed, the various public service professionals have different kinds of permission to get closer to strangers than normal social situations would allow. Patients take their clothes off and consent to intimate inspections of their bodies by doctors, actions that would be prosecutable in other circumstances. Social workers help service users to take off their 'emotional clothes' to expose thoughts, feelings and beliefs that are not always acceptable outside the social work encounter. It is part of what makes a social work encounter different from a social encounter.

Social work has a particular responsibility with regard to this emotional disrobing because of the powers that lie in the wings. Service users' honesty when all is laid bare can then be used in ways that might be at odds with their own interests. At the heart of this dilemma lies the fact that social work is as responsible to the broader community as it is to the individual service user, whose dealings with social workers are not privileged like those with lawyers and priests (Chapter 8).

Medicine has some parallel dilemmas; for example, the examination that reveals a condition that will increase the patient's insurance premium or restrict their ability to drive. Should the patient be warned of the possible consequences of a particular investigation (and, therefore, decline to submit themselves to it) or does the public at large have the right to know whether an individual poses a risk behind the wheel of a car? What complicates social work is the lack of clear social rules or protocols to govern the encounter; 'taking off emotional clothes' is, pointedly, a metaphor, a rather more subtle act than actually disrobing in front of a doctor. The doctor has curtains and a chaperoning nurse where appropriate, but what 'curtains' or 'chaperone' should a social worker deploy in order to safeguard the integrity of the emotional disrobing?

## Driving dilemmas underground

One response to these awkward ambiguities has been to try to manage them out of existence (Lymbery and Butler, 2004; Rogowski, 2010). The managerial response leads to the creation of an emotional distance that denies the service user the opportunity to become close to the social worker. Since there is a risk involved in closeness, why not remove the risk by disapproving of it? The imposition of targets for crime statistics is a similar attempt to rationalise a difficult situation; the intent is to 'manage' crime, whereas the consequence is that crimes become inconvenient and the efforts of law enforcement are directed at 'de-criming' acts (failing to register them as crimes) rather than recording them in order to secure a prosecution. Similarly, there is a danger that the notion of *the relationship* has become inconvenient in social work; emotional disrobing and the closeness that this entails is discouraged, even defined as unprofessional, by those who seek to define and control the profession.

As will be apparent from this and other chapters, driving dilemmas underground is the very worst of practices. The risks might be deferred but they are deepened. Social work must embrace the risks inherent in the closeness of the relationship between practitioner and service user. Social work is not synonymous with case management, though of course managing cases is an element of social work; the essence of social work is a commitment to social justice at the broad level and an engagement in meaningful relationships at the interpersonal level (Hennessey, 2011; Ruch *et al.*, 2010). Both of these goals inevitably involve conflict, difficult choices and moral ambiguities.

As explained in the introductory chapter, the organisation of the various dilemmas in social work practice into eight themed chapters is not intended to obscure the messy reality of practice, where there is much overlap. Each **singularity** is likely to involve a number of different kinds of dilemma. However, there is often a central dilemma, one that has the strongest profile, and in this chapter I will be focusing on those that cluster around the relationship between social workers and the service users with whom they work, using the term 'relationship boundaries' to describe this cluster of dilemmas. Let us consider different kinds of relationship dilemma.

## Personal feelings

Social workers bring their own feelings to the encounter with service users. Feelings can be strongly negative or positive, or a confusing mixture of the two. They can arise suddenly and soon, or might be slow to manifest. Social workers' feelings about service users and their situations might be related to the social worker's own value base – anger at the injustice a service user has experienced, revulsion at the racist attitudes of another. The feelings might have their roots in past experiences – sympathy for a person who reminds us of a previous well-liked and appreciative service user, annoyance at someone who makes the same kind of demands a previous service user made aggressively. The social worker might feel helplessness in the face of the magnitude of the service user's problems.

The term 'transference' is used in psychodynamic theory to describe strong feelings that we transfer from one person to another, where the one reminds us in some way of the other. A tender relationship with your grand-mother might transfer to similar feelings towards an older woman that you are working with. There might be a strong 'counter-transference' when this older woman does not respond in the way that is expected (that is, the way your grandmother would have), leaving you feeling angry, confused, even in some ways betrayed.

## Personal boundaries

Working closely with people means that the gap between personal bound-aries and professional boundaries can be difficult to create. I worked for many years as a community-based social worker and lived on the geo-graphical boundary of my 'patch,' the neighbourhoods where my clients lived. Some of the people I worked with as clients I would see at the week-end as shoppers in the local streets. Working over many years in the same area meant that I saw service users from different generations of the same family, and in chance encounters they were keen to tell how their families were getting on, to catch up with the news. And they would want to know how I was doing, too. We return to this self-disclosure theme later in the chapter.

Social workers in residential and day care settings often see their service users in intimate situations such as getting ready for bed or having a bath. Physical care like lifting, bathing and feeding brings professional and service user literally closer together and tests the personal boundaries that we normally consider as acceptable.

## Sexual attraction

It features little in the social work literature, yet sexual attraction is hugely important to human life (Bernsen *et al.*, 1994). Indeed, the question of sexual attraction is probably the one that is most buried, not just in social work writings but in supervision and everyday workplace chatter, because it is considered to be such a taboo topic. There is often blanket collusion in the idea that professionalism is about denying any questions of sexual attraction, especially if a second boundary is crossed (same-sex attraction, age gap attraction, etc.).

In fact it is unprofessional *not* to be aware of and *not* to discuss feelings of sexual attraction. If there is denial (whether conscious or not), decisions are made with a layer of important knowledge obscured. However, can the social worker feel confident that in raising the subject of sexual attraction (or, even more difficult perhaps, sexual revulsion), talking about it will not be mistaken as a readiness to act on it? For that is what the **wise professional** would counsel – that professionalism is not about denying the feeling but declining to act on it.

## Exploring dilemmas

**Sinéad** is a social worker in a learning disabilities team. She is due to lead a parenting skills group for the first time. The purpose of the group is to work with parents who are having behavioural problems with their children to the extent that there is a risk of family breakdown. The parents are either self-referred or referred by other professionals.

Sinéad was planning the group with a co-worker, Jack, but he has gone on long-term sick leave and the rest of the team is too stretched to help. Her first dilemma is a practice dilemma with an ethical dimension:

1. **Should I continue with this group even though it means I will be sole leader?**
A central practice dilemma that Sinéad must consider is what evidence there is to suggest that sole leadership of a group has a better or worse outcome than co-leadership. She knows that co-leadership is the dominant model in the UK, but that sole leadership is quite common in the US. In one English study (Doel 2006: 108), 87% of the 68 groups in the research were planned to be co-led; the percentage of single-led groups that failed to start (36%) was notably higher than the failed starts for co-led groups (13%). However, Sinéad knows herself to be very motivated and feels confident that if she had been in that study, hers would have been one of the 64% of single-led planned groups that did succeed.

However, she does feel that the group members' experience of the group will not be as rich as it would have been with a co-worker. She herself enjoys the variety that comes with two group leaders. That said, she takes a **utilitarian** view that the greater good is served by her continuing with the group single-handedly. It may not be as qualitatively good an experience as it would have been, but it will be better than no experience at all. Also, starting the group always leaves open the possibility that she can persuade another colleague to join her at some point.

▶

Just as Sinéad closes the door on one dilemma, another opens. She receives a referral from a health visitor that names her sister-in-law, **Ruth**. Sinéad has been aware that Ruth is having problems with her 13-year-old autistic son, Sinéad's nephew, Fraser, but the referral includes new information that she was not aware of.

## Relationship boundary dilemmas

2. **Should I accept Ruth, my sister-in-law, as a member of the Parenting Group?**
The initial dilemma faced by Sinéad centres on the nature of the information she has acquired about her sister-in-law via her work as a social worker. The health visitor did not know the family connection and Ruth had not thought of the possibility that Sinéad would have involvement in the group. Should Sinéad let Ruth know that she has this new information about Fraser? Fortunately, there is a phone call from Ruth who has put two and two together and has anticipated Sinéad's current dilemma. Ruth is very reasonable. She would really like to come to the group, feels she needs it, but fully understands the difficult position it puts Sinéad in. She is happy to leave the decision with her.

Sinéad gets on well with her sister-in-law, even though there was a messy separation with Sinéad's brother, **Fergus**, the father of **Fraser**. She can see the possible difficulties of the **dual relationship** – a group member who is also a family member – and her first feeling is not to risk it (Carney and McCarren, 2012; Reamer, 1999). What if group members feel she is favouring her sister-in-law? ... what if Ruth says things like, "Well, you know what Fraser's like" to her in the group, compromising her authority as group leader? What if ... ? Much easier to delete the risk by not inviting Ruth to the group in the first place.

Discussing the dilemma with her supervisor, it is evident that the risks of commission (such as those above) are more vivid in Sinéad's mind than the risks of omission. Her supervisor asks other *what if?* questions: what if the group can help Ruth with Fraser's behaviour? What if Ruth's physical health deteriorates (Sinéad had spoken about the effect Fraser's behaviour was having on Ruth) as a result of missing out on the possibility of the group's help? What if ... ?

Sinéad's supervisor helped her to consider Ruth's rights, in particular her right to help when it is considered necessary and it is available. Is it right that her relationship to the group leader denies her the possibility of a place in the group that an independent professional has judged would benefit her? There is no financial gain (to either Sinéad or Ruth), nor has influence been brought to bear to secure Ruth a special place. On the other hand, would Ruth's presence in the group compromise Sinéad's *objectivity* (one of Nolan's 1995 seven principles of public life) or be seen to compromise it by other group members?

Sinéad begins, now, to think of the possible advantages to the group process – her customary **utilitarian** thinking – of how the greater good might be satisfied by a decision to include Ruth. First, there will be two other single parents in the group, so Ruth's presence will strengthen that minority. Secondly, in the relatively small world of the community where Sinéad works there is always the prospect that a group member will have some other connection to another, and Sinéad had already planned to ask the group to explore this in the first session. In this group she will be a 'member' as well as the facilitator, she and Ruth declaring their own family connection. Sinéad can see how this could be a help as well as a hindrance. If her personal knowledge of Ruth's circumstances surface in the group, well this too is an opportunity to explore how these kinds of **dual relationships** (common in lots of other aspects of people's lives) can be welcomed and managed. Better to model a way of working with this than to avoid it. Better not to deny Ruth her rights to help and support.

---

Sinéad and her team have taken the decision that the group will go ahead with Sinéad as the sole leader and her sister-in-law, Ruth, as a member. She has met all the prospective group members in advance of the group.

The group consists of four couples (Tara and Darren; Marina and Jim; Parveen and Ali; Ellie and Dan) and three single parents comprised of two mothers and one father (Kirsty; Ruth; Sean).

Sinéad has a strong dislike of **Jim**, one of the fathers in the group. Knowing that she dislikes him, Sinéad has tried to be even-handed and has given Jim a lot of rope, repressing her feelings so 'they don't get in the way'. Jim puts people down with sarcasm and **Kirsty**, one of the single parents, particularly bears the brunt of this. Kirsty is not much liked by the rest of the group, who are wary of Jim and laugh along with him, perhaps because they would rather he turn his fire on Kirsty than them. **Darren**, especially, provides a ready sidekick. Sinéad feels out of control of the group, sorry for Kirsty and angry at the rest of the group for letting Jim get away with it. She is asked by her supervisor to put her dilemma into a question. Sinéad says:

### 3a. What should I do with my feelings about Jim?

Sinéad's supervisor asks her exactly what her feelings are. Sinéad starts to reflect on how Jim reminds her of a former partner. At one level she knew this as far back as the pre-group interview (where the possibility of groupwork is offered), but she had denied these feelings to herself and it is only through supervision that she now *realises* this knowledge and has given it voice. The supervisor asks Sinéad what she has done about her feelings so far, and Sinéad recounts how she is aware that she has tried to compensate for her dislike, failing to challenge Jim appropriately earlier in the group's life. Because of this she has failed Kirsty and has also failed the group as a whole (which now doesn't like itself because of the bad taste that scapegoating leaves); and, indeed, she has failed Jim. His dominance is doing him no service, as he is not getting any learning from the group.

Sinéad has already resolved part of her dilemma. By acknowledging her feelings about Jim and, more importantly, the consequences of trying to suppress that knowledge, she is being honest with herself and this transparency opens the door to a better analysis of what is happening in the group. Of course, it would not have been right to *express* her dislike of Jim, but nor was it good for her to *suppress* it. Had she had a co-worker it is possible that the co-worker could have confronted her early on to recognise the impact of her feelings about Jim. But, then, had she decided not to lead the group because of the lack of a co-worker, the group members would have been denied the *possibility* of the benefits of a group, even if at present they are being denied the reality of them.

The discussion has led Sinéad from a practice dilemma of what a good groupworker does when she has strong feelings of dislike for a group member and, also, when the group is experiencing scapegoating. But Sinéad now reframes her query into an ethical one:

### 3b. What *ought* I to do with my feelings about Jim?

The practice dilemma of *how should I … ?* might be resolved, for instance, by recourse to agency protocol or a professional code of practice. *What ought I … ?* requires Sinéad to make moral and ethical judgements. Procedures prescribe certain paths; moral philosophy opens up the choice of various different paths. The chosen path relies on reasoning, not just of the individual practitioner but the collective reasoning of the practitioner-in-the-team.

With Sinéad's feelings openly expressed, Sinéad and her colleagues decide that she *ought* to challenge the behaviour. She takes a

**consequentialist** path, reasoning that if she doesn't challenge this dynamic in the group, at best the group will fail to reach its potential and at worst harm will be done. There are elements of an **ethics of care**, also – a focus on ethical relationships *within* the group. The dilemma now moves back to a practice one: what groupwork practices are most likely to challenge Jim appropriately and engage the group as whole in a resolution? It is Sinéad's responsibility to lead the group to a way through, but not to 'fix it' herself; she must help the group towards a mutual resolution. It is not this book's purpose to consider the groupwork options in detail, but if you would like to explore these further you could turn to Doel (2004).

The successful resolution of one problem or dilemma does not, of course, mean the cessation of dilemmas altogether, though it probably limits them. In the course of Sinéad's Parenting Group other dilemmas relating to professional boundaries occur. Let us explore these dilemmas and consult with Sinéad, her supervisor and her colleagues about what she ought to do.

**Sean**, the only single father in the group, seems quite agitated. At the end of the session he lingers to talk to Sinéad alone and he explains that he has found out that his wife has cheated on him. They'd been hoping to get back together, but he's found out she's been seeing someone else. Sean asks Sinéad outright, "would you get back with someone if they had cheated on you?" There isn't time to discuss this with her supervisor or colleagues, so Sinéad asks her **wise professionals**:

**4.   Ought I to respond directly to Sean's question?**
Take a **consequentialist** approach to Sinéad's dilemma; in other words, consider the possible consequences (good, bad and indifferent) of a direct response to Sean's question and, then, the possible consequences (good, bad and indifferent) of refusing to respond directly to Sean's question. Does a consideration of these two lists help your decision? If you had an initial 'gut' decision about what Sinéad ought to do, has this changed in any way as a result of compiling the lists?

Let us take one path, the one where Sinéad decides she ought not to respond directly, and decide *how* Sinéad will reply; after all, she can't just turn away as though Sean hasn't spoken to her. She and Sean are in the room because he is a member of a parenting skills group and she is the leader of that group. They (the group, not Sinéad and Sean) have been talking for an hour and a half about personal and family difficulties, which has included some taboo topics, and they've been working together to give mutual support, aid and understanding. Sinéad needs to respond to Sean in a way that brings the group back into their private discussion and that also respects Sean's reasons for choosing not to give this information in the group.

> "I'm really sorry to hear this, Sean. It must be very upsetting and it can't have been easy for you to tell me about it. It's a complicated situation and I guess your decision about what to do will be based on a lot of different things. I wonder, now that you've told me, is this something you could share with the group, perhaps at the next session? Only if you feel ready to, of course. But I think the most important thing is not what other people might or might not do if they were in this situation, but to help you find out what you want to do, because I get a feeling that you're in two minds. I know that the group as a whole would be able to offer you a lot of support and ideas, much more than I can on my own, if you feel ready to trust them."

Sinéad has found a way to respond to Sean's personal question directly, though it depends on how 'directly' is interpreted. We would have to ask Sean what he felt about Sinéad's reply and await next week to see if he feels he can bring this topic to the group's attention; however, Sinéad has done her best to reply respectfully and to explain her reasoning. She sees the issues of trust and hope as central to Sean's dilemma and these are themes that have been emerging for the group as a whole.

———————

At the next session, **Parveen** and **Ali** are the last to leave. Parveen has been helping Sinéad to straighten up the room, being useful and also filling time whilst Ali has been on his mobile phone outside the building. As Parveen and Sinéad leave the building, Ali asks Sinéad if she'd like a lift and Parveen insists on it, too. Once again Sinéad must consult her inner **wise professionals**:

5. **Ought I to accept Parveen and Ali's lift in their car?**
   In this case the answer does seem as though it will have to be a *yes* or a *no*. When considering what to do, ought these circumstances to affect the decision?

   ➢ It is raining heavily and Sinéad has no umbrella.

   ➢ Sinéad has to take two buses to get home.

   ➢ Ali tells Sinéad their route and it turns out they pass right by her home.

   ➢ Sinéad gets on well with Parveen and Ali.

If you consider any of these circumstances to be material, *how* material are they? For instance, how softly does it have to be raining for it no longer to be a factor? If Sinéad only has one bus or only a short walk? If Parveen and Ali will be taken five minutes out of their way or fifteen minutes? ... etc. Or is the ethical question about whether Sinéad ought to accept or decline the lift not one that can be decided in a **casuist** way? Does Sinéad resort to **rule utilitarianism** and tell Parveen and Ali not to take it personally but she never accepts lifts – or 'agency policy' is never to accept?

If Sinéad is honest with herself, in the back of her mind she wonders whether any refusal on her part might be interpreted by Parveen and Ali as a kind of racism and this inclines her more to accepting than would otherwise be the case. She muses whether this situation is related to a concept of 'cultural friendliness' that she had been reading about; ought she, therefore, to respond differently in response to different cultural expectations (Engelbrecht, 2006: 257)?

---

**Tara** is Sinéad's age and has a similar family background. During the coffee break in the group, Tara often seeks out Sinéad and wants to confide with her. In the penultimate session, Tara tells Sinéad that she sees her more as a friend, not the first time that she has referred to their relationship as a friendship. Sinéad is uncomfortable with this, though she could see herself being friends with Tara if they had met in different circumstances. She can choose to ignore it for now and consult with her supervisor at their next session, or she can ask her **wise professionals** there and then:

6. **Ought I to question Tara's view of me as a friend?**
   If I do, can I do this without spoiling our relationship?
   Choose either a **consequentialist** approach (to construct two lists of possible consequences, one contingent on questioning Tara's view and the other on 'letting sleeping dogs lie'); or a **casuist** approach (to compile a list of factors that you consider might alter your judgement about whether to challenge or keep quiet). Does either of these approaches lead you to a conclusion? Is it the same or a different one in each case?

---

**Kirsty** has become a more accepted member of the group. She is still seen as a bit of an outsider, but is offered much more support by the group. Indeed, Sinéad has concerns about where Kirsty will get this support once the group ends. Kirsty is edgy during the final session and when people are leaving and saying their goodbyes, she starts to cry. She gives Sinéad her personal contact details, asks for hers, too, and requests a follow-up time with her. What ought Sinéad to do?

7. **Ought I to accept Kirsty's personal contact details?**
   **Ought I to give her mine?**
   **Ought I to follow through with her?**
   Unlike Sinéad's dislike of Jim, which brewed over time, or Tara's growing friendliness, both of which can be denied or ignored, the Kirsty dilemmas are immediate and, like Parveen and Ali's offer of a lift in their car, require a direct response. In this case, Sinéad's agency has a policy that employees do not give their personal details to service users.

   ➤ Is this policy ethical?

   ➤ How does Sinéad decide whether it is ethical?

   ➤ Are there any circumstances in which Sinéad's **wise professionals** would advise her to break with the protocol?

---

The group ends as planned and there is a successful evaluation. Sinéad is pleased that she decided to go ahead as sole leader and that she accepted the referral of her sister-in-law, Ruth, though she had felt self-conscious when she had not known what to do about the scapegoating of Kirsty. She is very pleased to have had access to good supervision, the embodiment of her wise professionals. As the group progressed, Sinéad noticed that one of the fathers, Sean, came to like her a lot. She thinks he finds her very attractive and she has discussed her own attraction to him in supervision.

Two months after the group finishes Sinéad goes to her local coffee shop, seats herself at a table with her coffee and sees **Sean** at the next table. They get talking across tables and he asks if he can join her at hers. At first the talk is of the weather and the like, but then they move to other things and discover common interests in music, cinema and politics. Sean buys Sinéad another coffee and tells her what's happened since the group. His son's behaviour is improved, and he's feeling good about things, helped by a promotion at work. He's got over his feelings about his wife, who is now in a steady relationship with another man. They have started divorce proceedings. He apologises for putting Sinéad in a difficult position when he asked her what she would do if she found out her partner was cheating on her – he accepts that it wasn't fair to ask her like that, outright, but he was in a very different place then. Sinéad finds herself liking Sean's company very much and feels drawn to him. Before he leaves he writes his phone number down and gives it to Sinéad saying he'd love to see her again but understands if she can't because it puts her in a difficult situation. Sinéad finds herself thinking about Sean a lot over the next few days and realises that she is very attracted to him and wants to meet up, but decides to wait until her next supervision session before making a decision.

She has her question ready for her supervisor:

### 8. Ought I to act on my feelings about Sean?

As Sinéad approaches supervision, if she is honest with herself (and she is) she really wants her supervisor to tell her what to do. She trusts her supervisor's judgement. At best Sinéad can be seen as seeking professional advice, at worst she is dumping the dilemma on someone else. But she remembers what her supervisor said when Sinéad last mentioned this: "I'm pleased you trust my judgement but it's my job to help you to trust your own," and she reminded her of the many dilemmas during the Parenting Group when Sinéad has had to do just that. Sinéad also realised that Sean had been doing exactly the same – wanting someone else to make the decision when he asked her whether she would get back with someone who had cheated on her.

In the supervision session, Sinéad is asked questions to help her to draw up a balance sheet of the pros and cons of whether to act on her feelings. You might like to write your own before reading Sinéad's.

*Act on your feelings – pros and cons*

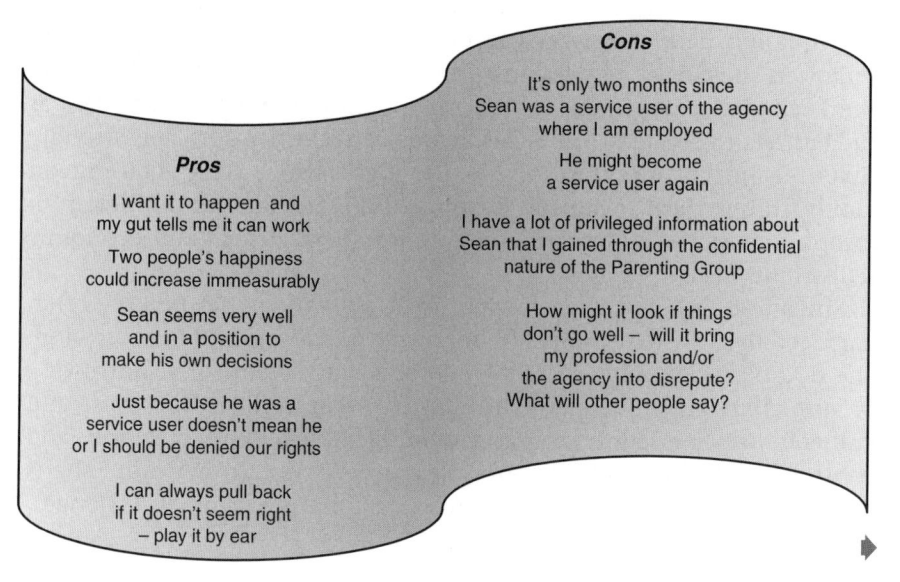

**Cons**

It's only two months since Sean was a service user of the agency where I am employed

He might become a service user again

I have a lot of privileged information about Sean that I gained through the confidential nature of the Parenting Group

How might it look if things don't go well – will it bring my profession and/or the agency into disrepute? What will other people say?

**Pros**

I want it to happen and my gut tells me it can work

Two people's happiness could increase immeasurably

Sean seems very well and in a position to make his own decisions

Just because he was a service user doesn't mean he or I should be denied our rights

I can always pull back if it doesn't seem right – play it by ear

The balance sheet approach of lists does not in itself provide an answer. There is no algorithm that can be applied to produce the 'right' result that moves Sinéad from an *is* to an *ought*. Indeed, the experience of presenting these kinds of dilemma to large audiences has taught me that some readers will be wondering why Sinéad thinks there is a dilemma here at all (some who think it's obvious she should act on her feelings and others who think that it is equally obvious that she most certainly should not), whilst other readers lie somewhere along this continuum (Doel *et al.*, 2010; see also Cooper, 2013). Jayaratne *et al.*'s (1997) study found that respondents were almost as likely to consider the same 'boundary behaviors' appropriate as inappropriate. For some the choice is a stark one: does Sinéad put personal happiness above consequences to her career?

The length of each list is not as material as the significance of particular items; is any single item a clincher, or a deal maker or breaker in terms of the weight it ought to carry?

The inclination to move towards one side of the balance sheet or the other cannot be separated from personal beliefs. Let us visit two different Sinéads and see how the worldview of each might lead her to weigh the lists of pros and cons.

**Sinéad.01** believes that people are fundamentally trustworthy and caring. Because of their experiences in life (oppression, poverty, lack of reliable love and care, rejection, etc.) some people need help to learn how to become autonomous adults, but almost everyone is capable of this. Sinéad is an optimist and has generally quite high expectations; she is sometimes disappointed, but not often. She believes in the equality of service users and professionals and that it is too often forgotten that many professionals are service users, too. She dislikes all the keypads on the doors to her office building and what she sees as the barriers to services. She is suspicious of authority and feels strongly that it is more important to do the right thing than focusing on 'doing things right' (Munroe Report, 2011). Sinéad.01's political philosophy views the state as the engine for social justice and economic redistribution.

**Sinéad.02** believes that service users are vulnerable people, often damaged by early experiences of deprivation, and in need of protection. She doesn't judge service users when she finds them to be untrusting or suspicious but understands this as an expression of their hurt and vulnerability. She sees herself as providing the necessary authority and control that is often missing in service users' lives. To her mind she is realistically pessimistic about the prospects for any meaningful change.

She likes the safety and privacy that the keypads on the office building afford, and she feels the agency's procedures and protocols offer
her additional security. Whilst it's important to do the right thing,
Sinéad.02's focus is on doing things right – for her the two are, after all,
the same. She doesn't see herself as having 'a political philosophy' as
such.

Each Sinéad is likely to place a different emphasis on the two lists
of pros and cons. All social workers need to be aware of how their
own philosophical make-up weights the factors they use to make their
judgements.

## Consequences

What are the consequences of the various actions that Sinéad is contemplating? If meeting Sean with a view to pursuing a relationship would risk
disciplinary action does this, therefore, mean that she *ought* not to do it?
Or, if she feels that she loves him, or will love him (and he her), ought
she to 'follow her heart'? Ought she to put personal happiness before her
career? If the rules get in the way of two people's happiness, ought she to
break the rules? Ought she to keep quiet? Who will find out and how?
Ought Sean to be involved in these conversations?

If Sinéad puts personal happiness before career and chooses to act with
integrity by informing her agency, and as a consequence has her employment terminated, does the ethical situation change the rights and wrongs
when we now discover that she is a highly regarded worker and that many
of her service users will suffer with a change in social worker? These include
a four-year-old child who is very close to her and whose family is relying on
her help to keep them together – and for many service users it will mean a
long gap in support, as posts are frozen and a new social worker will not be
recruited, thus adding to the burden on Sinéad's colleagues.

Is the ethical situation changed if Sinéad and Sean meet *six* months after
Sean has been a service user or a year later ... ten years later? Can Sean and
Sinéad never fall in love and live their lives together because Sean was a
member of a group that Sinéad led? But if at some point the passing of time
means that it is right for Sean and Sinéad to get together, what is this point
and how can something be wrong on Tuesday (a day short of the correct
length of time) and become right on Thursday (the day after the correct
length of time has been reached)?

# The Big Picture

## Dual relationships and corporate tax

In recent years global companies such as Amazon, Google and Starbucks have used legal loopholes to move their liabilities away from the countries where the profits are made to jurisdictions with minimal rates of tax (Murphy, 2011). This deprives the communities who pay for their goods of considerable income and has provoked outrage but little action. Enforcing ethical action increasingly relies on international cooperation. Company tax accountancy and law has its equivalent to the **dual relationships** discussed in this chapter in relation to social work; individual financial transaction accountants who, having worked with the government revenue service are employed by private accountancy firms, essentially to buy the inside knowledge they have gained about how the government tries to close the tax loopholes. There is frequent movement between big business and government; close but questionable relationships develop across boundaries that ought to be carefully managed. The ethics of dual relationships are carefully considered in social work and other professions; ought this to be the case, then, in the financial sector? In terms of fairness, consistency, utility and many other ethical principles, the revolving door of gamekeepers and poachers is unethical and illustrates an elite that chooses to use its power to construct its own 'moral' world, one that observers call corrupt.

# Guidance from Codes, Standards and Principles

The Italian code of ethics for social work (Cavaliere, 2014: 66) is clear that *'Nel rapporto professionale l'assistente sociale non deve utilizzare la relazione con utenti e clienti per interessi o vantaggi personali'* (Italian National Council, 2009, Titolo III, Capo II.2) (social workers must not use their relationship with service users for personal gain); and the Northern Irish code states, 'As a social worker, you must strive to establish and maintain the trust and confidence of service users and carers.' (NISCC, 2009: 4, code #2) The American code states, 'Social workers should respect clients' right to privacy. Social workers should not solicit private information from clients unless it is essential to providing services or conducting social work evaluation or research. Once private information is shared, standards of confidentiality apply.' (NASW 2008: 10) However, common with codes of ethics, there is little room for nuance nor information about how these exhortations are put into practice.

Some codes, such as the Australian (AASW, 2010: 16), detail the *reciprocal* rights to which social workers are entitled, such as the right to exercise professional discretion and judgement. Presumably, this includes judgement about how to interpret codes of ethics, in particular the sections that deal with relationships and disclosure.

For standards specific to social work with groups, visit the website of the International Association for Social Work with Groups (IASWG 2006: Core Values §1; Ethical Considerations §6).

## Consulting the wise professionals

Sinéad has frequently consulted her **wise professionals** during her journey through several dilemmas. At this point, perhaps they would ask us to interrogate further the idea of *disclosure*, a loaded term that suggests high risk and consequence. What if these situations are considered less as the risks of disclosure (and self-disclosure) and more as the opportunities for *reciprocity*, a kind of sharing?

### Self-disclosure or reciprocity?

Earlier I described my experience as a neighbourhood social worker, and how living on the geographical boundary of my 'patch' meant frequent encounters with service users. It is natural for people to want to catch up at these chance meetings and swap stories. If we view these conversations as 'risks of self-disclosure' we are likely to be tight-lipped, but what if they are turned on their side and seen as opportunities to reciprocate? After all, there is an expectation of reciprocity in a relationship, even a professional one.

What ought to be the degree of reciprocity? For instance, you bump into someone with whom you have worked about a year ago as their social worker and a conversation develops. Within which of these catch-ups would you feel OK to swap information?

1. She's seriously inconvenienced by changes in the local bus service timetable (*and you are too*).

2. He's just back from a holiday in Kendal in the English Lake District (*and, as it happens, you're just back from a holiday in Kendal, too*).

3. He's very happy because he's just become a grandfather (*and you have, as well*).

4. She mentions that she has moved house since you were working with her (*and you have moved, too*).

5. She mentions that her 24-year-old son has moved out at last (*and your 24-year-old son has moved back in*).

6. He hopes the local councillor gets re-elected in the council elections today (*and you support this councillor and her party, too*).

7. He mentions that he had always found you attractive (*and you found him attractive, too*).

8. She tells you that her father died of cancer recently (*as has yours*).

9. They (*you worked with the woman but her partner is new to you*) have just got together and she and her former partner have separated (*and you are with someone you have just got together with, having separated from your former partner*).

10. He's looking to extend his local involvement, but not sure how (*you are the secretary of the local history society and you're looking for new members*).

Try scaling the scenarios above – how likely it is that you would share your reciprocal news, 1 being least likely and 10 being most? What are the factors that make the difference between the lower, middle and higher ends of the scale; or are all your responses clustered in one part?

Your response to each scenario might be, 'Well, of course, it depends.' Fine – so what does it depend on? Are there material factors, such as how much time has elapsed since you worked with the person – and why might that make a difference? Would it be unprofessional if your response depended on, say, your mood on the day? On the other hand, can a decision about whether to reciprocate be *too* calculated? Can people tell when you are finely calculating what to share and what not to share, like a hack politician, and does this very calculation add up to a failure to share properly?

Some of the factors that you might weigh in the balance are how much you trust the person with information about yourself, what you think they might do with the information, even how much you like them. These might not seem professional reasons for making a decision, but they are what people do when deciding what and how much to share about themselves. Moreover, what research we have suggests that service users like and appreciate social workers who they can see as human beings, and that reciprocation is significant (Doel and Best, 2008).

So, our wise professionals make a judgement, but a not-too-calculated one, about when and how to reciprocate. All the time they are reflecting on their actions to see how the reciprocation is being received, not wanting it to feel as though it is a game of 'Snap'. The wise professionals stand invisibly to the side, monitoring the relationship.

# 8 SHARING INFORMATION AND CONFIDENTIALITY

Decisions about information and how or whether it should be shared are commonplace in both personal and professional lives and feature in many other chapters in this book, but their prevalence makes them no easier to resolve.

Let us first explore an illustration from a personal situation:

You see your best friend's husband at the theatre with another woman.

Do you tell your best friend or keep quiet? And what do you base your decision on?

First, there is a desire to explain the situation to yourself and to explore the possible social meanings. Observing their behaviour, the explanation that strikes you as the most obvious is that they are 'having an affair'. However, your choice of words to give meaning to your observations already begins to define it – 'having an affair'. Could it be that your friend and her husband have a very private arrangement, such that this is not therefore 'an affair'? Or perhaps your observations are incorrect. The intimacies that you see are, in fact, those of two people who have known one another for a long time. The theatre is, after all, a public occasion so this cannot be a secret 'affair', otherwise why risk exposing it? Perhaps your friend cannot use her ticket and, last minute, her husband has asked a long-standing woman friend to join him. Perhaps it is indiscreet of you to be making these observations in the first place. Have you yourself been observed observing and would this make a difference to what you do or say when you next meet your friend, if you know that the husband has seen you or not?

It seems that there is a complex array of factors in the mix of a decision: observations; interpretation of their meaning; openness to other interpretations. At the same time observations are being saddled into principles and these principles do not necessarily point in one direction, for they are frequently at odds with themselves. The principle of honesty alongside the right to privacy, for example. The principle of openness against the desire not to cause hurt or harm. What justifies the pain of truth if suspicions are correct? What justifies the risk of humiliation if they are not? So, when to let sleeping dogs lie and when to wake them?

## Exploring dilemmas

Information gained and used in professional circumstances has much in common with the kinds of dilemma illustrated above in a personal situation. In the rest of this chapter we will explore common themes that emerged at a conference of service users, students, social workers, practitioners and managers (held at Dundee University, Scotland, in 2013) where participants were asked to share a recent ethical or practice dilemma. Over a quarter of the 66 dilemmas included some element of information sharing and uncertainty about the bounds of confidentiality.

*Deciding what is problematic*

> **Ann's dilemma:** "A terminal cancer patient wanted me to document her life and chose to exclude her family from this activity. She wanted to prioritise her remaining time for contact with me and she didn't want her family to know this."
>
> Let us interrogate Ann's dilemma. First –

> ➤ What is 'the information' exactly?

It seems an obvious question, but what precisely *is* the information that is seen to be problematic or causing the dilemma? It helps to comprehend the nature of the dilemma if you understand the nature of the information that is seen as problematic. For instance, in Ann's example, is it the fact that the person doesn't want the documentation to be shared, or is it the fact that this task is being done with someone other than family members? How else might the information be problematic?

> ➤ What are the possible meanings or significances of the information?

In framing her dilemma, Ann notes that the service user wants to prioritise her remaining time for contact with her, but doesn't want the family to know this. What is the significance of this? The service user is not formally estranged from her family (it seems that they expect to continue to see her), yet can we assume that she is not very close to them because she prefers to spend her dying days in the company of Ann, a relative stranger? This seems an unusual request, one in need of explanation. Does it mean that there will be information in the documentation that is sensitive and will put some family members in a poor light? What is the purpose of the documentation and who is the service user thinking will access it once she has died? Will family members then become aware of the fact that they were excluded

▶

◀

from this process? What, then, are they to be told about it? Might they reason that she was not of sound mind, perhaps disorientated by the medication she was taking in her final days?

> ➤ What are the implications of sharing or not sharing the information?

Ann searches for possible explanations for the service user's wishes, but ought she also to explore the background to this request with the service user herself to help them both think through the implications? What situation might Ann be faced with if it transpires that the service user starts to reveal accusations of illegal activity against a family member, for instance of sexual abuse? Does Ann have a responsibility to share her concerns with the service user or is this an unthinkable burden for someone who is nearing death?

The responses to these questions help Ann to come to a point of decision. She hopes it will be the 'right' decision, but at least it will be a considered one, and one that she will be able to explain to others, should she be asked.

**Bryony's dilemma:** "During a group supervision session with a student group, information about a student in another agency was discussed in the group. This leaked out and was reported to the student in question."

Let's take the same steps as we took with Ann's dilemma.

> ➤ What is 'the information' exactly?

Bryony's dilemma differs from Ann's to the extent that the information is already shared – 'leaked', in her own words. The issue is what exactly is the nature of the confidentiality that has been broken, the information that is causing the dilemma? Is it the content of the information that implicates the student in question; or has the dilemma transformed to one of what to do with the knowledge that the student knows that information concerning him has been revealed in Bryony's group? Perhaps there are multiple levels of indiscretion.

> ➤ What are the possible meanings or significances of the information?

Information is often incomplete and, seen through a particular prism, often at the end of a chain of whispers. In Bryony's example, do we know that the student was explicitly named or have people put two and two together to

▶

◀

recognise the student – and does this make any difference? What potential significance might attach to the information itself; for instance, if it concerns a malpractice by the named student? Who told the student that information about him had been revealed and how might the revelation of the indiscretion be interpreted – for instance, was a group member genuinely hurt that her friend was being talked about or, rather, seeing an opportunity for some drama? Does this make a difference and, if so, why?

➤ What are the implications of sharing or not sharing the information?

Bryony is likely to be considering the implications of these apparent indiscretions for her group and her leadership. For instance, as the facilitator, did she discuss confidentiality fully with the group? The notion of confidentiality is complex and it seems there have been two kinds of breach: one within the group, as someone revealed information about another student not present; and another outside the group, as someone has subsequently discussed what happened inside the group with a person outside. Bryony will be concerned about the impact on the group's trust in itself and also its confidence in her leadership if she failed to nip the breach of confidentiality at the time. Perhaps the breach was couched in elusive hypothetical language, such as "If you knew that a student was doing X, ought you to do Y," which was then translated outside the group into a specific "Poppy asked the group what should be done about you doing X."

If the group has discussed the nature of confidentiality within the group and outside it, is the breach of this confidentiality a more culpable act than if the group had not been given this opportunity? Similarly, if the discussion in the group was framed in a hypothetical manner, is there greater culpability attached to the act of reframing the hypothetical into the actual and posing the breach as such? And does the notion of culpability have any impact on what ought now to be done?

➤ Who is involved?

As well as clarifying the nature of the information and its significances, it is also important to clarify who is involved. This is often not simple, as Bryony's case reveals. Within the group there is the student who talked about (or alluded to) the other student – let's call the first **Poppy** and the second **Ramon**. Then there is the student in the group who told Ramon about Poppy's possible indiscretion, **Sonya**. And now we learn that Sonya wouldn't have done this if she had not been egged on by another student in the group, **Terri**. The information concerns Ramon's relationship with **Ursula**, his supervisor at his placement in the Voluntary Services Organisation. The

▶

information has implications for that organisation. And, of course, Bryony and the rest of the student group are also players in this scene.

We can see the complexities in this diagram of the relationships:

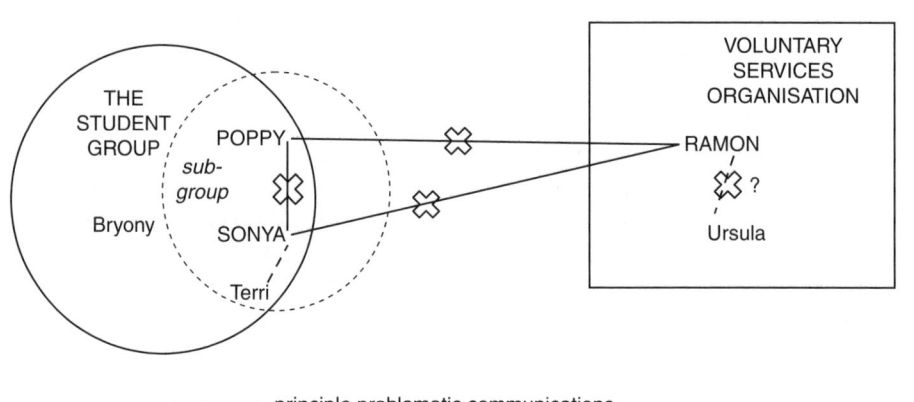

—————— principle problematic communications

– – – – – other significant communications

✖ (possible) breaches of confidence

**Figure 8.1** Bryony's dilemma in a picture

The words we use are illustrative. Is it a complete *breach* of confidentiality, reckless and crass, or a mild *indiscretion*, tactless and misjudged? Is it a deliberate and culpable act or one that is misinterpreted and unintended? Does it form part of a pattern of failures to respect confidential boundaries or is it a surprising lapse? And how severe and far reaching have the consequences been?

Do we attach greater or lesser significance to the breaches of confidentiality of happenings *within* the group (i.e. Sonya telling Ramon of something that was said in the group's space) or to breaches from *outside* the group (i.e. Poppy's disclosure in the group of information about Ramon)? What helps us to decide their relative values?

As the facilitator of the student group and as an experienced practice educator (field instructor), Bryony has the formal and professional responsibility to take the lead in clarifying the information, to locate where breaches of confidentiality have been made, to consider different courses of action and to decide which one to follow, or at least which to propose.

Bryony might call on the advice of others. In particular, if she has a groupwork supervisor or is a member of a practice educators' development group, this is exactly the kind of situation she might present (with suitable anonymities) for others to reflect on. However, are there persons with whom she ought not to confer about a decision? To what extent should the group itself discuss the dilemma and decide what should happen? It offers potentially very significant learning and empowerment for the group. Moreover, since all the group members are likely to be aware of the situation would a failure to discuss the dilemma be ignoring the elephant in the room?

Bryony must find ways of recognising her own feelings and, where necessary, find somewhere to park them. For instance, Poppy makes good contributions in the group and Bryony has liked her since the first session. Sonya, however, is unforthcoming and Bryony doesn't feel she knows her, and Terri is someone Bryony instinctively dislikes. She sees Terri as passive aggressive, using manipulative behaviour in the group to exert backroom control. Bryony does not know Ramon, but has met Ursula in practice educators' groups and likes her. Bryony is aware of all these feelings, but what *ought* she to do with them?

### Using a moral philosophy lens

> **Charlie's dilemma:** "The service user informed me of his intention to commit suicide when his terminal illness became too difficult and requested me not to inform his family."

Charlie's dilemma is whether to follow the service user's request for the family to remain ignorant of his intent to commit suicide. **Kantian** ethics would at first suggest that Charlie respects the client's self-determination, laying heavy emphasis on self-actualisation and the value of his wishes. So there is no dilemma? Well, Charlie might ask whether the client is 'reasoned', in Kantian terms. Of course, this begs the further question of how to determine 'reasoned'.

Charlie the **utilitarian** would not consider confidentiality to be absolute, nor the wishes of an individual sacrosanct. However, the scales to weigh the greatest happiness for the greatest number are not at all straightforward. Would the family be happier knowing or not knowing this information? Does the potential distress for the service user provoked by telling the family outweigh any potential 'happiness' the family experiences from being included in this knowledge? As a **rule utilitarian** she might *always* follow the wishes of a dying person which, from her point of view, limits the number of situations that present as a dilemma.

With her greatest concern focused on the *relationship* between her service user and his family rather than his individual wants and rights, Charlie might seek to explore the possible hurt he might cause his grieving family as she pursues a course of action inspired by an **ethics of care**.

Time has passed, and Charlie's client has died. In fact, he did not take an overdose and his family never knew of his intention (but perhaps they had suspected). If Charlie had had this foreknowledge ought it to have influenced her decision about what to do? Perhaps more often than we are aware, decisions are based on judgements of the likely consequences, and these judgements are in turn based on the sum total of our experiences so far – on our perception of the likelihood of C following A and B. This **consequentialist** approach is improved when unspoken analyses are made explicit and therefore subject to a range of possible consequences. When weighing the consequences of different actions, social workers seek those that cause least harm to the individual service user, benefit most people and make best use of resources (Banks, 2004).

*Timing*

> **Deepa's dilemma:** "Certain service users expressed a wish not to work with me because I'm a student. There's a need to be honest about my status as a student, but this leads to a dilemma about how to work with disengaged service users if I share this information from the start."

Deepa's dilemma lies between the question of honesty (about her status as a social worker) and the practical advantage of authority (which she sees as diminished if she is honest about being a student). Though honesty is highly prized it is not necessarily a first principle. We understand the difference between an act of commission, telling an outright lie – Deepa answering 'No' to the direct question, 'Are you a student?' – and an act of omission, failing to mention her status if its salience has not been queried. We all reveal information about ourselves at times when it seems appropriate or indeed propitious; indeed, there are circumstances when making an unsolicited declaration of one's status as a student in the very first exchanges would seem strange. Timing is all.

Most important is to find ways to explore with the service user what it is that concerns them about working with a student and to open a dialogue that addresses these concerns. Some may be valid, such as a concern that Deepa will not know what resources are available or will lack the authority to access them. By acknowledging some of the possible disadvantages, the service user might allow potential advantages, too – the student's fresh approach, the fact that they have more time than a worker with a full caseload, etc.. Already, by attending to the service user's concerns rather

◀

than trying to defeat them with counter-arguments, Deepa is giving the service user an experience of a professional who listens and who will be good to have on their side, student or not.

Deepa's situation has much in common with the dilemmas of self-disclosure which we considered in the previous chapter.

*Elite knowledge*

> **Ellie's dilemma:** "Risk decisions were being taken without access to the full information, because of certain police procedures; yet this information was then being shared, despite the procedures."

Ellie's dilemma has many dimensions. The first relates to the paradox that rules and protocols about keeping certain knowledge confidential to one situation or arena can conflict with the practice task of gathering all the available intelligence in order to arrive at the best decision. A secondary dilemma, contingent on the first, is that this paradox exerts pressure on those involved so they face the dilemma of whether and how to break the rules, or at least find ways to massage them (see the next chapter). In this way an 'information elite' forms of those people who are privy to the knowledge in contrast to those who are excluded. In addition to the inequality, it is dysfunctional because those admitted to the elite are not necessarily the people with the most significant and trustworthy information; rather it is their perceived loyalty to the others in the elite that admits them.

Suppose that Ellie finds out that there has been information sharing that has broken protocols (or even laws) – what ought she to do with that information? Ought it to make a difference if the sharing of this information has led to a better and safer decision for the service user (in other words, a **pragmatic** approach)? Or is the knowledge that elite information sharing is taking place of more far-reaching significance than any particular gain that collusion might bring in this one instance? Will the manner in which she has come by this information affect her decision (after all, Ellie is not one of the elite, so will the finger be pointed at her for accessing the information improperly?) From an information-sharing dilemma Ellie is moving into one concerning whistleblowing (see Chapter 9).

> **Frank's dilemma:** "The combination for a client's safe had been changed without notifying the client or the voluntary organisation working with the client. It was changed by the social work department who didn't want me to tell the client why the combination had been changed – it was because of thefts by home care staff."

▶

◀

Frank's dilemma is a variant of the elite information sharing we saw in Ellie's. In this case the *motivation* for elite sharing seems especially pertinent and we might look to **virtue ethics** for some guidance: the desire of a public agency to protect itself and its reputation from the knowledge that some of its employees have been stealing. Frank might not consider this to be a moral reason to keep the information within the elite group. On the other hand, does the possible distress that knowledge of this thieving might cause the client justify a 'need to know' response – that the client needs to know the new safe combination, not the reason for it? Or is the truth always the right course and does a **Kantian** respect for the individual call for the truth?

> **Giorgi's dilemma:** "I chose not to inform the service user of the full picture (that her child would be weighed at the meeting), knowing that if I did then the client would be unlikely to turn up. I didn't lie to her, but I didn't present her with the complete information so that we'd get a satisfactory result regarding her son."

This is a further variant of elite knowledge – choosing not to share information with a less powerful person (the service user taking her child to the clinic), this time for the perceived greater good. Giorgi's justification is twofold: first, that he chose this course of action because in his judgement it furthered the best interests of the child; second, that he didn't actually tell a lie. But he has identified it as a dilemma.

His **wise professionals** might ask Giorgi how he has come to this judgement and whether the undeniable paternalism of his action is justified, even if 'it works'. If the service user had asked Giorgi outright whether her child will be weighed would he have lied, and so is the fact that he did not tell an untruth merely circumstantial? Perhaps Giorgi would query why the service user would choose to absent herself unless she had something to fear – the same argument used by those who would advance the use of electronic surveillance: that only those up to no good have any reason to object. Does the service user have a *right* to know that her child will be weighed at the clinic? Does she have a right to refuse the weighing when it is proposed, in the way that a person might claim the right to privacy from surveillance? Will she feel she has been manipulated by Giorgi when she turns up for the clinic appointment and it is proposed that the child is weighed, and what will the service user have learned from this experience – that professionals are not to be trusted? – rather than the possibility of learning through dialogue why the weighing is considered necessary and discussing the possible consequences of not keeping a record of her child's weight?

▶

In most cases honesty *is* the best policy, not just for ethical reasons but for pragmatic ones, too. Others frequently have more than an inkling of the knowledge that the elite thinks is just theirs, and people learn to trust those who have confidence in them or, if not confidence, respect for their right to know.

> **Helen's dilemma:** "I supervise parental contact visits and the parent becomes agitated by comments made by the child and demands to know where these comments are coming from. I know but I'm not sure whether to say."

Social workers promote social justice and one of social work's objectives is to break down elites, so it is especially uncomfortable when they themselves are part of that elite. A significant aspect of Helen's dilemma is her 'accomplice' role: part of the information elite, but fearful of possible consequences if she aims to be inclusive and share her knowledge. The principles sketched with Giorgi's dilemma apply to Helen's. The parent probably has a good idea from where the comments emanate and the query might be more about testing Helen than confirming the parent's own suspicions. For Helen's **wise professionals** this is an opportunity to talk with the parent about boundaries of confidentiality and why these boundaries are drawn, and to open up discussion with the parent about her fears and concerns regarding the information and its significance; in contrast, Helen's less wise professionals will 'hmm' and 'haa', look uncomfortable, attempt diversions and give half-answers, all of which will undermine the parent's confidence in her, as well as Helen's confidence in herself. Once again, honesty is a good policy. In Helen's case, the honesty is channelled into a directness with the parent about how information will and will not be shared, and why.

### Public and private knowledge

> **Isha's dilemma:** "We were in McDonalds, me and a child who is accommodated. The child recognised an adult and pulled at their jumper. The adult looked at me and then said to the child, 'Hi, I thought you were living at your gran's?' I didn't know how or whether to explain my presence as the social worker."

In addition to the confidentiality aspects, Isha's dilemma is an example of the issue of professional boundaries that we explored in the previous chapter. A fast-food outlet is a public place so it is reasonable to expect Isha to have discussed with the child what they ought to say if they meet someone the child knows. This allows a rehearsal for the child to do their own explaining, based on what they had prepared themselves with Isha.

This earlier conversation might be a good trigger for the child to talk more generally about how they describe their situation to others, such as school friends and, therefore, how they seem themselves.

*Value clashes*

> **Janice's dilemma:** "A client asked me for advice about how to hide his savings from HMRC [the government tax collecting service] as he was claiming means-tested benefits. My agency's policy is one of strict confidentiality, but the client's actions are contrary to my own values."

Any action to defraud the tax revenue service is, of course, illegal, though the service user might be seeking to emulate the multinational companies that secrete their profits somewhere else – avoidance rather than evasion. Information gained by social workers is not privileged as it is with priests or lawyers, so the agency's policy of strict confidentiality appears to be 'trumped'. Even so, Janice has a dilemma about whether information about a possible intention to commit an offence should be reported or whether she should just omit to assist the service user. Do you try to avoid a clash with the service user's values or can the relationship be strengthened by talking openly about these differences? (See Chapter 4).

*Information about possible illegal activity*

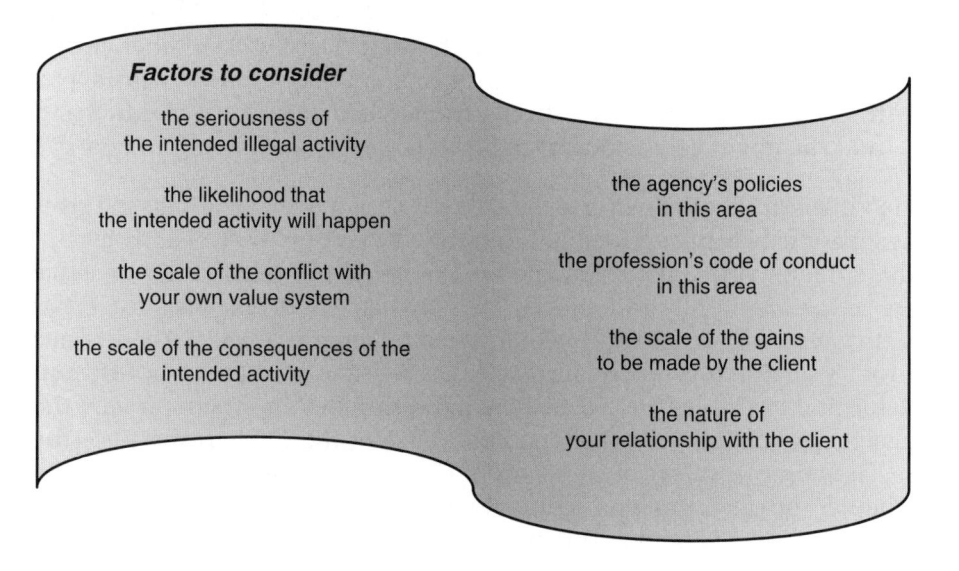

**Factors to consider**

the seriousness of
the intended illegal activity

the likelihood that
the intended activity will happen

the agency's policies
in this area

the profession's code of conduct
in this area

the scale of the conflict with
your own value system

the scale of the consequences of the
intended activity

the scale of the gains
to be made by the client

the nature of
your relationship with the client

◀

### Keeping information to yourself

> **Karen's dilemma:** "I was talking to a link worker and I mentioned about an inappropriate sexual comment made from one adult client with learning difficulties to another, and he then told the client's mother who was upset by this."

The **wise professionals** have generally praised the virtue of honesty, but perhaps they would counsel a difference between the careful sharing of honest information and the unconsidered repetition of information (sometimes called gossip). Karen ought to reflect on why she chose to repeat the information and what she expected the link worker to do with it. Was there an inherent good in relaying the information about the 'inappropriate' sexual comment (who defines 'inappropriate'?) and, if so, what was the nature of this good? The wise professionals might consider it unvirtuous to indulge powerful feelings by holding or withholding information and spreading vicarious, even malicious, interest in other people's lives. This conflicts with the virtuous idea of taking action for some purposeful good. The loose exchange of information can be as unethical as the withholding of information or its restriction to a tight elite. Karen ought to reflect on why she is spreading information and whether this is wrong.

### Your role in creating the dilemma

> **Liu's paradox:** "I'm worried that the help I give the mother in her supervised visits with her children is so good that it masks the true picture. I worry about the mother's unsupervised care of the children and that she might get custody of them based on misleading information."

Liu's dilemma is paradoxical, expressed in the worry that the help she gives in supervised visits is so good it masks the true picture. We feel fairly certain that athletes who use performance-enhancing drugs to do better in a race are acting unethically and, indeed, they are liable to disqualification. What if they receive psychological help in order to 'enter the zone'? There seems to be a view that psychological and physical assistance are ethically different. Returning to Liu, her help is truly empowering in that it is improving the experience that both mother and child have of the supervised visits – the social work equivalent of 'entering the zone' – yet she is right to wonder whether the other function of the visits, to assess the mother's capabilities, is being distorted and that this enhancement will not be possible when Liu is absent.

▶

Like most, perhaps all, dilemmas, the ethical and the practical are entwined. It would, surely, be unethical for Liu to withdraw her supporting role in the supervised visits, yet perhaps just as unethical to fail to consider how the mother can learn how to improve her own care of the child when social work assistance is not on hand. This is the difference between dependence and empowerment and, as such, it becomes a practice dilemma with which all social workers are familiar: how to help clients to transfer the learning from their social work encounters to the rest of their lives. Some methods, such as task-centred practice, have been found to be more effective than others at achieving this transformation (Doel and Marsh, 1992; Marsh and Doel, 2005). Certainly, Liu – like all social workers – has an ethical responsibility to seek knowledge about which methods of practice are most effective and empowering and to develop her skills accordingly (Trevithick, 2012).

### 'Catch-22'

**Mahmoud's paradox:** "Drug-addicted clients need to be open and honest about relapses if treatment is to be successful. But there's one I'm working with just now where this means disclosing an offence which I should then report, which stops other service users from being honest, which then stops their treatment."

Mahmoud's drug-addicted clients need to be honest about relapses for treatment to work, but if they are honest it can lead to withdrawal from treatment. The concept of *catch-22* was first popularised by Joseph Heller (1961) in his novel of the same name, and refers to circumstances when the one solution is made impossible because of rules inherent in the situation (in Heller's book, you could be discharged from the army if you could prove you were insane, but by wanting to be discharged from the army you proved your sanity). Even more absurdly, the hero in Heller's novel discovers that catch-22 does not exist, but because everyone believes it to exist it has tremendous power and, moreover, because it does not exist it cannot be repealed! This Kafka-esque world is not unfamiliar to social workers. Mahmoud's best policy might be to discuss the effects of this paradox with fellow workers (who are likely to have experienced it, too) in order to agree a strategy to revise the agency's protocols.

**Natasha's paradox:** "The client believes it is shameful for other people to know your business, so she will not allow information to be shared with others. But help would only be forthcoming from Housing Services if the details of her personal circumstances could be passed to them. Without this help, the client would have to go back to an abusive husband, risking herself and the children."

This is also a *catch-22*, where one belief (that it is shameful for other people to know your business) leads to an inescapable outcome (that the housing department is denied the information needed to allow her to escape her abusive husband). The child abuse scandal in Rotherham, northern England, was sustained by shame, a collective belief that the shame of being a victim was worse than the shame of perpetrating abuse. Ruzwana Basir, a past President of the Oxford Union, has spoken out about her experience of child abuse, and was vilified rather than lauded by some in her community. It perpetuates a destructive catch-22, when the victims of child sexual abuse feel unable to speak because they will be ostracised by their communities, but the consequence of not sharing the information is their continued appalling abuse. (See Das and Kulkarni, 2006a: 84–8 for an excellent account of the dilemmas an Indian social worker faces in this context.)

Once again an ethical dilemma is entwined with a practice dilemma – how to work with belief systems that undermine the well-being of the person who owns them? A variant of this is the Marxist notion of *false consciousness,* illustrated in the voting patterns of marginalised people who vote for political parties that uphold the powerful elite. Social work practice dilemmas often call on individual conscientisation and systemic policy change. What does this mean in practice? For Mahmoud it indicates an understanding with individual service users that they might have to stop short of complete honesty about offending, whilst also confronting his agency about the way the existing policy binds everyone unreasonably. Social workers frequently have to work at these different levels – individual, organisational and political – to achieve lasting change. For Natasha, the focus is likely to be more with the individual service user to acquaint her with the rules of confidentiality in public service in the hope of reassuring her that the (shameful) information she gives to the housing department will not leak back into her own community. And it is a reminder to public servants about why confidentiality and privacy are so important.

### The place of policies

**Owen's dilemma:** "I'm the key worker for a 16-year-old boy who abused other boys and is now moving into a residential care unit. I'm not sure who should and shouldn't know about his past – the care staff, the other residents, the residents' families … ?"

◀

Sometimes there are clearly stated policies to guide or even prescribe a course of action. For instance, Owen's agency is likely to have a policy to help decide who should know about the past abuse by the 16-year-old boy. Much will depend on how common it is for someone with the boy's history to be joining the unit and this in turn will influence the established norms and expectations.

Having a policy can increase feelings of security, but it ought not to excuse a failure to think about the issues. Sometimes a policy feels wrong in the particular circumstances and professionals need to know how to challenge and refine such policies (see the following chapter for a further development of these ideas).

If you were a worker in Owen's residential unit, what policies do you think *ought* to be in place to decide what happens to information about a new resident's history? How would you balance the individual's rights to privacy and the community's need to know of potential risks? Obligations to the community are more developed in societies that are not individualistic. In South Asian countries, for instance, *not* to share knowledge with the community can be as offensive as breaking privacy in individualistic societies. Breaking trust with the community by guaranteeing an individual's confidentiality could have hazardous consequences for that individual (Das and Kulkarni, 2006a).

## The Big Picture

### Elite knowledge sharing and the Establishment

In the previous chapter's Big Picture we considered the revolving door of high-level tax accounting personnel from government tax authorities to large private companies and back. This same example illustrates the concept of elite knowledge sharing that we have explored in this chapter; complex knowledge about tax (and its legal avoidance) is secreted in the hands of relatively few people, all of whom have a vested interest. Those who have been engaged in closing loopholes have the best knowledge about how to open them and the result is a worsening of the tax intake from multinational corporations, which in turn results in poorer funding of public services. Indirectly, this elite knowledge sharing has a more profound impact on the lives of ordinary people than the elite information sharing that takes place in professional groupings, but this top echelon elite, the Establishment, is so powerful that the very knowledge of their information sharing is, itself, elite.

## Guidance from Codes, Standards and Principles

'Social workers, in handling the information collected in the form of documents, pictures, computer files, etc., must inform clients of the purpose and use of the information as well as the limitation of confidentiality in detail. Client consent must be obtained prior to the disclosure of information' (Korean Association of Social Workers: 4). How might this injunction help the various social workers', students' and service users' dilemmas reported in this chapter? In many ways it illustrates the limitations of the kind of guidance given in formal codes of ethics. The Aotearoa New Zealand code does attempt to illustrate the limitations to client confidentiality. For instance, 'In an emergency, a decision to provide client information to responsible third parties may be in the client's best interests. In such an instance, it is the [social worker's] duty to fully inform the client as soon as is reasonable after the event of what information was divulged and to whom' (ANZASW, 2015: 5). Even with this illustration, many questions remain to be explored, such as what is a 'responsible' third party?

'Codes of ethics are seen as the first tangible commitment to being ethical,' state Keeney et al. (2014: 5) – but are they? Is it possible to act ethically without a code of ethics in place and does a code of ethics automatically suggest ethical practice? (Butler, 2002). 'Tangible' means visible to an audit but not necessarily realised off the page. This is a concern with codes of ethics, that they might lead observers to mistake the written word with practice; like the proliferation of the use of the word 'quality' in mission statements and the like, when the services themselves are being cut and are demonstrably not improving in quality. The NASW (US) code of ethics grew from a page of 14 general statements of principle in 1960 to 27 pages of ethical prescriptions – this does not mean that American social work is 27 times more ethical now than it was in 1960.

## Consulting the wise professionals

### A framework

We have already heard from the **wise professionals** on a number of occasions in this chapter, in particular to present a framework within which to interrogate dilemmas (see pages 116–118):-

➤ What actually is the information?
    The way a dilemma has been framed might not be the most helpful or accurate way to picture it. A diagrammatic format like the one on

page 119 can help to expose which lines of communication are possibly compromised and, therefore, exactly what is the information that might be problematic.

> Who is involved?
> A mental map (or another diagram on paper) of who is communicating with whom and which communications are seen as problematic helps chart an ethical course of action.

> What are the possible meanings or significances of the information?
> It is important to be open to all possible interpretations of the information, not just the ones that at first seem obvious, and to treat what you see and believe with philosophic doubt.

> What are the implications of sharing or not sharing the information?
> Professionals operate in a world where an understanding of the possible consequences of an action is important, so pragmatic concerns must be weighed alongside values and belief systems about the rights and wrongs.

Try practising this framework with one or two of these dilemmas which, like all the others in this chapter, came from social workers, service users, students, educators and managers who were invited to share recent dilemmas:

**Parvez's dilemma:** "A much-needed carer threatens to withdraw her support for her mother if she is not informed of her medical information. Her mother does not want any personal information revealed to her daughter, but also will not countenance accepting any support from domiciliary services."

**Queta's dilemma:** "A young girl tells me she wishes to see her dad, but she doesn't want her mum to know of her wish. She eventually tells her mother, who is then very annoyed with me because I had not let her know."

**Rab's dilemma:** "Should I have found a way round telling my mother that I was the informant about her wanderings and fallings? It led to a breakdown in our relationship."

**Suzy's dilemma:** "One agency made a referral to mine; then new information led to an argument between the agencies. The referring agency made a complaint against me and my agency made me write a letter of apology to the family, even though it wasn't me who supplied the new information."

Try using the framework with your own information and confidentiality dilemmas. This process needs time away from the heat of a particular situation, so that you are responding rather than reacting to the circumstances of the dilemma. Discovering how you best find this place – whether it is a space in the physical world or one in your own head, or both – is an important step to internalising the wise professionals and *becoming* them.

# 9   RULES, DISOBEDIENCE AND WHISTLEBLOWING

## Duty to obey; duty to rebel

Is it ever right to disobey the law and does it make a difference whether the law in question is in a totalitarian or democratic society? In some political philosophies the duty to civic obedience is dependent on the government's commitment to promoting the 'common good' (Plamenatz, 1938); and the corollary is a duty to overthrow a government that is not promoting the common good. However, it is far from straightforward to decide what is 'common' or 'good' about the 'common good'. The philosopher John Locke (1632–1704) considered the nature of *tacit* consent; that, for instance, by travelling in a country you tacitly accept its laws. By working in an agency do you tacitly accept its policies?

Political obligations are not absolute: the Nuremberg defence ('I was only following orders') was disallowed.

> Our ultimate obligation to obey the law is a moral obligation and not a legal obligation. It cannot be a legal obligation, for this would lead to an infinite regress – since legal obligations derive from laws, there would have to be a law that says we must obey the law. What obligation would there then be to obey this law? If legal obligation, then there would have to be another law . . . and so on. If there is any obligation to obey the law it must, ultimately, be a *moral* obligation. (Singer, 1973: 3, my italics)

It is no longer 'Why ought I to obey the law?', but 'When ought I to obey the law?' and 'When do I have an obligation *not* to obey the law?'

**Utilitarians'** views of obligation are merely forward-facing, in terms of what has the best consequences, whereas most people see obligations as having some backward-looking relevance to previous undertakings that might or might not have been given.

## Protocols, procedures and policies

**Rule utilitarians** develop general rules to govern behaviour designed to produce the happiness for the greatest number of people using rule-of-thumb principles. Protocols are the playing fields on which action takes place and, from an ethical standpoint, we ought to ask whether it is level and designed to arrive at a fair decision. The fairness of protocols are often called into question; at a national level, the protocol for general elections in the UK can see a single political party grab an absolute majority of seats in the UK parliament with less than 37% of the overall votes cast (as happened in 2015). Some argue from a **pragmatic** stance that this system produces strong government and this outweighs the unrepresentative nature of that government.

A problem with protocols is the potential to replace ethical thinking with a step-by-step routine in which the players turn to a manual for instruction, rather than their **wise professionals**, and the manual is not capable of the precision needed for each **singularity**. The danger is of social work losing its moral agency to procedural expertise, and the power that accrues to procedural expertise lies with the rule makers. Balancing the benefits of routines that provide stability and equality of service with the discretion and flexibility of professional autonomy is a challenge to any public service, social work in particular. Policies forged in the heat of a public inquiry can have unforeseen consequences that outweigh the initial benefits; for example, a 'no touch' policy can result in an impoverishment of relationships with long-term costs to the quality of social care.

## Whistleblowing

One form of 'disobedience' is whistleblowing, the term given to the exposé of poor-doing or even wrongdoing, most often associated with an individual or small group revealing what it believes to be poor practices, sometimes even wholesale corruption (Ellis and Dehn, 2001; Hunt, 1998). Despite legal protection in some countries, such as the UK's Public Interest Disclosure Act 1998 and charities like Public Concern at Work, the act of whistleblowing is likely to provoke strong feelings and many dilemmas, ethical and practical. It is the anticipation of these feelings that can make it difficult and inhibit it from occurring (Mansbach and Bachner, 2009).

Another perspective on whistleblowing is as a form of disclosure (Chapter 7); it is concerned with the handling of information, but in circumstances that are much more exposing than most of the dilemmas of disclosure. There are close links, too, with the dilemmas of confidentiality (Chapter 8) though, again, the whistleblower's stakes are usually higher.

### Loyalty – look to your own

Whether in football, politics or the family, much value is attached to the idea of loyalty (Dolgoff *et al.*, 2009). From Macbeth/Duncan to Heseltine/ Thatcher, the ousting of a leader through an act of disloyalty rarely ends happily for the one seen as treacherous. Disloyalty to an in-group breaks many social codes and can be seen as a moral failing. Solidarity, by contrast, is the virtue of lending support to another group (for instance, 'the miners marched in solidarity with the nurses'). Loyalty is often hierarchical (dogs are loyal to their owners) whilst solidarity is usually non-hierarchical.

Loyalty springs from a strong need to belong and for the protection of a larger grouping. Criticism inside our own group is allowed, but there is an expectation to close ranks in the face of out-groupers, however defined (adults, men, white people, another team, a different organisation, a rival company). There are strong imperatives *not to wash dirty laundry in public* and to exercise solidarity against possible exploitation by others who see weakness through fractures. Breaking this taboo risks banishment from the in-group, a lonely social death.

If the in-group is a collection of people or an organisation where much energy and trust has been invested, or where there is dependency (for emotional warmth, safety, a salary), then the motivation to ignore its wrongdoings or to try to explain them in the best light is strong: *you don't bite the hand that feeds you.*

A **virtuous** social worker is a loyal one. But loyal to what?

## Conformity – when in Rome

Closely linked to loyalty is conformity, when individuals feel strong peer pressure, even coercion, to alter their beliefs and behaviour to bring them in line with group or organisational thinking (Janis, 1972; Turner and Pratkanis, 1998). Social experiments such as Asch's (1952) exposed this process, in which the pressure of primed group members, 'confederates', all giving the same incorrect answer led the single genuine participant to give the same incorrect answer in three out of four cases. It takes a strong mind to point to the nudity of *the Emperor's new clothes.*

Conformity can lead to complicity or to subversive rebellion, still an act of conformity and as such rendering the person complicit and submissive. The subversive act allows the retention of some pride but, because it is unknown to the powerful decision-makers it has no impact on that decision. Cumulative acts of subversion can overturn established powers, but 'covert activism' (Greenslade *et al.,* 2015) is essentially a **pragmatic** rather than an ethical response.

## Doubt – physician, heal thyself

Referees blow their whistles to indicate a foul, or the game's end, and the term 'whistleblowing' nicely conveys this sense of *enough is enough.*

Whistleblowing is usually a definitive and purposeful act taken after deliberation rather than in a moment's rush. Referees have the advantage of clear rules that direct their actions and, though there might be disagreement about what has been observed, the referee is the recognised authority on the pitch with sanctions for those who do not respect this authority.

When a worker cries foul, the rules are often not self-evident. There might be a whistleblowing procedure in the agency's protocols, but the process that has led to the blowing of the whistle is typically heavy with doubt: is there an obvious explanation for the practice that you think is unacceptable, something that you are 'missing'?; are your standards unrealistic in this context?; how about your own practice – will it stand up to scrutiny? Self-doubt comes from the worry that once the spotlight is switched on it will shine not on the practices of others but on your own; that your head is above the parapet; that you are in the line of fire rather than those sensible enough to keep low.

I have advocated philosophic doubt throughout this book as a way to connect with the wise professionals, but it is this professional predisposition to subject a singular hypothesis to critical examination, to doubt it, that can also inhibit blowing the whistle, an act which requires supreme confidence.

## Fear and loss

Fear of being wrong is significant in whistleblowing, though most fears are perhaps associated with anticipated consequences, especially the potential losses – job, profession and career, friends and colleagues, respect.

Fear of the unknown can prevent a person from whistleblowing. Who knows what the future holds for the whistleblower? Exile in a Moscow airport or refuge in an Ecuadorean embassy were not the outcomes of first choice for Edward Snowden or Julian Assange. Kay Sheldon, a whistleblower at the Care Quality Commission, had good reason to be fearful as it later transpired that a secret dossier was being compiled regarding her mental health, to be used to attempt to discredit her. Her concerns were vindicated, but no one was held to account for the victimisation she experienced. Margaret Hodge, MP and Chair of the Committee on Public Accounts, underlined the impact of fear in this statement:

> You only have to look at my Committee's work on everything from GP out of hours services to tax avoidance to see how vital whistleblowers are to protecting taxpayers' money. It is extremely worrying, therefore, that half of workers stay silent about misconduct, possibly because they fear what will

happen if they speak out. Government must do more to support those workers. (Committee of Public Accounts, 2014)

We will consider **consequentialism** (deciding the ethics of whistleblowing by weighing the consequences) in the example dilemma later.

## Power – you can't fight City Hall

Decisions about the ethics of whistleblowing are rarely made amongst people with equal power. In the most well-publicised incidents of whistleblowing, the individual ('a maverick') against the organisation, it is always clear who has the most power.

The whistleblower is not powerless, nor is the organisation against which the whistle is blown all-powerful; often it is the loss of prestige and reputation that most motivates agencies to fear whistleblowing and, reasonably, to defend themselves from mistaken or mischievous whistleblowing, aware of the common belief that *there's no smoke without fire*. Some whistleblowers are relatively powerful collectives, such as *The Guardian* newspaper, though they seldom match the resources of their adversaries (phone hacking in Rupert Murdoch's media empire; global organisations failing to pay their UK taxes). Power ought not to enter the ethical equation in whistleblowing but it does, with an expectation that the most powerful side will win. Ought the judgement about the likelihood of success to be a factor in deciding whether to blow the whistle?

## Motive – enough is enough

One of the more interesting questions around whistleblowing is *why?* We instinctively desire to understand the motives that lie behind the act of whistleblowing. If an individual is set to gain from an act of whistleblowing ought that to influence our judgement of the ethical balance?

> The French government decided to renovate *La Santé,* a notorious Paris prison, after the publication of a whistleblowing diary written over seven years by the prison's chief medical officer. This triggered a parliamentary enquiry. The whistleblower received death threats after the publication of her diaries and has been barred from entering the building ever since. (Reported in *The Guardian,* 22 July 2014, p. 15.)

If the whistleblower in the *La Santé* case received royalties from the sales of her diaries (there is no suggestion that she did) would this make any difference to the validity of the claims of her whistleblowing? Does the fact that there were seven years between the commencement of the diaries and the public revelation of their content affect our confidence? Ought the moral character of the whistleblower to be relevant to our judgement about the strength of her claims?

The motivation for a whistleblower might be 'to do good'. Interestingly, the term 'do-gooder' has become a term of reproach, even abuse, often preceded by 'so-called'. Is the whistleblower a 'so-called do-gooder' whose self-righteousness leads them to conclude that they are in the right when all around them are wrong? Does the whistleblower have a strongly **deontological** sense of the right thing to do and a duty to do the right thing?

The circumstances in which most whistleblowers find themselves are much more fluid and ill-defined than those of the referee at a football match. The logic that has driven to a disclosure is likely to have been **defeasible**; that is, contingent on various and varying factors, open to refutation and interpretation with an *all-things-being-equal* conclusion, the best move at this point. Do the possible cataclysmic consequences of the whistleblow justify what might well be such an indecisive conclusion? The experiences from *La Santé* and elsewhere suggest that time passes before individuals decide that something is wrong and even longer before they take action.

It seems that whistleblowers need these characteristics: a loyalty to ideals and standards; a willingness not to conform and the confidence to stand alone; an ability to move from doubt to decision and to act on the basis of (strong) probability; courageousness; motivation by other things than self-interest; and a strong internal locus of power. The media's concoction of the whistleblower invariably lauds or demonises the individual – the Edward Snowden and the Julian Assange – in tune with the general obsession with heroes or traitors as mavericks against the system, when the reality is that successful challenges to bad practice might more likely be achieved through collective action.

## Exploring dilemmas 1

**Stan** is a student social worker on a bachelor's course. He has just completed his first placement in a criminal justice setting. He is a confident, able 30 year old with personal experiences of caring. He passed the placement, but subsequently he was found to have extensive service user files in his possession. Stan had thought the service user was being discriminated against by the agency and had taken the materials to put before a solicitor. He had taken these at the end of the placement with the permission of the service user but not the agency. The materials

▶

◀

contained a range of third party information including, as it happens, the home address of the judge in the case.

The case involved contested contact and custody. Stan's service user was the father, a working class man receiving benefits, whilst the mother was an affluent professional. Stan argued that his responsibility to promote the child's rights to parental contact and his service user's well-being and rights were greater than his responsibility to follow agency procedures. Stan listed a number of instances of alleged discrimination (against himself whilst on placement) and how he had attempted to intervene on the service user's part but had been told he was wrong or over-attached or had deficient assessment skills.

*Fitness to Practise protocol*

What are the protocols to balance the rights and wrongs in Stan's case? The programme responsible for the governance of social work education has a protocol to convene a panel to decide a student's professional suitability, their *fitness to practise*. This covers areas that lie outside practice competence or academic ability and relate to behaviours and attitudes, integrity and values. The Fitness to Practise panel is composed of three or four members drawn from inside and outside the school of social work and includes a representative from an agency that provides social work placements but has not been involved with the student. The members are drawn from a regular pool of people who have training to prepare them for this role. Before it convenes, the panel reads a report prepared by an investigating group and Stan's report in response. The leader of the investigating group and Stan (accompanied by his student representative) are present at the panel to answer questions.

In Stan's case the usual members have been replaced by a panel of moral philosophers:

> **Rose** takes a **duty-based** approach with some aspects of **rule utilitarianism**.
> **Selina** follows the **consequentialist** ethical tradition.
> **Spencer** is a **virtue ethicist**.
> **Rajesh** is a feminist moral philosopher who focuses on the **ethics of care**.

(You might want to refresh your knowledge of moral philosophy by turning to pages 11–17 and the Glossary, page 183, but it is possible to make sense of what follows without this refresher.)

▶

Beneath the explicit questions that the panel puts to Stan there are implicit questions (subtext) that relate to their moral view of the world.

As the members convene, Rajesh has a question for the panel itself:

1. **"Who ought to be involved in judging the rights and wrongs of Stan's actions?"**

Subtext: "What is our moral authority?" Rajesh is concerned about the relational aspects of the case and, before any deliberations can take place, he is keen to explore who gets the right to make the decision about Stan's future. Rajesh does not have the power to change the protocols themselves, but he does have the authority to question whether they are likely to be experienced as fair, especially by Stan, and whether there are other parties who ought to be included.

He notes that service users as a whole are a group who have an interest in the outcome but who are not represented. Although the particular service users in this case might find a voice via the investigating group's report, is Rajesh right to question whether there ought to be a service user educator on the panel to provide a general perspective? If Rajesh feels strongly that the composition of the panel is flawed, ought he to continue to participate in it?

The panel, including Rajesh, decide to continue. Stan, his student representative and the leader of the investigating team are invited in. Spencer asks Stan:

2. **"What was your motivation for these actions?"**

Subtext: "Is Stan a 'good' person?" Spencer is trying to establish what kind of person Stan is – is he 'good'? If he has acted from good intentions this makes his actions good, no matter what their consequences. Let us imagine responses from three Stans:

| STAN.01 | STAN.02 | STAN.03 |
|---|---|---|
| "I was keen to see justice done and though I knew it was taking a risk with my own future and career, it was the right thing to do. If I'd known there were other personal details in the case files I would have tried to remove those." | "I felt sorry for the father who was powerless against the education and wealth of the mother. I felt sorry for the kid, too, who really wanted to see his dad but had been cowed by his mother into denying it." | "There was no way I was going to get my way other than to take the files. I was angry the way I was being ignored and disrespected by the agency, so I was left with no alternative but to take the matter into my own hands." |

◀

How might the different Stans influence Spencer's reflections on whether *Stan is a good person*?

Spencer asks a supplementary question:

**3.  "How were you found out?"**

Subtext: "Again, is Stan a 'good' person?"

| STAN.01 | STAN.02 | STAN.03 |
|---|---|---|
| "Well, I wasn't 'found out' as such. I'd been having qualms and wanted reassurance that I had done the right thing, so I mentioned it to my tutor, expecting to get confirmation, well, hoping – but it turned out rather differently." | "I didn't know how I could get the files back to the agency, hadn't really thought about that and I knew I couldn't keep them indefinitely, so I had a word with Jean from Admin and she said she was sorry but she'd have to tell Sunia, the team leader." | "A couple of pints loosened my tongue and I guess you could say I was bragging to a friend about 'beating the system' and she told her tutor – 'snitched' is one word for it. As you can imagine, we're not talking." |

Spencer and the other panel members are building a picture of Stan, essentially a moral picture of what kind of person they judge him to be. This is particularly important for Spencer because of his allegiance to **virtue ethics**, and also for Rajesh to an extent. We learn that Stan.03 has a friend who felt it was her duty to tell someone what she knew. Does this give us a clue about what she thinks about Stan.03 and ought this to colour our view?

Is Spencer's question a valid one – ought it to make a difference, the way the situation was revealed?

Selina asks Stan:

**4.  "Whose 'good' were your actions promoting?"**

Subtext: "Have Stan's actions added to the greater good?"

In whose interests is Stan acting? In one sense he is acting in the father's interests, but perhaps he is acting in his own, to the extent that he is satisfying his own desires (for justice, etc.). See the Stans' responses on page 142.

Developing this theme, Selina now poses the question as harm and asks Stan:

**5.  "Has anyone been harmed by your actions?"**

Subtext: "Have Stan's actions subtracted from the greater good?"

Selina wonders whether Stan's actions might be taken as an example that would in the greater scale of things prove harmful, for instance if it sets an

▶

◀

| STAN.01 | STAN.02 | STAN.03 |
|---|---|---|
| "I'd like to say I was acting in the common good, in that my actions weren't just about helping the father to get a fair hearing and proper redress, but there's a broader benefit, a bit abstract, in opposing discriminatory practices." | "I took this risk solely for the father and the son, so it was for their good. I felt they were getting a raw deal and this seemed to be the only way to get some justice for them." | "I didn't think of it in terms of whose 'good', only that I'd have found it difficult to live with myself if I'd not done something about the situation. It's about having a sense of pride." |

example whereby other students start to act on their own moral judgement and ignore agency protocols.

| STAN.01 | STAN.02 | STAN.03 |
|---|---|---|
| "I can see that my practice teacher and the team leader at the agency might feel harmed, in the sense of being undermined. That might harm the trust between the uni and the agency but I sincerely hope that isn't the case. It really wasn't my intent." | "Although I knew that the mother would be opposed, I don't think my actions did her any harm and there was certainly no ill intended towards her. In the long run I hope she sees it's not caused harm, in fact it's been good, for her son." | "The only possible harm is to myself if this panel decides to remove me from the course. No one else has been harmed by my actions as far as I can see." |

Rose has been sitting with her arms folded, looking unimpressed. She challenges Stan directly:

6. **"What gives you the right to steal from the agency?"**
　　　　　　　　Subtext: "Where does Stan believe that his duty lies?"
By accepting a placement, has Stan tacitly agreed to the agency's protocols and practices – what Singer (1973: 49) calls quasi-consent? Singer uses the example of a group of people going to the pub and, in turn, buying a round of drinks. When it comes to the last round, the last person is expected to buy the round. He or she has not consented to this, but has given tacit consent by accepting the drinks in the previous rounds. Has Stan tacitly agreed to the agency's practices? Or, by not consenting explicitly, is he excused? The service user consented to the removal of the file. Does that count? Ought it to count?

　　Stan might rephrase words from Thoreau's (1866) essay on *Civil Disobedience*, '[W]e should be men [*sic*] first and subjects afterwards' into '[W]e

▶

should be people first and professionals afterwards.' Thoreau's essay continues, 'It is not desirable to cultivate a respect for the law, so much as for the right [thing to do]'.

| STAN.01 | STAN.02 | STAN.03 |
|---|---|---|
| "I definitely don't see it as stealing as I had the intent to return them, so in that sense they were being borrowed. I'd like to see what I did as in the tradition of the Dissenters. I see disobedience as a plea for reconsideration." | "Well, whose notes are they anyway? I don't know the legal position, but morally surely they are the service user's and he has a right to them, even though it should have been him who made the request. But he consented to their removal." | "The only alternative to acquiescence was dissent. Under duress, I took the files as it was the only course of action left to me by that time. I didn't have any personal gain so I don't see how it could be described as theft. There was no financial gain involved." |

Rose reminds Stan that there is a requirement in the agency's code of practice to protect service user's records. The student representative comes in, "Yes, but he *was* protecting them. He didn't damage them, he returned them intact. From his point of view he was protecting the records not just as physical objects but as what they are supposed to do, their *purpose*. At the very most, he was borrowing them and he considers they belonged to the client."

Rose has another question:

7. **"In a few years' time, if and when you are a team leader and a student on placement decides to take extensive case files home, what would you do about it?"**

      Subtext: "Do you understand the principle of universalisability?" If Stan is acting from a moral principle, then he must accept that if and when he becomes a team manager and one of the students on placement in his team takes a case file home because they consider that the service user has been discriminated against, Stan must accept this as a legitimate act. To do otherwise means that Stan is acting from a selfish principle, not a moral one.

Spencer feels that Stan was acting with **beneficence** because he was seeking to do good and he sees this is a critical factor in determining his culpability or not. Rajesh agrees that, at the very least, Stan was acting from a principle of **non-maleficence**; that is, seeking not to do harm.

| STAN.01 | STAN.02 | STAN.03 |
|---|---|---|
| "It would be hypocritical of me to act against this future hypothetical student, given that I have done exactly the same now as the student. I'd want to remind myself of that." | "In principle, yes, but I'd like to be the judge of that situation in the future – you can't just take a file, there has to be a good reason for it and I would want to be the judge of that." | "I would look on the act sympathetically, but it's hard to know what kind of person I will be then and how my different role might make me act differently." |

Rajesh asks Stan:

**8.** **"Did you agonise much about this decision?"**

Subtext: "Did you act from an ethics of care?"

| STAN.01 | STAN.02 | STAN.03 |
|---|---|---|
| "Yes, I thought long and hard. I wanted to talk about it rather than come to the decision on my own, but I didn't want to put anyone in that difficult position. In the end it was my care for the father's situation that pushed me into the decision." | "I didn't see it as a dilemma as such – more a risk, in that I was risking my place on the course. I knew it was the right thing to do, so to that extent it wasn't a dilemma. Any agonising was whether I could afford the risk and what might happen to me." | "It was the obvious thing to do. All other doors had been shut in my face by the attitude of the agency and my practice teacher. I was painted into a corner with no alternative, so I'd say no, I didn't agonise over it." |

Ought it to make a difference what other avenues Stan tried before he decided on this course of action? Rajesh's question aims at understanding Stan's own abilities with moral reasoning, not just whether he acts from an ethics of care.

Before they leave, the student representative, a student of moral philosophy, puts her question to the panel:

**9.** **"Isn't Stan's action an example of good practice, as the regulatory body for social work\* allows confidentiality to be overridden if there is a risk to a service user?"**

Subtext: "He acted from an ethics of care"

◀

*\* In the UK: Health and Care Professions Council in England; Scottish Social Services Council in Scotland; Care and Social Services Inspectorate in Wales; Regulation and Quality Improvement Authority in Northern Ireland.*

---

In the deliberations following the departure of Stan, his representative and the investigating leader, Selina asks the panel:

10. **"Has anyone been harmed by Stan's actions?"**
    Rose is firm in her belief that Stan's duty was to follow the rules and that personal judgement is not central to morality. Selina believes his example might ultimately be harmful if students start to think they can act on their own will. Spencer wants to know what Stan wanted to do with the notes and, indeed, what he did do with them; on balance he thinks the action was a good one. Rajesh feels that at least one of the Stans made a good case for disobedience in this case.
    The panel members are finding it difficult to come to any agreement and the emotional temperature is rising.
    Rajesh asks:

11. **"Ought our emotional responses to be a factor in our determinations?"**
    After initial resistance from the other panel members they agree to an honest statement of how Stan's case makes them feel.

    ➤ Rose feels *anger* with what she sees as Stan's arrogance and, as he is one of her students, *embarrassment* about his actions.

    ➤ Selina feels *sympathy* for Stan's actions, but *frustration* with the way he has conducted himself.

    ➤ Spencer feels *uncertainty* about Stan and *confusion* about his actions.

    ➤ Rajesh feels *compassion* for Stan's situation and *solidarity* with his actions.

The four members of the panel have found it problematic to come to an agreement not because of a disagreement about the facts but because they focus on different aspects of Stan's case. We will not necessarily change an individual's moral reasoning, but it will always help if each one can understand the basis for the disagreements.

Spencer, using a hypothetical formulation similar to Rose's Question 7, asks the panel to consider:

▶

◀

## 12. "If we were the service user, the father, what would we have wanted Stan to have done?"

─────────────

Finally, the four members sum up their positions regarding Stan's actions.

*Rose*

"I can say that I wouldn't want him in my agency as I couldn't trust him to act responsibly."

*Selina*

"On balance, I think more good than harm came out of Stan's actions. However, I'm not convinced about how much he troubled to weigh these 'goods'."

*Spencer*

"In all his other work he has acted with probity and integrity and the service users have given positive feedback about his work. It's possible that he over-identified with the father in this one case, but he is a student and he is learning."

*Rajesh*

"There is evidence that he acted from a duty of care and he acted out of deep concern".

## 13. Does it make a difference how the story is told and re-told?

"Did you hear about the student who tried to whistleblow discriminatory practice and was nearly chucked off the course?"

"Did you hear about the student who stole some files from his placement?"

Rightly or wrongly, in the Age of the Inquiry (Stanley and Manthorpe, 2004) and the viral nature of social media (see the next chapter), the recounting of events has a significant impact. Will social media see Stan as a hero who fought for the rights of his service users and now finds himself victimised for his moral stance? Or will he be cast as a maverick, a chancer, even a bit

▶

of an idiot, who is untrustworthy and egocentric, acting on his own estimation of right and wrong without thinking of the consequences?

## Alter egos

We have played with a conceit that the panel members were professional moral philosophers rather than social work tutors and agency staff. In fact, these moral philosophers all have alter egos as social workers who think much the same and who ask similar questions. They're not called moral philosophers and they are unlikely to be explicit about their ethics, and may be unaware themselves of having an ethical 'stance'. When the moral philosophers get together they know what to expect, but a social work panel is puzzled by these differences and attribute them to other factors – culture, coming from another setting, cussedness, etc.. So, it is important to try and tease out the subtext of questions and statements. This does not bring automatic harmony, but it will illuminate why there is disharmony and, therefore, how to improve communication and arrive at better decisions.

## The outcome

The outcome at the panel was that one member voted to remove Stan and two to give him leave to stay on the course, and one abstained. Stan's progress depended upon him preparing an additional reflective assignment on the topic of confidentiality and whistleblowing.

## Exploring dilemmas 2

**Sarah** qualified as a social worker two years ago. She had first worked for a not-for-profit organisation, *The Hearth,* that provided day centre services for homeless people and for people with drug and alcohol problems. Sarah liked her work as it was varied; one minute she'd be advocating for a service user at an immigration tribunal, the next facilitating a women's group and then making sandwiches or doling out the upmarket leftovers donated by the nearby Pret a Manger – avocado and smoked salmon for the homeless. As a non-Catholic she felt some unease at the iconography around the place, but by and large the Catholic volunteers didn't 'push' religion, although one volunteer, on hearing that Sarah was not a Catholic, was bemused about what her motivation for this work could possibly be.

After two years at *The Hearth*, Sarah decided she wanted mainstream statutory experience and she successfully applied for a position as a social worker in a mental health trust.

She arrived at the office at 8:45 on her first morning to find it locked. At length, at 9:15, someone arrived to open up the building. It transpired that Sarah's new supervisor was on holiday, so she was given a pile of case files to read and catch up on. She had no allocated desk, so she sat at her supervisor's vacant seat.

On return from holiday, Sarah's supervisor, **Rasheeda**, was apologetic and welcoming. Sarah found her very personable and decided that the first impressions had just been unfortunate ones. However, halfway through their first meeting together, Rasheeda congenially confessed that she must let Sarah into a secret – there was a pile of unallocated work because of the chronic short staffing and Sarah would need to complete the assessments on 40 service users before the end of the month, just three weeks away.

Sarah, not really knowing what to say as this was her first supervision session, took the list of cases that Rasheeda handed her.

Let us pause to consider how relevant to Sarah's situation are the strong emotions discussed earlier in the chapter (pages 134–138). First, *loyalty*. Sarah is torn between the loyalty of an employee to the agency which provides the wherewithal to practise her skills and, of course, her salary; and, on the other hand, loyalty to social work, which requires her to uphold its professional standards. She feels a strong urge to *conform*. It is her first few days in an unfamiliar workplace where she has yet to establish any reputation or trust. She is uncertain what she should expect of herself, given the free-flowing nature of her previous job, and this leads to *doubts* that she perhaps might not have what it takes to survive in a statutory mental health setting. She has been asked to perform these assessments in the time available, so surely it must be considered a feasible task? She *fears* that if she raises her concerns she will be seen as incompetent or as a troublemaker. Rasheeda is her supervisor and line manager – does she have the *power* to require her to follow instructions? If Sarah refuses to comply, how will her *motivation* be construed? She understands her motivation as wishing to uphold good practice and to do the right thing; but it might be construed as unwilling to compromise, as more keen on having her own way than

◀

her employer's and not willing to take any risks for the sake of the organisation.

**Angela**, one of the support team, gathers the relevant files and puts them on Sarah's new desk. After she inspects two of the files, Sarah doubts that it will be possible to see all of these people and make appropriate assessments before the end of the month, especially with the handicap of being unfamiliar with the formal mental health assessments; but, still, she later wonders whether she has misjudged the throughput in a statutory agency and that perhaps she should expect to be able to manage this. She reflects some more, does some calculations with her diary and comes to a more confident conclusion that it will not be possible.

When she calls on Rasheeda she has a feeling that Rasheeda is expecting her.

| | |
|---|---|
| *Sarah* | It's not physically possible to see all these people to complete these assessments before the end of the month, certainly not possible to conduct a proper assessment. I need some coaching, too, as I've not done these formal assessments before. |
| *Rasheeda* | Well, you don't actually have to see them all, not straight away. The thing is, just do a paper assessment on the basis of the information you read in the file and then do the actual face-to-face contacts when you can, over the next few months. You just have to have the paperwork up to date by the 31st. |
| *Sarah* | ?! |
| *Rasheeda* | (*Registering Sarah's disbelief*). You see, the thing is, if we don't get these assessments done by the end of the month, the Trust will be fined – very likely in the order of anything up to a million pounds. Yes! Do you want to be responsible for costing the Trust a million? I don't!<br><br>It's just a paper exercise, games-playing, we have to do it all the time. The service users will get their proper assessments in due course and they don't have to know anything about it. No one does. |
| *Sarah* | Are you certain that the Trust will be fined a million pounds? You seem rather vague about the sum. |
| *Rasheeda* | Does it matter how much exactly it is? Either way it will be a lot. Also, I don't want to go around asking too many specific questions because it's only going to arouse suspicions, isn't it? |

▶

| | |
|---|---|
| *Sarah* | Why don't we come clean and let the Trust know the situation? We could use it as a bargaining chip – you know ... 'This is what happens when you don't staff properly.' |
| *Rasheeda* | You say 'we', but it'd my head on the block, not yours. You've only just arrived and you're not complicit. I've had to keep this ship afloat pretty much on my own and at long last I thought I'd have an ally. |
| *Sarah* | Well, why don't *you* come clean with the Trust. Say it's been an impossible task with all these vacancies and HR taking so long with applications. Ask for some locums to help out – the Trust must have saved a lot of money not paying salaries on the vacancies. |
| *Rasheeda* | Do you know how hard it's been for me as a Muslim woman to have achieved a position as a manager in this city? And, if I'm not seen to take this on the chin, how it'll be generalised – 'They just can't hack it, these women, these Muslim women.' They know – up there – what the situation is, they just don't want it to be known that they know, so we have to sort it, quietly. As long as we sort it there'll be no questions, I know that. And I've been promised two new posts in the next financial year. We'll lose those if we don't play ball. |
| *Sarah* | It just doesn't seem fair to put me in this position. When I applied for this job there was no mention of these outstanding cases or how it was intended they be dealt with. If I'd known, I'll be frank, I wouldn't have accepted the position, so it feels like a breach of contract. |
| *Rasheeda* | I agree that it's not fair, Sarah. Also, it won't be fair to our service users if the service they receive is even worse next year because of the fine on the Trust's finances and the withdrawal of the promise of new posts. As to your contractual arrangements, these are to follow the instructions of your line manager, me. It's me who will take responsibility for it all – I'll be the one signing them off. It'll all be in good faith because I know you'll be doing the real assessment, let's call them the final assessments, eventually. So, to my mind, it's just a question of timing. These we can consider to be interim assessments. |

1. What *ought* Sarah to do?

2. At this point what *would* you do as Sarah?

◀

Are your responses to the two questions above the same or different?

*Consequentialist moral reasoning*

The problem has been posed by Rasheeda in terms of consequences – the financial consequences to the Trust if these assessments are not completed and signed off by a target date. There are other possible consequences of not completing the assessments:

1. The Trust's reputation is damaged when it becomes known that it has not been able to fulfil its statutory responsibilities.

2. Services to the Trust's users are worsened as a result of the crisis in its finances that result from the fine.

3. Two new promised social worker posts are lost.

4. Sarah is exposed to harassment and bullying as a result of her stance.

5. Sarah gets a reputation for disloyalty and troublemaking – with possible consequences for her future career and job prospects.

6. Rasheeda's job is put at risk.

7. Women in general and Muslim women in particular are seen as incapable managers and not in control.

Any other potential consequences to add?

Consider your amended list and work through each consequence in turn using a scale of 1–10, where '10' is what you consider to be an extremely serious consequence and '1' not at all serious. Place the list in descending order from highest scores to lowest. Does this order match your sense of which are the most *important* factors? If it does, it is perhaps an indication that your thinking tends to be consequentialist. If there are some disjunctions between the seriousness and the importance of the points in your list, take a while to consider what these differences are and what they might indicate. It can be illuminating to compare your list with other people's and discuss why you have made similar or different judgements.

There are possible consequences of *not* whistleblowing, too. For instance:

1. Subsequent discovery of the subterfuge leads to disciplinary action against Sarah and Rasheeda.

2. The Trust does not learn from its current bad management and poor practices.

▶

◀

3. Inaccurate assessments are made in respect of the Trust's service users.

4. Now that Sarah is complicit, Rasheeda continues to make unreasonable workload demands on Sarah.

5. Sarah's relationship with the two social workers who are subsequently appointed is undermined by the dishonesty of Sarah and Rasheeda's secret of the paper assessments.

Follow the same schedule as you did for the earlier list, adding further possible consequences and ranking all of them, and reflect on what the ranking tells you about yourself and your moral reasoning.

*Religious moral reasoning*

Rasheeda's initial framing of the dilemma is **consequentialist**, but Sarah's subsequent ethical reasoning need not follow that path. Let us conjure a Sarah who is guided strongly by her Christian faith, so it is this to which she first turns for ethical direction. One of the most important tenets of Sarah's religious faith is 'Do to others as you would have them do to you' (Matthew 7.12 – sometimes known as 'The Golden Rule'). She does not take a literal view of the Christian teachings and recognises that even The Golden Rule might be modified; for instance, one person might derive sexual pleasure from certain masochistic practices that others would abhor, but she believes that it is generally good moral guidance.

So, if Sarah lives by The Golden Rule, how ought she respond to Rasheeda's request? She feels certain that if she were in Rasheeda's shoes she would not be asking a new worker to perform unseen assessments; but if Rasheeda were her (Sarah), perhaps she would have no problem with this? The Golden Rule does not give Sarah any clear guidance. However, there are other principles key to Sarah's religious faith, not least her duty to live honestly. She ponders whether it might be possible to construct the case file entries so that they make no explicit reference to the service user being seen in person, so the record would be textually honest. However, she concludes that the assessments would not be honest in spirit. She considers the longer-term effect on her 'moral score card' of this kind of dishonesty and decides that it would not help her entry into heaven (thus, interestingly, combining religious ethics with **consequentialism**).

Sarah might talk with Rasheeda about The Golden Rule and discover that Rasheeda, too, lives by a similar **maxim** from Muhammad's teachings, '*Aheb li akheek ma tuhibu li nafsik*' – 'Wish for your brother what you wish

▶

◀

for yourself.' Again, this identical outlook might, ironically, not help them to reach agreement because their wishes are so different.

## A compromise?

Rasheeda and Sarah agree a day's cooling off for them both to consider the situation. They meet again the next day.

> *Rasheeda*    What about if we both take the 40 cases between us and do as many as we can in person, then complete whatever remains as paper exercises, 'interim'? I'll sign them off, so it's my name at the bottom – with a commitment to us both visiting the unseen service users as soon as we can after the 31st?
>
> *Sarah*    ...

3. **How ought Sarah to respond to Rasheeda's compromise?**
   Ought she to engage at all in seeking a compromise position and, if so, what ought this compromise to be? Is the one offered by Rasheeda satisfactory and if is, why? Ought she to reject any negotiation with Rasheeda?

4. **If Rasheeda continues to refuse to let her own manager know of the situation, ought Sarah to blow the whistle?**
   Sarah has a choice to refuse the instruction to write the assessments without visiting the service users but not blowing the whistle – not alerting others to the situation, either inside or outside the mental health trust. What are the ethical and practice issues around that particular decision?

*Involving others – cat out of the bag*

So far we have considered Sarah's ethical dilemma as hers alone: ought she to whistleblow or not? However, there are alternative paths. Ought Sarah to approach her trade union or her professional body, so the decision is not made alone? Unions were created not just as a form of collective bargaining for better wages but also to provide collective protection, and professional associations like the British Association of Social Workers are independent from the practice in any one particular agency and can provide protection for social workers. The difficulty is that once uncertainties have been shared, those privy to this information are also complicit. You can't 'half dive' into

▶

◀

a pool. Social workers give service users a similar warning at the beginning of a new group, that any disclosures of criminal activity cannot just rest in the group.

### 'Soft' whistleblowing – safety valves

A small group of social workers meets every few months with the local councillor who is the Chair of the Social Services Committee. It is an informal gathering, held in the evening in a local pub. The social workers use the occasion to give the councillor a front-line perspective on the department – how policies and procedures are *actually* experienced by workers and service users. They are not reporting serious malpractices or corruption and they are positive as well as critical about the experience of working there.

Are these workers being disloyal to their managers? Does it undermine collective means of giving voice to the workers? Or is it a practical way for those responsible for the provision of social work (in this case, local politicians) to feel the pulse of current realities, unmediated by the spin of management? It could be all of these, but if it is to improve the service, the relationships between councillor and professionals must be trusting and built on an **ethics of care**. This kind of soft whistleblowing can act as a valve that safely allows pressures to surface and be worked with; the challenge is to avoid an ethos of 'behind closed doors'.

### In what circumstances would you whistleblow?

Take the following dozen situations and decide whether there are grounds to whistleblow. How seriously would you view the situation about which you have become aware and would you expect to take action? Your responses might be 'it depends'. If so, what does it depend on?

1. A social worker becomes engaged to a person who until two months ago was a service user of the agency that employs the social worker.

2. A social worker over-claims mileage allowance in order to fund a group for services users.

3. A social worker refuses to work with a same-sex couple because it contravenes their religious beliefs.

4. A social worker invites a service user to pray with them.

5. At the request of a 25-year-old man who has lost use of his arms, the social worker masturbates him.

▶

◀

6. A social worker appears on local television with a service user to publicise the service user's plight.

7. A social worker gives advice about where a service user can purchase cannabis.

8. A social worker becomes aware that a colleague has borrowed money from a service user.

9. A social worker qualified in the use of hypnosis uses hypnosis with a service user.

10. A social worker invites a homeless service user back to their home to stay.

11. A social worker discusses the details of a service user (without using their name), to complain about their boss to other friends on Facebook.

12. A social worker is working as a dancer in a lap dancing club in their own time.

adapted from Doel, *et al.* (2010)

# The Big Picture

## Conscientious objection

Acting on your conscience has a noted history, in particular the notion of conscientious objection (Singer, 1973) and non-violent civil resistance such as Gandhi's campaign of *satyagraha*, which translates roughly as 'insistence on truth'. Should you obey a bad law if the law has been passed by a democratically elected government and what kind of opt-out ought to be allowed for individuals with particular moral objections? How 'democratic' is a law passed by a government with only 37% of the popular vote (the share of the vote for the majority party in the 2015 UK general election). How far can a government go in persecuting a minority of its people before it breaks its legitimacy? Were those who refused to pay the poll tax in Scotland in 1989 right? Ought the 'bedroom tax' to be obeyed or does it tax ethical principles of equality and fairness to a degree that breaks the call on obedience?

'Staff who blow whistle on abuse and misconduct left with no protection' stated a report on the lack of support given by the UN to whistleblowers (*The Guardian*, 14 September 2015, p. 24.) Out of 447 claims to the

UN's ethics office from people alleging they had experienced retaliation for whistleblowing, only four cases were upheld – hardly an encouragement to expose wrongdoing. Most whistleblowers resigned rather than endure the lengthy investigative process.

## Guidance from Codes, Standards and Principles

The Australian code of ethics states, 'Social workers will appropriately challenge, and/or report, and/or work to improve, policies, procedures, practices and service provisions', continuing with a bulleted list to describe possible contingencies, and concludes, 'Social workers are advised to ascertain what, if any, whistleblower protection options are provided in their state or territory.' (AASW, 2010: 32)

The ninth of BASW's 17 ethical principles reads:

**Being prepared to whistleblow**
Social workers should be prepared to report bad practice using all available channels including complaints procedures and if necessary use public interest disclosure legislation and whistleblowing guidelines. (BASW, 2014: 14)

Of all the national codes of ethics available in English, Norway's goes into the most detail about unacceptable conditions and how whistleblowing should be undertaken, including protection from retaliation for whistleblowers (FOKUS, 2009: 15–16).

Increasingly, organisations have whistleblowing policies, probably including the mental health trust where Sarah worked (see earlier dilemma). In the UK there are criteria for whistleblowing policies at a national level (National Audit Office, 2014a, 2014b). However, there can be a 'startling disconnect' between policies and practices, (the words are used by a report from Margaret Hodge's 2014 public accounts committee in relation to the generally good whistleblowing policies of the UK government and the contrasting way they are operated in practice), underlining the limitations of codes of ethics.

## Consulting the wise professionals

Perhaps we need look no further than the words of Margaret Hodge, some of which we have already encountered (page 136), for the view of a wise professional. Her words are spoken more with taxpayers' money in mind than ethics, but they are worth repeating:

Government's uncoordinated, piece-meal approach to whistleblowing is simply not good enough and it is completely unacceptable that almost two-thirds of those who speak out receive no response at all from their management. The longer this goes on, the more likely it is that patterns of wrong-doing will be missed – undoubtedly resulting in taxpayers' money being mis-spent or even lives being put at risk.

(Committee of Public Accounts, 2014)

The wisest professionals look for, and find, an abundance of paths. It is important to position yourself so that you give yourself choices about which paths of moral reasoning you take. When the dilemma is framed in one set of terms (e.g. the **consequentialist** approach of Rasheeda in the dilemma example earlier) there is a tendency to follow unquestioningly that same path of moral reasoning. However, because the first signpost is pointed in that direction, it is not necessarily the *right* signpost to follow. The more powerful people or institutions in any situation are likely to set the signpost down the path that most favours them, rather than to offer a choice of paths. In the final chapter I will offer a 'moral compass' that enables social workers to make their own decisions about which paths of moral reasoning are best or right.

# 10    SOCIAL MEDIA

The growth of social media is a phenomenon that will continue to have a profound impact on our personal and professional lives. To some extent ethical dilemmas arising from social media are not dissimilar to those we have considered in other chapters, such as confidentiality, the use of information and the boundaries of professional and personal relationships. The question is, does the nature of social media now amplify these dilemmas (and, indeed, possibilities) to such an extent that they have become *qualitatively* different?

There are parallels with other aspects of human life. For example, war has always been violent and destructive, but it can be argued that developments in technology during the twentieth century (the tank, fighter jet, nuclear bomb and the industrialisation of civilian death in concentration camps) have transformed not just the quantitative element of war but the qualitative one as well. So, does the extent and immediacy with which information can be shared and the numbers of people who can be linked at the click of a mouse, change the *qualitative* nature of the dilemmas associated with social media, not just the quantitative aspects?

We must remind ourselves that technological social media are in their infancy and that appropriate social norms and etiquette take time to evolve to keep pace. The law is also playing catch-up. For instance, the growth of 'revenge pornography' (the sharing of sexually explicit pictures of former partners without their consent) has led to UK legislation that will make it a criminal offence with imprisonment of up to two years; indeed, the social media occupy an increasing proportion of police time.

Social media leave a transparent audit trail and a permanent record, unlike previous forms of social communication, such as 'the grapevine', all of which could be denied and whose provenance was far from clear. Most people have at least one moment or incident in their life that they are happy to have forgotten. Now there is every chance that it will be captured digitally and, worse, endure through digital time. (Ironically, the long-term durability of electronic data is questionable. Whilst the photograph in the shoebox might fade a little over half a century, digital photos might become inaccessible as application software becomes obsolete). So, we are still deciding how to tame this new power; indeed, contemplating whether it is capable of being tamed.

Another important factor is the psychology of electronic communication. In theory there is a much greater opportunity to mediate thoughts and feelings through written words (they can be deleted and replaced before they are dispatched, in the way that the spoken word, once spoken, cannot); and yet the distance created by the typed word seems to disinhibit some people. This can lead to venting spleen in ways unmediated by voice tone (the telephone) and facial tells (tête-à-têtes and meetings).

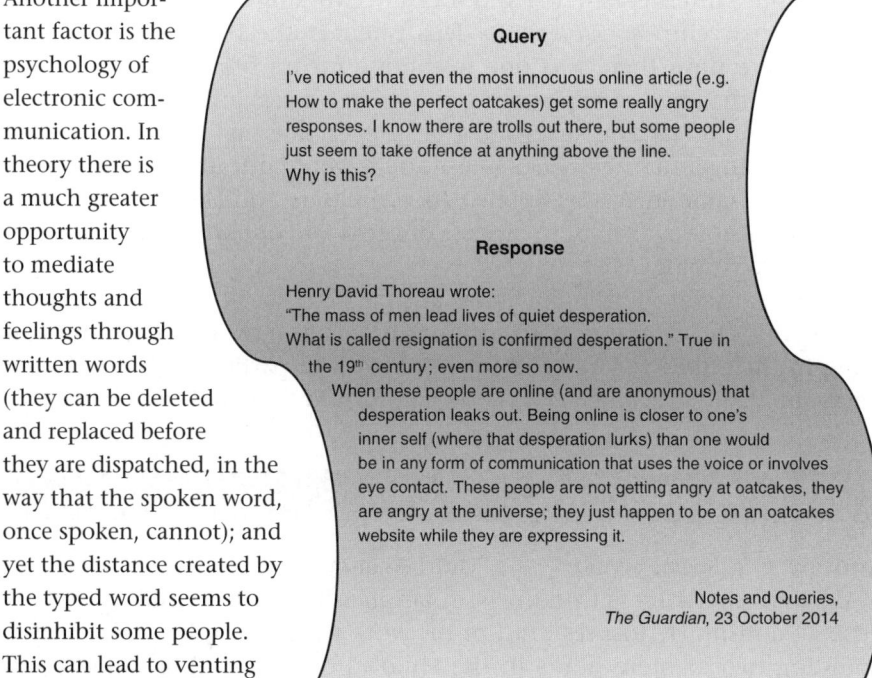

**Query**

I've noticed that even the most innocuous online article (e.g. How to make the perfect oatcakes) get some really angry responses. I know there are trolls out there, but some people just seem to take offence at anything above the line. Why is this?

**Response**

Henry David Thoreau wrote:
"The mass of men lead lives of quiet desperation. What is called resignation is confirmed desperation." True in the 19th century; even more so now.
When these people are online (and are anonymous) that desperation leaks out. Being online is closer to one's inner self (where that desperation lurks) than one would be in any form of communication that uses the voice or involves eye contact. These people are not getting angry at oatcakes, they are angry at the universe; they just happen to be on an oatcakes website while they are expressing it.

Notes and Queries,
*The Guardian*, 23 October 2014

You can probably still remember your first 'flame mail', whether sent or received.

These kinds of concern are not restricted to social work. A report noted that:

Hundreds of police employees have been investigated for breaching social media guidelines at forces across England and Wales during a five-year period. Police officers and civilians made racist and threatening comments on Facebook and Twitter, sent 'friend' requests to victims of crime and uploaded images of colleagues in 'compromising positions'. (*The Guardian*, 19 August 2014, p. 9)

It also reported that just under 10% of cases ended in resignation, dismissal or retirement. The report, however, did not differentiate between civilian employees and professionally trained police officers.

Also of ethical interest is what this same report described as 'excessive and inappropriate use of internet during working hours, in particular online auction sites, internet banking and social networking sites.' I was a student in a busy city centre social services department in the 1970s where, hard to contemplate now, there was one telephone for an office of *nine* people. Apart from the obvious explanation (scarce resources), management's logic was based on a fear and suspicion that if everyone had a telephone they would be using it for their personal use and it would intrude into work time. Exactly the same logic was applied to computers and the internet when they first became available. The fears, concerns and opportunities transcend time and technology.

As we consider specific dilemmas arising from social media, we should also be mindful of the opportunities that social networking systems can bring to the public at large and to social work in particular (Ledesma and Casavant, 2011; Oakwater, 2012). We will turn to these positives later.

## Exploring dilemmas

**Andrew** is a social worker in a Multi-Agency Support Team (known as MAST). His speciality is working with families in which a child has a diagnosis of autism. He focuses most of his work with the child's carers, often spending two or more hours in the child's home providing support and direct advice to the carers, helping them respond to the child and develop strategies that are most likely to meet the child's and the family's particular needs. He gets good results and he is much liked and appreciated by his clients and colleagues.

Andrew has been working with **Sandra** and **Danny**, whose child **Ethan** is autistic. They have noticed improvement in Ethan's behaviour since Andrew started to work with them as a result of his support and practical advice, but Andrew has had to cut back hours since one of the MAST team has left and the post is not being filled because of financial cuts. Sandra and Danny start an online petition to raise awareness of autism and, more particularly, to reinstate the lost post so that Andrew's talents can be used to the full and he doesn't have to cover for the other position.

➢ Ought Andrew to start the online petition as a co-sponsor with Sandra and Danny?

➢ Ought Andrew to dissuade Sandra and Danny from creating the online petition?

➢ If Sandra and Danny start the petition, ought Andrew to sign it?

How principled or how pragmatic is your personal response to internet opportunities and demands? For example, are you a subscriber to

▶

◀

organisations such as *38 Degrees, Avaaz.org* and *Change.org* and, if so, when you receive petitions how carefully do you scrutinise each one? Do you forward petitions to colleagues? Are there any circumstances in which you would forward a petition to a service user?

## Seven other examples

Let us consider some examples of dilemmas related to social media and social work. With each statement, make a note of your immediate response to the statement before reading on. When you reach the last, return to your brief notes and see whether your response has modified and, if so, how and why.

**1.** A service user asks if they can 'friend' you on Facebook.

(*Make a brief note of your first response before reading on.*)
How might your response to this question vary depending on which part of the social work service you work in – for instance, if you work with children and young people, or in community-based settings? Or might you (or the agency that you work for) have a blanket policy that you do not 'friend' or engage with any service user on Facebook, full stop?

Policies are useful shortcuts that mean you don't have to spend a lot of time explaining yourself or working out whether this circumstance justifies that action, etc.. Just as a parent might have a 'policy' of no sweets before tea time, so the agency might have a policy that its workers do not engage in Facebook friendships with service users. What are the principles that such a policy might be based on and are these principles ethical or practical ones, or both?

In fact, professional befriending has a long established tradition: probation officers were required as part of their role to 'advise, assist and *befriend*' those under supervision (Probation of Offenders Act, 1907). Before electronic social media, relationships developed and withered without the explicit act of 'friending' and 'unfriending'. The act of declaring someone a friend (or by ignoring a request, not a friend) makes it difficult to maintain the fluidity and nuance that characterises most relationships. Regular culling of friends might be necessary as the Friends list gets unwieldy. This illustrates the discussion early in this chapter, that social media are having a *qualitative* impact on many long-standing notions, such as befriending and what it is to be a friend.

In the absence of a specific agency policy about friending, what ought to guide you in your decision about whether to accept a service user's request to 'friend' you? It is probably easier to think of circumstances where you would deny the request, so think of circumstances where you might accept. For instance, perhaps when you are leaving your job, or the service user is discharged from the service; or if the service user becomes a volunteer at the centre where you work, or even a paid member of staff; or they agree to be a co-trainer with you; or they know other people that you are already friends with on Facebook.

**2.** A colleague asks if they can 'friend' you.

(*Make a brief note of your first response before reading on.*)
Let us first ponder how electronic social media have changed, or added to, the meaning of 'ask'. It is difficult to imagine a colleague asking, face to face, "Will you be a friend?" or committing the request to paper in a letter; but electronic communication has introduced strict binary categories that were not previously present: categorically a friend, or categorically not a friend. So, in this system, if you are not 'a friend' are you 'not a friend'? Like 'like' and 'dislike' in some other internet platforms, there is no room for agnostics.

However, it is easier to ignore an electronic request than one made in person or on the telephone, and to quietly unsubscribe from requests to **'discover X's favorite websites!'** Perhaps there are differences in perceived etiquette between those who are regular users of social media and those who are not, with the former much more comfortable with unsubscribing, unfriending and the like, and the latter feeling that this is snubbing behaviour and a social taboo.

If you are already 'friends' with some colleagues, what is the difference between colleagues who are friends and colleagues who are not – what principles help you make these decisions? If you work or are placed in an agency where there are volunteers, do the same rules apply to your response to paid colleagues or are they different? In either case, why? So, what factors would influence your decision about whether to accept the colleague's invitation to 'friend' on Facebook? Here are some possibilities:

> Differences and similarities (in age, gender, professional background, length of time in the team, etc.)

> Power and seniority (is the colleague a peer, a supervisor, a supervisee?)

> Local culture (are other people in the team or agency 'friends'?)

> Policy (does the agency have a policy about colleagues' relationships?)

➤ Consequences and meaning (what do you think the colleague's invitation signifies? Is it like being asked for a drink after work?)

➤ Attraction (personal, not necessarily sexual. Do you like him/her?)

➤ Your personal feelings about privacy versus your desire not to be left out

➤ Trust (is this someone who will share their data and yours in a responsible manner?)

By now you are familiar with the ethical theories introduced in Chapter 2. Which ethical theories are supporting the various factors in the list above, do you suppose?

**3.** A service user texts you.

(*Make a brief note of your first response before reading on.*)
There will be readers who wonder why this is considered to be a dilemma, but for completely different reasons: those who see texting service users as integral to their work and those for whom it is a no-no.

Texting permits a different type of intimacy between social workers and service users, perhaps a more casual connection that has advantages and disadvantages. It could make service users feel able to cancel appointments rather more readily as they don't have to tell the social worker to their face. Texting means service users can contact social workers out of hours. You may not get the message until you turn on your work phone in the morning, but does it feel 'right' that texts can be left with you at midnight? How long after a text was sent would you expect to respond to it? Texts are open to misinterpretation, especially with abbreviated language.

On the other hand, a text to a service user is a very useful, not too obtrusive way of reminding them about an appointment or sending a word of encouragement when you know they are doing something they feel anxious about. One social worker notes:

> "I had a situation with a suicidal service user – she wouldn't pick up calls or speak, but kept in touch with me via text, through which I was able to get her to go the GP and have an admission to hospital. I'm not sure that this would have happened without the texting – she simply wouldn't pick up the phone or open her door."

Would you think it right to give some service users your work mobile phone number (thereby inviting the possibility of texts) whilst denying it to others? If so, what criteria would you use to decide which service users are in and which are out, and would this be fair?

**4.** A colleague wants to connect with you via LinkedIn.

*(Make a brief note of your first response before reading on.)*
How ought we to respond to online professional associations? I was asked by a family member in the early days of LinkedIn to 'connect'. It seemed a harmless thing to do, especially as my relative was at an earlier stage in their career when it would have seemed churlish to deny them. Then requests came from known people with whom I was happy to connect. Then requests were received from unknown people, who were at first scrutinised a little, but when the scrutiny started to become onerous and rather arbitrary, I accepted requests in blanket fashion with the hope that none would turn out to be a child molester (and, anyway, if they did, would that reflect on all those with whom they were professionally connected via LinkedIn)?

Again, we are developing new behaviours with only old social mores as a guide. This particular internet journey was taken with no guidance or explicit precedent. Social media creep in without our explicit consent or awareness, and this itself is an ethical issue. Less passive users of LinkedIn perhaps target their connections more rigorously, leading to jobs and new opportunities, and if our acceptance of requests to connect helps people to achieve more success do we have a moral duty to accept in order to further their happiness? Or is this just another commercial internet company that has found a way to exploit the human desire to join the in-group? In my ethical audit ought I to be concerned that LinkedIn's UK sales are booked through an Irish company, and that despite employing 180 people in Britain, LinkedIn only paid £532,000 in taxes in 2014, whilst the division's London directors were paid twice that sum, £1.2m? In the equation of right and wrong, ought this knowledge to influence whether I choose to join? (*The Guardian,* 28 January 2016). Researchgate.net has infiltrated another niche since this chapter was first drafted, such is the proliferation of activity.

**5.** One of the children in the residential care facility where you are on placement tells you she sent a 'snapchat' of herself naked to a boy in the same home.

*(Make a brief note of your first response before reading on.)*
*Snapchatting* – sending images with text (or instead of text) via mobile phones – is common amongst younger people and 'naked selfies' have also become part of youth culture. The girl's behaviour might, then, be

likened to wearing a mini-skirt in the 1960s, no doubt shocking then to those born before 1920, but viewed by the mini-skirt wearer as part of the self-expression of youth. In theory, snapchats self-destruct in a matter of seconds and if someone tries to screen-grab them the sender is notified; however, hacking into accounts isn't difficult, so there are risks attached to this activity.

Expressing yourself on social media connects you to a larger, more unknown audience than has ever been possible. Previously, only famous people could experience such amplification of themselves; now social media have made a reality of Andy Warhol's 15 minutes of fame. The general human need for attention is exaggerated in some people and at some developmental stages such as adolescence, and social media afford almost unlimited attention – postings on YouTube, for example, offering an opportunity to go viral.

As with real world behaviours, online behaviours need careful exploration to fully understand their meaning and consequences. The potential numbers involved in online behaviours is a real complication, but the fundamental issues – control of your actions and protection of who you are and who defines you – are guided by the same principles in both worlds. Children are especially vulnerable because they do not yet have a fully developed sense of who they are and they are dependent on the adult world for so many aspects of their lives. Should social media be likened to smoking a cigarette, drinking alcohol or driving a car: something restricted to adults only? Indeed, the digital age of consent in Europe is 13 (with proposals possibly to raise this to 16). Though you are not allowed a Facebook account until you are 13 years old, it is difficult to police – and what ought you to do if your 12-year-old niece requests you to be a 'friend'? What protections ought to be afforded to minors in the world of social media? And how ought the adult world to respond to misuse of social media by children? Social work is often at the brunt of these broad social issues with decisions needing to be made in real situations.

**6.** You are a member of an international online community of practice and you are concerned about one of the member's ethical standard of practice.

*(Make a brief note of your first response before reading on.)*
Distance brings with it a confusing mix of safety and uncertainty. The relative anonymity of distance, perhaps secured by adopting an alias or avatar identity, can be liberating. Social obligations weaken when the community is diffuse and far away and when it revolves around a single concern. When you are in conversation with another person in the same

room at the same time, you can read the subtext of their communication – through their body language, eye contact and other nonverbal communication – but you are also more constrained by the social obligations that personal contact entails.

With distance, lines of responsibility and accountability loosen and blur. For instance, if a fire breaks out in the room you ought to try your best to extinguish it or, failing that, ensure that everyone in the room leaves quickly and safely. What happens when you see a fire in the room where others are Skyping? Certainly you ought to alert those in the distant room, but how does your status as witness, rather than agent, change your moral responsibilities?

The 'fire' in the case of this example dilemma in an online community of practice is perhaps more of a smouldering cinder; if you were physically in the room you'd be able to smell something was not right, but it is this metaphorical 'nose' that might be distorted or absent in the online community. So, you are likely to be confounded on two fronts: the first is the difficulty in sniffing out the evidence and the second is the uncertainty of where your responsibilities lie once you have located it (McKenna and Green, 2002).

A community of practice brings professionals together in an online forum around a specific topic of mutual interest (Wenger, 1998). For the sake of this example, let us take an online forum of social groupworkers all of whom facilitate groups for people with mental health problems. The group comprises social workers from many countries and has already engaged in illuminating discussions about what mental health means, with significant variations about how it is viewed.

> Over time and place, the behaviours that we associate with mental illness have variously been described as mad, creative, eccentric, evil, feeble minded, magical, wise, anti-social, and the list continues. To some it is a disorder of the psyche, to others a spiritual state, an existential crisis, a neural malfunction or a mutant chromosome, and to others a social phenomenon or learned behaviour. The causes and meanings of 'mental illness', and therefore the response it requires or respects, are almost wholly culturally determined. (Doel, 2012: 175).

How, then, to determine what might be *an ethical standard of practice* in these circumstances?

Subsequently, one of the groupworkers in the online forum posts his success in funding a new group using monies that were acquired from overclaiming expenses on another project. Another groupworker in another continent thinks this is unethical practice and that he ought not to have done this. Is she right? The first groupworker declares that it is common practice in his country and that it's the only way to get the necessary resources and that groupworkers from wealthy nations are in no position to judge. Can it be ethically sound in one country and not ethically sound in another – is this justifiable **moral relativism**? If the second groupworker continues to consider this to be unethical practice what ought she to do?

The weakening of lines of responsibility brought about by distance perhaps explains why so many people who were aware of abuse in children's homes (in Rotherham, for instance) felt no responsibility to find out more and act on this knowledge. In this case, distance was not geographical but social, cultural and professional. It is a case where professional distance put the children at risk.

7. You become aware that one of your service users is experiencing cyberbullying.

*(First, take a moment to make a note of your own first thoughts and frame these first thoughts as a question to yourself.)*

*Responses from eight different social workers*

The first thoughts of eight different social workers, framed as a question, are recorded below. Subsequently there is an exploration of what these first thoughts might tell us about the social workers involved and potential consequences for the service user.

| | |
|---|---|
| *Clara* | What is my role in relation to the service user? |
| *Dion* | What is my relationship like with the service user? |
| *Ed* | Are there any differences between face-to-face bullying and cyberbullying and if so, what are the significances of the differences? |
| *Fay* | Who else might be involved, either in the cyberbullying itself or to provide action or support? |
| *Gina* | Is this going to end up like that last case of cyberbullying I worked with? |
| *Hassan* | What are the risks to the service user? |
| *Isobel* | What does the law have to say about cyberbullying and what are my legal responsibilities? |
| *Jean* | How can the service user's human rights best be served? |

Of these eight first thoughts, which comes closest to your own?

If each of these eight social workers acts upon their own first thoughts, it is likely that each of their next steps will be different. For instance:

| | |
|---|---|
| *Clara* | I'd want to be clear whether it was considered to be part of my job to work with this situation. It can be a minefield and it might |

be better to get the service user to report it to the police if it seems an offence has been committed. I don't think it is my role, so I'd refer her to the police.

**Dion**
I'm assuming that the service user, let's call her Gemma, has told me herself about the cyberbullying and this indicates we have a good relationship because it's a very personal thing to talk about and it's probably taken courage and trust to reveal it to me. I'd find out more about what Gemma wants to happen now. How much support does she have from family, for instance, and has she shared this with anyone else. But, yes, I ought to help her because cyberbullying can ruin people's lives and she's shown trust and confidence in me. So, I'd sit down with Gemma and work out the next steps together.

**Ed**
I haven't come across cyberbullying in my work but I've read about cases in the media. I work with drug addicts and they experience a lot of bullying, but it's literally in their face, personal. I imagine cyberbullying builds up over time and, of course, it can be anonymous, though I suppose the user is likely to have a good idea of who it is. I'd expect the user to bring it up in one of our support groups, so it wouldn't just be me and the user, we'd have the experience and opinions of other users, too. I'd be interested to know if any of the other users had experience of cyberbullying, but most don't have mobiles and the like. So, the next step would be to take the issue to the next group meeting.

**Fay**
There's a strong chance that the person who's doing the cyberbullying is a service user as well and they, too, might be experiencing bullying. If the service user is a child or juvenile it's best taken up with the parents and the school support services (the cyberbullying is more than likely to involve a number of other school kids). If it's someone the child doesn't know (someone they got in contact with online) it's probably best to get the police in. All things considered I don't think it's a social work thing, so I'd be referring on.

**Gina**
I had a case of cyberbullying just a month or so ago, a girl in residential care. It was all very complicated and in the end the police got involved, but no one was charged. It was all a bit of a waste of time. The trouble is her behaviour had brought a lot of it on herself and it became difficult to know who was bullying who. So I suppose I'd be rather sceptical of this new case and I'd put my kid gloves on rather than go rushing to the rescue. I'd want to talk to the other people and professionals in the service user's life to get a bigger picture.

*Hassan*    Cyberbullying can lead to depression, mental health problems and even suicide so it needs to be taken very seriously. Cyberbullying can be much more insidious than face to face and, of course, it can involve a lot more people, as stuff gets shared. I know a case where someone got a big group of people to 'unfriend' someone. As soon as the evidence of cyberbullying came to my attention I'd want to do a risk assessment to find out what the risks were for the service user – and risk assessments should include social networking. This covers them and, to be honest, it gives me protection, too.

*Isobel*    I'm a newly qualified social worker and I'm not that sure what I ought to do if I meet these circumstances. A friend of mine experienced what I suppose you'd call cyberbullying and I saw what an impact it had on her, though she wouldn't report it even though myself and her other friends were trying to encourage her. It'd be a different situation with a service user, rather than a friend, so I'd definitely want to know where I stood legally and so the first thing I would do is to talk to my supervisor about my legal responsibilities – and the agency's.

*Jean*    I see someone who is suffering and whose human rights are being violated. I ought to help her or him. First thing to do is to find out more details about the cyberbullying and then provide support to deal with it. I see someone else who also, in their own way, is suffering (the bully) – why are they doing this and what lies behind it? I think if we can reach out to them they can change.

Are the ethical stances of the social workers discernible from these comments? For instance, Clara's position is close to the Stoics', for whom **virtue** was the discharge of **duty** – the ultimate good is to know one's role and to fulfil it (Feinberg, 1969). Dion is motivated by conscientiousness – a matter of conscience – which in Kant's thinking is the only motive of genuine moral worth. Dion illustrates what **Kant** described as the 'infinite worth' of all persons, and the bully perhaps offers an example of Kant's 'crooked timber of humanity'.

An **ethics of care** is present in Ed's emphasis on the supportive relationships he would seek to bring to the dilemma. Isobel's position is rule governed, similar to the classic three-tier classification of rules: the required, the permitted and the forbidden (Feinberg, 1969). Her **rule utilitarianism** provides her with a quick and easy response – required actions are 'right', permitted actions are 'all right' and forbidden actions are wrong. Hassan has a **consequentialist** approach, concerned about the possible outcomes of not taking action and wanting to weigh up the pros and cons via a risk assessment. He is also concerned about the consequences to himself. Jean's response reflects the theory that there is a universal moral equality, that no matter how individuals differ in other ways, they are all equal in respect of their supreme moral importance, again a **Kantian** approach. In the twentieth century this became enshrined in laws such as the Human Rights Act (Androff, 2015). Jean also shows sympathies with **redemptive ethics**. Gina is a sceptic, though this should not be confused with **philosophic scepticism**.

## Philosophic scepticism

In fact, none of the eight social workers has engaged in a process of philosophic scepticism. However, if they all joined together and listened to one another, the journey to philosophic scepticism would have begun. How readily do *you* expand on your first thoughts, your gut feelings, to explore other ways of interrogating a dilemma? Each of the eight responses has its own logic, derived from the individual social worker's beliefs, attitudes and experiences. None of these responses is immaterial, nor is any one of them so primary that the others ought to be excluded from judgement.

What is important for work with service users is not necessarily which of these responses comes first to the social worker's mind, but how comprehensively the social worker interrogates *other* possibilities. One of the benefits of considering these dilemmas 'on the page' is that it helps to expose any habitual thinking – any of your thought processes that follow defined tracks rather than a response to each new situation: *le chemin se fait en marchant* (the path is made by walking it). Or perhaps you feel an affinity with the First Nation concept of **surrender** (see page 60).

------------

Now you have considered all seven dilemmas return to the notes you made when first reading each one. Have your initial responses changed and, if so, how and why? If there are no changes, what circumstances relating to any of the dilemmas would change your initial response?

## Social workers' responsibilities and social media

Thus far social media have been presented as problematic and the source of numerous complex ethical dilemmas for social workers. However, we should ask what *opportunities* social media present for social workers to understand and work with ethical dilemmas – and whether these opportunities present dilemmas.

Social media offer pools of information and support for service users that are an alternative to formal, professional sources. Professionals can be sceptical about the credibility and simplicity of online information, but it is often presented in more accessible ways, by people for people in similar circumstances. Individuals who are marginalised in the physical world can move to the centres of virtual worlds and can seek and find others in similar situations, even though these others exist at a distance. They might work through dilemmas in their own lives with the assistance of this greater resource. These sites can enable people who have personal and social problems to have a degree of social life and can expose people to views and opinions they might never have encountered. Social networking can raise awareness in the wider community; for example, *#NoMakeUpSelfie* was a (controversial) awareness-raising campaign for cancer – women took a photograph of themselves without make-up, posted it on Facebook and gave a donation to cancer research. It went viral and raised over eight million pounds for charity.

We might ask whether social workers *ought* to engage with social media. There are at least two levels at which this question can be understood. The first relates to a much broader notion of the social distance, or proximity, between social workers and the people they work with. If the typical social worker tends to be social media naïve and the typical service user is generally savvy, does the social worker have a duty to close the gap? In fact, this stereotype is changing as new generations of social workers are trained. Cooner (2013: 2) conducted a poll at a UK university in which 90% of MA and 96% of BA final-year students reported having an active Facebook account. This figure rose to 100% in 2015. I am not suggesting that social workers should feel they have to tweet, snapchat and text, or engage in internet memes like planking, but that they ought to know, for instance, about the importance of privacy settings on Facebook and how they are used. To use another analogy, it is not necessary to engage in promiscuous, paid-for sex to know about the risks and advise on the precautions. The evidence suggests that when social work students are involved in carefully constructed Facebook groups for educational purposes the results can be encouraging, with those new to the medium finding it helpful (Cooner, 2014; Facebook for Educators). 'To prepare for twenty-first-century social work, students must access learning opportunities to critically assess their SNS [Social Networking Sites] use, so they can ensure their online behaviour does not breach confidentiality, bring the profession into disrepute or transgress personal/professional boundaries.' (Cooner, 2013: 2)

Finally, ought social workers to consider the social media needs of their service users as part of their work with them? (Westwood, 2014) We have so far considered social media as, on the one hand, a possible danger and a vehicle for cyberbullying and, on the other, a way in which services users can support one another. To what extent should social media figure in social workers' assessments with service users? This is not necessarily a dilemma, as such, but it is certainly an issue for policy and practice.

## The Big Picture

### Social media and exposure

In 2015, 33 million people had their names and identifying details exposed by hackers. They were users, current or past, of a website expressly advertised as an invitation to have an affair (Ashley Madison – slogan: 'I'm looking for someone other than my wife'). If there is moral culpability in this story where does it lie? Is the exposure a come-uppance for users of the website who ought not to have been cheating their partners? Is the website to blame for encouraging people into bad behaviours? And what is the 'bad behaviour' – the dishonesty, the breaking of trust, the sexual liaison or all three?

Is there anything worse or better about finding potential lovers via an internet site rather than in a club or the workplace? Does the commercial element of the transaction, the fact that payment is made to the internet site for access to partners, have any bearing on the morality of the case? The hackers are creating transparency and honesty which are taken as good things, so are their actions *good*? The hackers' motivation stemmed from the website's failure to properly delete their information after they wanted to expunge their presence on the site. Seen through the lens of **redemptive ethics**, these ex-users are people who ought to be forgiven for what they now understand was a mistaken transgression. Does the website carry the heaviest moral responsibility because it took money from people for a service (deleting information) that it failed to deliver? Indeed, is there something morally dubious about monetarising personal relationships?

One aspect of the little-discussed ethical issues posed by social media is the fact that they are profit-making commercial companies. To open accounts with them, even if they are free, is to support their practices and the values they espouse. Other online companies such as Amazon and Google have become notorious for their tax avoidance and/or employment practices. Ought you to enquire after the tax and employment policies of the social media companies to which you subscribe and ought this to affect your willingness to support them?

What, too, of the long-term effects, professional and personal, of the drive to immediacy, the culture of 'always available', that social networking encourages? Will it prove detrimental to physical and mental health, so that we will in the future look back on Facebook as we currently regard the sugar companies and much of the processed food industry, as responsible for a massive deterioration in health? With that knowledge, what ought to be done?

## Guidance from Codes, Standards and Principles

Reviewing 11 English language social work codes of ethics, I found only the Australian code made specific reference to social media or social networking and then only briefly, in relation to professional boundaries and in the 'sexualised conduct' section in the 'Glossary of terms' (AASW, 2010: 22, 45).

The American code (NASW, 2008: 5) states:

1.03 (e) Social workers who provide services via electronic media (such as computer, telephone, radio, and television) should inform recipients of the limitations and risks associated with such services [*but not the opportunities – my observation*];

and later:

1.07(k) Social workers should protect the confidentiality of clients when responding to requests from members of the media (NASW, 2008: 7).

Ethical issues arising from the kinds of situation discussed in this chapter must be inferred from the existing discussion in the US and other codes.

Nolan's (1995) seven principles of public service are: selflessness; integrity; objectivity; accountability; openness; honesty; and leadership. In what ways might these relate to the kinds of dilemma we have discussed in this chapter and do developments in social networking require any additional principles of public service that are qualitatively different from Nolan's?

## Last word from the wise professionals

As you know from previous chapters, the **wise professionals** are the very best professional within each of us, the ones who encourage us to ask *what ought I to do?* questions and who guide us through the ensuing tangles.

What have we learned from the dilemmas in this chapter? First, that each practitioner has an habitual starting point that frames their initial response and helps that individual to shape each new situation. The situations vary but the framework likely does not. These frameworks reflect the personality, values, beliefs, working environment and professional experience of the particular practitioner.

It is important to be aware of the existence of habitual frameworks in order to interrogate them and expand them to include other possibilities. Social media can be harnessed to this effect (Cooner, 2013b). This, in turn, can reframe the first response into a more rounded judgement. Ultimately some action must be taken (or not taken), but the judgement about what this *ought* to be has grown into one that is based on the different possible questions that could and ought to be asked in order to lead to a decision about which of the paths is the best. 'The best' has become the balanced sum of all these judgements, not the habitual one.

To return to this chapter's opening concerns about the qualitative difference in the scale of social media dilemmas, we *can* use the same ethical theories as we used for other kinds of dilemma in this book to negotiate the ethical mountains of social media. Social networking is a tool and, like any tool, if used with ethical precision it can be a great aid; used without ethical forethought it can be dangerous. It is crucial that social workers are competent and qualified to use this tool and to advise service users on its dangers and benefits.

# 11 MORAL CRUSADES, PANICS, GUARDIANS, LUCK AND COMPASS

Time box

Titus Oates fabricated a plot by English Catholics to assassinate the king, Charles II – The 'Popish Plot'. Plots against Protestant monarchs were credible and the accusations proved expedient for various Whig politicians as well as popular with the Protestant mob. The growing wave of moral panic resulted in the executions of 15 entirely innocent people. It took three years before the backlash set in and popular sentiment turned against Oates. Under the Catholic king, James II, he was tried for perjury, pilloried and imprisoned, only to be rehabilitated to a pension on the accession of the Protestant William III.

## Moral crusades and panics

A moral panic is an 'exaggerated or misdirected public concern, anxiety, fear, or anger over a perceived threat to social order' (Krinsky, 2013: 1); a panic often occurs when a moral crusade launched by moral entrepreneurs manning the moral barricades runs out of control (Goode and Ben-Yehuda, 2009: 67). The Popish Plot (time box above) is one of countless examples of the hysteria that can grab hold of large groups of people, even whole nations, usually aimed at a minority group: Catholics in the Popish Plot, Jews in the 1890s French Dreyfuss Affair, people with HIV-AIDS in the 1980s and young people in general in the ecstasy drug scares of the 1990s. As I write, the latest is Donald Trump's call for all Muslims to be turned away from the US. Moral panics, like economic bubbles, are a regular if volatile feature of social life, flaring and collapsing with no apparent rhyme nor reason.

Social workers work with the kinds of marginalised group that are targeted in moral panics. Ought social workers to use their position to stand in solidarity with threatened minorities – if there had been social workers at the time of the English Restoration, ought we to have expected them to have defended the Catholic minority from persecution and oppression? The social cleansing evident in many totalitarian regimes is far removed from the values of social work, but to what extent did social pedagogues in Nazi Germany collude with the state in removing disabled children from their families, even actively promoting the institutionalisation of 'degenerates'? How resistant is contemporary social work in the face of authoritarian regimes? Indeed, how resistant is the profession to current policies that contravene social work values by increasing inequality and deepening poverty?

Crusades and panics are often seen as unfathomable episodes, but perhaps they tell us something of more fundamental significance. Clapton *et al.* (2013: 197) suggest that 'many of the anxieties that beset social work are best understood as moral panics'. Indeed, social work can become caught up in a moral crusade not as a bystander but as an active moral agent. An example of a damaging moral crusade in which social work played a central role is the 1980s hunt for 'satanic cults' in the UK, when a belief that devil-worshipping covens were ritually abusing children had devastating consequences. Social workers 'rescued' large numbers of children from their families even though evidence for organised cults was never established.

What ethical position, then, ought social workers to pursue in the face of moral panics? There are at least two aspects of moral crusades and panics that pose a dilemma for social workers. The first is whether to play an active part in opposing the specific victimisation of the targeted group. Social work's moral mission to work for social justice and to empower marginalised groups would suggest that the profession ought to bring its authority to bear against the moral panic. As I write, my home city is mobilising as a 'City of Sanctuary' against the moral panic confronting the Syrian, Afghan and Iraqi migrants attempting to cross into Europe. Social media, often accused of feeding these panics, in fact enable 'folk devils' (Cohen, 1972) to defend, build allies and hit back. Choice, competition and fragmentation of the contemporary media can mobilise opposition to moral panic. Perhaps the Popish Plot would have been snuffed out early if modern social media communications had been available! The question for social workers is how actively they ought to participate in City of Sanctuary-type movements and ought they to be involved specifically *as* social workers? I would argue that international migration is a significant social issue and social work ought to respond. Any *social* issue is a *social* work concern.

A second dilemma for social workers is more nuanced and concerns social work's role as a critical commentator on social policy and social anxieties (Ungar, 2001). Social work has a duty to be aware of the subtext of social phenomena such as moral panics. What obligation, then, has social work in exposing this subtext and acting on it? For example, this is the gist of the message that 'greets' the traveller on boarding a train from Sheffield to Manchester:

> 24 hour CCTV is in operation for your safety and security. Please read the safety notices displayed in the carriages. Do not leave luggage unattended. If you see any suspicious behaviour please report it to the on-board staff immediately.

This is not, in itself, a moral crusade nor yet a panic, but it does provide the steady background hum of threat and fear from which panics arise. The public space of the train is presented as one of danger, not sociability; other people are potential killers, not providers of social protection. What purpose does this constant drone of fear serve? Sociologists like Cohen (1971) have pointed to its role as a diversion to sustain the status quo. Whilst the populace trembles at the remote chance of death by terrorism, the actual deaths by inequality are ignored ('Stark inequality kills more than 200,000 people early a year [in the UK]' – *The Guardian*, 10 September 2015, p. 6). Some social workers might see this kind of knowledge as political and therefore not part of professional practice. However, if your service user's life is cut short by stark inequality and your profession's statement of ethics requires you to promote social justice, how can it be right not to act on this knowledge? No longer, therefore, the dilemma of to do or not to do, but the challenge of *how?*

Can a moral panic ever be used for good? Would the greater good justify the moral panic? For instance, a moral panic around the dangers of people with schizophrenia killing random people in the community might bring about better resources for mental health services. However, moral panics cast people as unvirtuous – untrustworthy, dangerous or vulnerable to harm – in order to invoke fear. The deliberate stirring of fear is wrong, so it is difficult to cast the engineering of a moral panic as a good, whatever the motivation and the outcome. Practically speaking, a moral panic is like a wild fire, the path and extent of its destruction impossible to predict.

Sometimes fear and anxiety in the social realm is backed up by 'evidence' from the scientific sphere:

> One day we hear about the danger of mercury, and run to throw out cans of tuna fish from our shelves; the next day the food to shun may be butter, which our grandparents considered the acme of wholesomeness; then we have to scrub the lead paint from our walls. Today the danger lurks in the phosphates in our favourite detergent; tomorrow the finger points to insecticides, which were hailed a few years ago as saviours of millions from hunger and disease. The threats of death, insanity and – somehow even more fearsome – cancer lurk in all we eat or touch.

The paragraph above, written over 40 years ago (Rabinowitch, 1972: 5), is surprisingly current.

## Moral guardians

The creation of a moral panic may be unethical, but can moral *crusades* ever be justified and, if so, ought social workers to lead them? In more general terms, might social workers be seen as moral guardians of society?

A social work community that is under-confident, searching for its identity and in need of a guiding light might be well served by a notion of moral guardianship. In which case, what aspects of social work and public policy should be 'moralised'? In the past, social work's precursors used public anxieties over dangers to children in late Victorian England to create the NSPCC and the Children's Charter (Clapton *et al*. 2013). Ought social workers to campaign about the dangers of internet grooming of children and assume a position of moral guardianship of those children?

If we were to consult the **wise professionals**, they would likely be cautious about moralising a particular aspect of social work or public policy. To claim moral guardianship is to assume the high ground and the aphorism tells us that 'pride comes before a fall'. It is one thing to aspire to moral guardianship and another to claim it publicly and openly. Perhaps this is an instructive case of honesty not being a good; by the honest act of claiming moral guardianship, it is lost.

In the introductory chapter I was casual about the distinctions between ethics, values and morals, but perhaps those differences now reveal their significance. A strong, transparent position on ethics – that social workers should work to the highest ethical standard – does not provoke the qualms that arise from moralising practice and claiming moral high ground, which suggest superiority. Moral crusades invariably require their corollary, their own folk devils. Can a moral crusade on behalf of children at risk of being groomed through internet sites escape demonising the perpetrators? Crusades invariably need an enemy as well as a mission.

The **wise professionals** would respond to a moral panic the way they have been responding to the dilemmas in this book. They would stand to the side of the panic with the aim of seeing it for what it is, the subtext and social meaning of it. They would defend the victims of the moral panic, even if at the same time they would condemn the actions of some groups that are the target of the panic (such as paedophiles). They would make allies of individuals and groups who similarly seek to douse moral panics, such as the City of Sanctuary movement mentioned earlier in this chapter. The wise professionals would want social workers to be active in these social movements *as* social workers: in this way, social work begins to reshape its own identity, makes itself known to its public, and takes a hold of its own future.

## Moral luck

The journeys we have taken through the stories and dilemmas in this book have been predicated on a belief in *agency*. Agency is the power of individuals and groups to make choices that, in turn, make changes. It is a very human need to know that we can and do make a difference and that there are patterns in events that improve our choices with experience.

However, in the equation between intended cause and randomness, it is possible that we underestimate the proportions – that the tipping point, the one-way-or-the-other-ness of events is greater than we care to allow. When a moral judgement is made of someone where a significant aspect of what that person has done has depended on factors beyond their control, we speak of 'moral luck' (Williams, 1981). Let us consider examples from social work to consider the four kinds of moral luck identified by Nagel (1979).

*Resultant luck*

> Two social workers each want the best for their service user: one makes a decision to support the service user to remain in their own home, and the service user thrives happily; the other makes the same decision with their service user, who suffers unhappily. Is a good act a good act by virtue of the good intention (Kant's 'jewel shining by itself'), untouched by any notion of moral luck? In the moral world as it is exists rather than the one Kant would have for us, the social workers will likely be judged differently dependent on the outcomes. Again, if both social workers uncharacteristically completed the wrong paperwork, only the one with the poor outcome is likely to face blame.

*Circumstantial luck*

> Two social workers qualify together with distinction from the same course: one takes up employment in a well-run, well-resourced agency and has the opportunity to perform exemplary practice; the other is employed by an organisation which has covert corrupt practices in which the worker becomes unknowingly complicit, resulting in the loss of his professional licence. Had that worker been employed in the same agency as his fellow graduate, he would have practised exemplary social work.

Is it easier to be ethically minded, in your professional practice as well as your personal living, if you are fortunate enough to live in a corner of the globe where there is lawfulness and plenty?

### Constitutive luck

Who we are and the kind of person we are is largely a matter of luck. So, one social worker is courageous and runs into the service user's home in order to intervene in a physical confrontation during a domestic violence incident; and another social worker is cowardly and runs away. Why would the actions of the first social worker be judged morally superior to the latter, given that the first has the good luck to be blessed with courage and the latter has not?

### Causal luck

The 'problem' of free will centres on just how much control we really do have over our actions. If free will is necessary for us to be considered morally responsible for our actions, then the question of how much free will we can exercise is important when weighing moral responsibility. How responsible any social worker can be judged is circumscribed by how much they exercised free will.

In short, people's actions depend much more on moral luck (the chance of their personal qualities and circumstances) than is admitted, yet we are inclined to assess the moral quality of their actions as though moral luck were not a factor (Nelkin, 2013). Many people accept that the links between actions and consequences is hard to pin down, but at least we can and ought to be judged on our intentions; yet to what extent does the nature of intention (benevolent, spiteful, etc.) also depend on luck? Nagel (1979: 68) came to a conclusion that 'in a sense the problem has no solution'. In the end we are left with a series of events 'which can be deplored or celebrated, but not blamed or praised'. Perhaps this morally neutral world would be an improvement on the rush to judgement which characterises the moral world as it is.

## Moral compass

A problem might not have a solution, as Nagel (1979) suggested but, still, there might be *better* ways of looking at a problem. Is it possible, then, to devise the equivalent of a compass to guide us around the moral landscape, a way of tracking towards 'ethical north'?

Below is a grid charting two dimensions of practice. The north–south axis is the degree to which an action or situation is ethical; west–east is the degree to which it is effective. Of course, both of these terms 'ethical' and 'effective' beg exploration. We hope that the dilemmas in this book have helped with the ethical dimension and, undoubtedly, the effectiveness axis is not divorced from the ethical (can ineffective practice be ethical?). The professional compass aims to help its owner delve into these two dimensions in order to achieve a greater under-standing of the possible choices. Wherever you decide your particular dilemma lands on the grid (and of course this is subjective), the aim is to consider how you might edge towards the A1 square – to a position that is both more ethical and more effective. What would that look like? Think of the moral compass as the **wise professionals** in a board game format.

Try using the compass with some of the dilemmas in this book and some dilemmas of your own. For instance, where would you track each stage of Sarah's dilemmas in Chapter 9? What actions could you advise Sarah to take in order to edge her choices towards the A1 square?

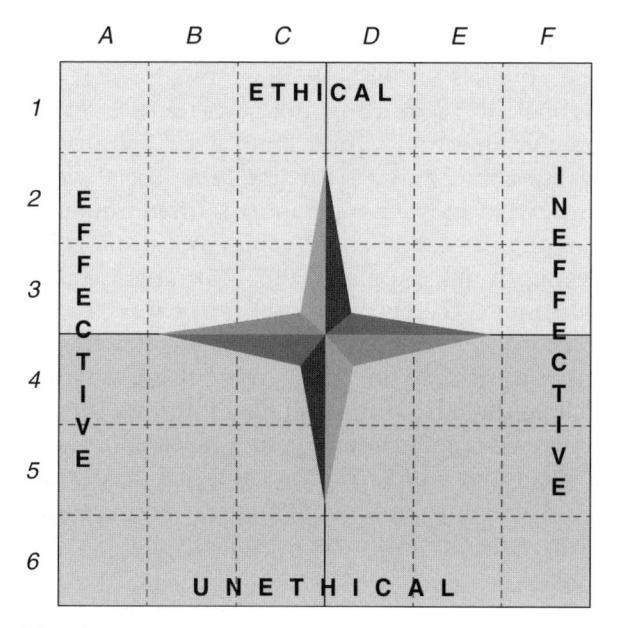

**Figure 11.1** Moral compass
(Doel, 2010: 97)

## Becoming a better social worker

A belief in the possibility of *agency,* the ability to will freely, survives most calls to determinism and so the question *'What makes a good social worker?'* and, indeed, *'What kind of social worker is the best social worker?'* remain questions worth asking.

The dilemmas in this book have taught us that the personal and the professional are integral, so professional integrity is bound with personal integrity, set in a political context. Many decisions are made with *'convenience to self'* at their heart (Joseph and Fernandes, 2006: 30, emphasis in the original): I know I shouldn't support a company that abuses its workers and is taking jobs and livelihoods away from my local high street, but it is so convenient to buy online that I ignore those other 'goods'. First and fundamentally, what I ought not to do is pretend that this is ethical behaviour or attempt to justify it through corrupted moral reasoning. Justifying decisions that are based on convenience to self and denying this through spurious moral reasoning dishonours ourselves and others, none more so than service users. When we have the personal integrity to recognise what is *not* ethical behaviour but personal convenience, we have opened the door to the possibility of changing our behaviour. At core, public and professional service is the will to act against one's personal convenience and interest, wrapped around the trust and care that I discussed at the conclusion of the first chapter. My hope is that now, having worked with the material in this book, it is a knowing (not naïve) trust and a considered care.

Perhaps the core question is not about good social workers and best social workers, but about how we become *better* social workers? 'When it comes to change, what moves people most is often not an argument from principle, not a long discussion about values, but just a gradually acquired new way of seeing things' (Appiah, 2007: 73). This is the counsel of the **wise professionals** – to recognise each **singularity** for what it is, a moment of decision when there is a choice between better and worse alternatives. What is surprisingly difficult is recognising singularities for what they are, unpicking them from the everyday routines. It is crucial, then, to discover your own wise professionals: your inner wisdom; a supportive peer group; a good supervisor – most likely a combination of these can provide your own ethical reference group. Staking out and securing the time to consult with your wise professionals is probably the best social work skill you can develop.

# 12 GLOSSARY OF ETHICAL AND OTHER TERMS

**a priori**
A statement that is taken and understood as truthful in itself with no need for further proof or justification.

**beneficence**
Seeking to do good.

**case-based ethics** – see **casuism**

**casuism**
Treating each situation case by case rather than applying principles or a strict rule book.

**categorical imperative** – see **Kantian**

**consequentialism**
When giving moral weight to any action, the primary concern is to understand the likely consequences of the action; this is a **teleological** approach.

**defeasible**
A proposition that depends on various and varying factors that are subject to refutation, and that lead to an inconclusive *all-things-being-equal* outcome, open to various interpretations.

**deontological**
Duty-based ethical theories in which principles are accepted as 'givens'; acting morally is doing your duty regardless of consequences and according to absolute rules that are always valid – for instance, that it is always right to tell the truth and, therefore, it is your duty to be honest.

**dilemma – ethical and practice**
Using a strict definition, an ethical dilemma is a choice between two ethically undesirable courses of action. In this book I use an inclusive definition that incorporates the everyday use of the word; i.e. a choice between courses of action where the balance between what is right is complex and

open to dispute. An ethical dilemma is where 'right' is used as a moral adjective and a practice dilemma is where 'right' is used a factual description (most effective), but frequently the same dilemma has a complex mix of ethical and practical uncertainties.

### dual relationships
The boundary issues that can arise when social workers have more than one kind of relationship with a service user (professional, social, commercial, etc.). Dual relationships can also refer to situations where social workers are also service users.

### duty-based ethics – see deontological

### emotivism
A belief that all ethical statements are merely expressions of the speaker's emotions, their likes and dislikes, and moral argument is to some extent meaningless.

### ends and means
Part of Kant's categorical imperative is to treat people as ends in themselves, not means to an end. This links with social work values concerning human dignity and the moral worth of every individual.

### ethics of care
Derived from feminist theory, ethics of care place relationships at their heart and recognise that for large parts of their lives humans are dependent on the care of others. Rather than seeing emotions as a challenge to rational moral reasoning, the ethics of care embrace feelings as central to ethics.

### existentialism
As existentialism focuses on *what is* rather than *what ought to be*, and is associated with moral subjectivism (i.e. morality is a matter of individual choice), philosophers query whether an existentialist ethics is possible.

### intuitionism
'Goodness' is something that we know intuitively, so it cannot be defined or inferred from any facts or propositions. However, from this knowledge of what is good it is possible to derive principles of obligation.

### Kantian
In Kantian ethics, good actions are those done from a sense of duty – motivation is all-important. Duties that are unconditional (*musts*) are called **categorical imperatives**. These are universal, applying to everyone in every circumstance. There is respect for people as rational beings.

**land ethics**
A thing is right when it preserves the integrity, stability and beauty of the biotic community.

**maleficence**
Seeking to do harm.

**maxim**
A general principle underlying any action, similar to an axiom; e.g. 'Do to others as you would have them do to you.'

**meta-ethics**
Meta-ethics focuses not on what is moral, but on what morality itself is – the status and meaning of ethical values and qualities.

**moral agent**
A person who is actively being and doing in ways they consider to be ethical.

**moral relativism**
The question as to whether ethical and moral judgements ought to differ from time to time and place to place; or whether there are moral absolutes that transcend era and location. A moral relativist asserts that there can be no universal consensus on what is right or wrong.

**narrative ethics**
Using stories to reveal ethical issues.

**non-maleficence**
Seeking not to do harm.

**ontological**
Ontology is the philosophy of being and the nature of existence and reality. Ontology describes the world as it is, not as it ought to be.

**philosophic scepticism**
Questioning the possibility of certainty of knowledge and being open to doubt and alternative perspectives. It can be used as a formal method of philosophical enquiry. Socratic dialogue is an attempt to reveal truth through dialogue and reciprocity.

**phronesis**
A form of practical reasoning, a kind of wisdom born from practical engagement with the world, 'street wise'. Phronesis is a personal virtue, one gained through the development of self-understanding.

**pragmatism**
A belief that the best solutions are those that work in practice and are the most accommodating; a strong belief in compromise rather than sticking to principles.

**principlism**
A reliance on guiding principles about how to act, adapted to the particular profession in question. Principles are broader than rules.

**redemptive ethics**
A strong belief in the possibility of change and the value of forgiveness; people who have committed wrongs can learn from these experiences and become better for them. Redemption plays a large part in much religious ethics, as in 'the road to Damascus' when the Christian-hater Saul converts to become the Christian saint Paul.

**relationship ethics** – see **ethics of care**

**relativism** – see **moral relativism**

**rule utilitarianism**
Personal judgement is not central to morality; obedience to a system of social rules is. Following these rules exonerates a person from the consequences, since they have 'played by the book' rather than used their own judgement.

**scepticism** see **philosophic scepticism**

**singularity**
A moment in time with potential significance.

**situation(al) ethics**
The ethics of each case ought to be determined by consideration of each person in their own unique situation; love is the central motivation in Fletcher's (1966) model.

**Socratic dialogue** see **philosophic scepticism**

**surrender**
Surrender is the ability to let go, central in holistic cultures (such as aboriginal and First Nations) where value conflicts are subsumed in the solidarity of the community and the individual's will is gifted to a collective wisdom.

**teleology**
Weighing good and bad in terms of what follows from an action (sometimes termed **consequentialism**); whether a lie is good or bad depends on the end goal and what happens as a result.

**universalisability**
Unconditional principles that can and ought to be applicable to all people. See also **Kantian**.

**utilitarianism**
Whatever brings about the greatest total happiness, or the least unhappiness.

**value patterning**
The particular values or ethical principles that are regularly given priority by an individual.

**virtue ethics**
An individual's character is what matters. It is necessary to cultivate a virtuous life in order to flourish as a genuinely rounded human being.

**wise professionals**
See pages 8 and 178 for an exposition of the wise professionals.

# APPENDIX

**Guidance on Conduct and Ethics for Students in Health and Care Professions** (HCPC, 2012; reproduced from the HCPC website: http://www.hpc-uk.org).

1 You should always act in the best interests of your service users.

> ➤ You should respect a person's right to have their interventions carried out by a professional and not a student.

> ➤ You should not exploit or abuse your relationships with service users.

> ➤ You should treat everyone equally.

> ➤ You should not do anything that you think will put someone in danger.

> ➤ If you are worried about a situation which might put someone at risk, you should speak to a member of the placement team or your education provider.

2 You should respect the confidentiality of your service users.

> ➤ You should keep information about service users confidential, and only use it for the purpose for which it was given, unless the information raises concerns about a situation where someone may be at risk.

> ➤ You should not knowingly give any personal or confidential information to anyone who is not entitled to access it.

> ➤ You should remove anything that could be used to identify a service user from confidential information which you use in your assessment.

> ➤ You should follow local policies or guidelines if you want to use information that may identify someone in your assessments.

> ➤ You should follow local policies or guidelines on confidentiality produced by your education provider or placement provider.

3 You should keep high standards of personal conduct.

> ➤ You should be aware that conduct outside of your programme may affect whether or not you are allowed to complete your programme or register with us.

> ➤ You should be polite with service users, your colleagues and the programme team.

> ➤ You should make sure that your personal appearance is appropriate for your placement environment.

> ➤ You should follow your education provider's or placement provider's policy on attendance.

4 You should provide any important information about your conduct, competence or health to your education provider.

> ➤ You should tell your education provider and placement provider about any existing health conditions or changes to your health which may put your service users or yourself at risk.

> ➤ You should tell your education provider if you are convicted of, or cautioned for, any offence.

5 You should limit your study or stop studying if your performance or judgement is affected by your health.

> ➤ You should get help from a doctor or an occupational health professional if you are worried about your health.

> ➤ You should be aware that you may put your service users or yourself at risk if your performance or judgement is affected by your health.

6 You should keep your professional knowledge and skills up to date.

> ➤ You are responsible for your own learning.

> ➤ You should think about and respond positively to feedback you are given.

7 You should act within the limits of your knowledge and skills.

> ➤ You should only carry out an unsupervised task if you feel that you have the appropriate knowledge and skills.

> ➤ You should make sure that you are appropriately supervised for any task that you are asked to carry out.

➤ You should ask for help when you need it.

➤ You should make sure that you do not claim that you have knowledge and skills which you do not.

**8** You should communicate effectively with service users and your education provider and placement providers.

➤ You should take all reasonable steps to make sure that you can communicate appropriately and effectively with service users.

➤ You should communicate effectively and cooperate with colleagues to benefit service users.

➤ You should communicate effectively and cooperate with the programme team and placement team.

➤ Where appropriate, you should share your knowledge with colleagues.

**9** You should get informed consent to provide care or services (so far as possible).

Informed consent is when someone has all the information they need, in a format they can understand, to make a decision about receiving care or services.

You should do the following (so far as possible).

➤ You should make sure that before you carry out any intervention, the service user is aware that you are a student.

➤ You should make sure that the service user has given their permission for the intervention to be carried out by a student.

➤ You should explain the intervention you are planning to carry out.

➤ Before you carry out any intervention, you should explain any risks associated with it.

➤ You should follow your education provider's or placement provider's policy on consent.

**10** You should keep accurate records on service users.

➤ You should make sure that any information you put in someone's record is accurate and clear.

➤ You should protect information in records from being lost, damaged, accessed by someone without permission or tampered with.

**11** You should deal fairly and safely with the risks of infection.

> ➤ You should make sure that you take all appropriate steps to deal with the risks of infection.

> ➤ You should follow your education provider's or placement provider's policy on managing the risks of infection.

**12** You should behave honestly.

> ➤ You should not pass off other people's work as your own.

> ➤ You should make sure that you reference other people's work appropriately.

> ➤ You should make sure that you truthfully and accurately fill in any documents.

> ➤ You should not let any improper financial reward influence the advice and services you provide, or the products you recommend.

> ➤ You should follow your education provider's policies on ethics when carrying out research.

**13** You should make sure that your behaviour does not damage public confidence in your profession.

> ➤ You should be aware that your behaviour may affect the trust that the public has in your profession.

> ➤ You should not do anything which might affect the trust that the public has in your profession.

# REFERENCES

AASW (2010), *Code of Ethics*, Canberra: Australian Association of Social Workers.

Adams, P. (2012), *Planning for Contact in Permanent Placements*, London: BAAF.

Akhtar, F. (2012), *Mastering Social Work Values and Ethics*, London: Jessica Kingsley.

Andersen, M. L. and Hill Collins, P. (2015), *Race, Class, and Gender: An Anthology* (9th edition), Boston, MA: Cengage Learning.

Androff, D. (2015), *Practising Rights: Human Right-Based Approach to Social Work Practice*, Abingdon: Routledge.

ANZASW (2015), *Code of Ethics*, Aotearoa New Zealand Association of Social Workers.

Appiah, K. (2007), *Cosmopolitanism: Ethics in a World of Strangers*, London: Penguin.

Appleton, C. and Adamson, C. (2016), 'The concept of integrity in relation to failing and marginal students' in A. Bellinger and D. Ford (eds), *Practice Placement in Social Work: Innovative Approaches for Effective Teaching and Learning*, pp. 181–202.

Asch, S. E. (1952), *Social Psychology*, Englewood Cliffs, NJ: Prentice.

Asimov, I. (1955), 'Franchise' in *If: Worlds of Science Fiction*, New York: Quinn Publications.

Aubert, V. (1980), 'Chance in social affairs' in J. Dowie and P. Lefrere (eds), *Risk and Chance*, pp. 74–97, Milton Keynes: Open University Press.

Ayer, A. J. (1936), *Language, Truth and Logic*, London: Gollancz (2nd edition: 1946).

Banks, S. (1995), *Ethics and Values in Social Work*, 1st edition, Basingstoke: Palgrave Macmillan.

Banks, S. (2004), *Ethics, Accountability and the Social Professions*, Basingstoke: Palgrave Macmillan.

Banks, S. (2006), *Ethics and Values in Social Work*, 3rd edition, Basingstoke: Palgrave Macmillan.

Banks, S. (ed.) (2010), *Ethical Issues in Youth Work*, 2nd edition, Abingdon: Routledge.

Banks, S. (2012), *Ethics and Values in Social Work*, 4th edition, Basingstoke: Palgrave Macmillan.

Banks, S. (2014), *Ethics*, Bristol: Policy Press.

Banks, S. (2016), 'Everyday ethics in professional life: social work as ethics work', *Ethics and Social Welfare*, 10(1): 35–52.

Banks, S. and Nøhr, K. (eds) (2012), *Practising Social Work Ethics around the World*, Abingdon: Routledge.

Barnard, A., Horner, N. and Wild, J. (2008), *The Value Base of Social Work and Social Care,* Berkshire: McGraw Hill.

Barsky, A. E. (2009), *Ethics and Values in Social Work,* New York: Oxford University Press.

BASW (2014), *The Code of Ethics for Social Workers: Statement of Principles,* British Association of Social Workers.

BATSW (2002), 'Declaration of Ethics for Social Workers, Bombay Association of Trained Social Workers: Mumbai' in J. Joseph and G. Fernandes (eds), *An Enquiry into Ethical Dilemmas in Social Work,* pp. 116–23, Mumbai: College of Social Work.

Bauman, Z. (1993), *Postmodern Ethics,* Oxford: Wiley.

Beckett, C. and Maynard, A. (2005), *Values and Ethics in Social Work,* London: Sage.

Bell, L. and Hafford-Letchfield, T. (eds) (2015), *Ethics, Values and Social Work Practice,* Milton Keynes: Open University Press.

Bem, D. (1980), 'The concept of risk in the study of human behaviour' in J. Dowie and P. Lefrere (eds), *Risk and Chance,* pp. 1–15, Milton Keynes: Open University Press.

Benson, A. M. (2011), *Volunteer Tourism,* Abingdon: Routledge.

Beresford, P. (2010), 'Re-examining relationships between experience, knowledge, ideas and research: a key role for recipients of state welfare and their movements', *Social Work and Society,* 8(1), accessed at: http://socwork.net/sws/article/view/19/56 on 3 March 2016.

Beresford, P. and Croft, S. (2001), 'Service users' knowledges and the social construction of social work', *Journal of Social Work,* 1(3): 295–316.

Beresford, P. and Holden, C. (2000), 'We have choices: globalisation and welfare user movements', *Disability and Society,* 15(7): 973–9.

Bernsen, A., Tabachnick, B. G. and Pope, S. (1994), 'National survey of social workers' sexual attraction to their clients: results, implications, and comparison to psychologists', *Ethics and Behavior,* 4(4): 369–88.

Biestek, F. P. (1957), *The Casework Relationship,* Chicago: Loyola University Press.

Bourdieu, P. (1991), *Language and Symbolic Power,* Cambridge: Polity Press.

Butler, I. (2002), 'A code of ethics for social work and social care research', *British Journal of Social Work,* 32(2): 239–48.

Butterfield, L. D., Borgen, W. A., Amundsen, N. E. and Maglio, A-S. T (2005), 'Fifty years of the critical incident technique: 1954–2004 and beyond', *Qualitative Research,* 5(4): 475–97.

CAIPE (2012), *Interprofessional Education in Pre-Registration Courses,* Fareham: CAIPE.

Cairns, K. (2008), *Attachment, Trauma and Resilience,* London: BAAF.

Cantacuzino, M. (2015), *The Forgiveness Project: Stories for a Vengeful Age,* London: Jessica Kingsley.

Carey, M. and Green, L. (eds) (2013), *Practical Social Work Ethics*, Aldershot: Ashgate.

Carney, J. and McCarren, K. (2012), 'Social work education in non-sexual dual relationships', *Journal of Social Work Values and Ethics,* 9(2): 10–20.

CASW (2005a), *Code of Ethics,* Canadian Association of Social Workers.

CASW (2005b), *Guidelines for Ethical Practice,* Canadian Association of Social Workers.

Cavaliere, F. (2014), 'The British code and the Italian code of ethics for social work: a lingua-cultural comparative analysis', *ESP Across Cultures,* 11: 57–73.

Clandinin, D. J. and Huber, J. (2010), 'Narrative inquiry' in P. L. Peterson, E. L. Baker and B. McGraw (eds), *International Encyclopaedia of Education,* 3rd edition, New York: Elsevier.

Clapton, G., Cree, V. and Smith, M. (2013), 'Moral panics and social work: towards a sceptical view of UK child protection', *Critical Social Policy,* 33(2): 197–217.

Clark, C. L. (2000), *Social Work Ethics: Politics, Principles and Practice,* Basingstoke: Palgrave Macmillan.

Clark, C. (2006), 'Children's voices: the views of vulnerable children on their service providers and the relevance of services they receive', *British Journal of Social Work,* 36: 21–39.

Cohen, S. (ed.) (1971), *Images of Deviance,* Harmondsworth: Penguin Books.

Cohen, S. (1972), *Folk Devils and Moral Panics: The Creation of the Mods and Rockers,* London: Routledge.

Committee of Public Accounts (2014), *Whistleblowing. Ninth Report of Session 2014-15,* London: House of Commons.

Cooner, T. S. (2013a), 'Using Facebook to explore boundary issues for social workers in a networked society: students' perceptions of learning', *British Journal of Social Work* (2013): 1–18.

Cooner, T. S. (2013b), *Social Work Social Media APP,* accessed at: https://itunes. apple.com/gb/app/social-work-social-media/id656114442?mt=8&ign-mpt=uo%3D4 on 3 March 2016.

Cooner, T. S. (2014), 'Using closed Facebook groups to teach social work skills, values, and approaches for social work media', in J. Westwood (ed.), *Social Media in Social Work Education,* pp. 29–39, Northwich: Critical Publishing.

Cooper, F. (2013), *Professional Boundaries in Social Work and Social Care: A Practical Guide to Understanding, Maintaining and Managing your Professional Boundaries,* London: Jessica Kingsley.

Crowe, J. (2004), 'Is an Existentialist Ethics possible?', *Philosophy Now,* 47: 29–30.

Dalai Lama (2013), *Beyond Religion: Ethics for a Whole World,* London: Rider.

Das, C. and Kulkarni, A. (2006a), 'Culture and ethics' in J. Joseph and G. Fernandes (eds), *An Enquiry into Ethical Dilemmas in Social Work,* pp. 78–91, Mumbai: College of Social Work.

Das, C. and Kulkarni, A. (2006b), 'Person vis-à-vis profession' in J. Joseph and G. Fernandes (eds), *An Enquiry into Ethical Dilemmas in Social Work,* pp. 92–103, Mumbai: College of Social Work.

de Beauvoir, S. (1947/1986), *The Ethics of Ambiguity,* New York: Citadel Press.

Dickens, J. (2012), *Social Work, Law and Ethics,* London: Routledge.

Doel, M. (2004), 'Difficult behaviour in groups', in *Groupwork,* 14(1): 80–100.

Doel, M. (2006), *Using Groupwork,* Abingdon: Routledge.

Doel, M. (2010), *Social Work Placements: a Traveller's Guide,* London: Routledge.

Doel, M. (2012), *Social Work: The Basics,* London: Routledge.

Doel, M. and Best, L. (2008), *Experiencing Social Work: Learning from Service Users,* London: Sage.

Doel, M. and Marsh, P. (1992), *Task-Centred Social Work,* Aldershot: Arena.

Doel, M., Allmark, P., Conway, P., Cowburn, M., Flynn, M., Nelson, P. and Tod, A. (2010), 'Professional boundaries: crossing a line or entering the shadows', *British Journal of Social Work,* 40(6), 1866–89.

Doel, M., Kachkachishvili, I., Lucas, J., Namicheishvili, S. and Partskhaladze, N. (2016), 'Creating social work education in the Republic of Georgia', in I. Taylor, M. Bogo and M. Lefevre (eds), *International Handbook of Social Work Education,* pp. 96–106, London: Routledge.

Dolgoff, R., Loewenberg, F. M. and Harrington, D. (2009), *Ethical Decisions for Social Work Practice,* 8th edition, Belmont, CA: Thomson Brooks/Cole.

Dominelli, L. (2002), *Anti-Oppressive Social Work Theory and Practice*, Basingstoke: Palgrave Macmillan.

Dominelli, L. (2004), *Social Work: Theory and Practice for a Changing Profession*, Oxford: Polity Press.

Dubois, B. and Miley, K. (1996), *Social Work: An Empowering Profession,* Harlow: Allyn and Bacon.

Durkheim, E. (1957), *Professional Ethics and Civic Morals*, London: Routledge.

Ellis, P. and Dehn, G. (2001) 'Whistleblowing: public concern at work' in C. Cull and J. Roche (eds), *The Law and Social Work*, Basingstoke: Palgrave Macmillan.

Engelbrecht, L. (2006), 'Cultural friendliness as the foundation for the support function in the supervision of social work students in South Africa', *International Social Work,* 49(2): 256–66.

Facebook for Educators, accessed at: https://en-gb.facebook.com/FBforEducators/ on 3 March 2016.

Feinberg, J. (1969), *Moral Concepts,* London: Oxford University Press.

Flanagan, S. (2015), 'How does storytelling within higher education contribute to the learning experience of early years students?', *Journal of Practice Teaching & Learning* 13(2): 162–184.

Fletcher, J. F. (1966), *Situation Ethics: The New Morality*, Philadelphia: Westminster Press.

FOKUS (2009), *Ethical Guidelines Fokus (Code of Conduct),* Oslo: Norwegian Union of Social Educators and Social Workers.

Freire, P. (1970/2000), *Pedagogy of the Oppressed,* London: Bloomsbury Publishing.

Frost, N., Mills, S. and Stein, M. (1999), *Understanding Residential Child Care,* University of Michigan.

Frost, R. (1916), 'The Road Not Taken' in *Mountain Interval*, New York: Henry Holt and Company.

Gaine, C. (2010), *Equality and Diversity in Social Work,* Exeter: Learning Matters.

Gardner, P. J. and Poole, J. M. (2009), 'One story at a time: narrative therapy, older adults and addictions' in *Journal of Applied Gerontology,* 28(5): 600–20.

GASW (2005), *Social Work Code of Ethics:* Georgian Association of Social Workers, under construction at: http://gasw.org/ka/component/content/article/132. html.

GASW (2007), *Social Work Professional Standards:* Georgian Association of Social Workers, under construction at: http://gasw.org/ka/component/content/ article/132.html.

Gill, A. A. (2012), *The Golden Door: Letters to America,* London: Phoenix.

Goode, E. and Ben-Yehuda, N. (2009), *Moral Panics: The Social Construction of Deviance,* 2nd edition, Malden: Wiley-Blackwell.

Gray, M. and Webb, S. (eds) (2010), *Ethics and Value Perspectives in Social Work,* Basingstoke: Palgrave Macmillan.

Greenslade, L., McAuliffe, D. and Chenoweth, L. (2015), 'Social workers' experiences of covert workplace activism', *Australian Social Work,* 68(4), 422–37.

Hardcastle, D. A. (2011), *Community Practice: Theories and Skills for Social Workers,* Oxford: Oxford University Press.

Hardwick, L. and Worsley, A. (2011), *Doing Social Work Research,* London: Sage.

HCPC (2012), *Guidance on Conduct and Ethics for Students in Health and Care Professions,* accessed at: http://www.hpc-uk.org/assets/documents/10002c16g uidanceonconductandethicsforstudents.pdf on 3 March 2016.

Heath-Kelly, C. (2012), 'Counter-Terrorism and the counterfactual: producing the 'radicalisation' discourse and the UK PREVENT Strategy', *The British Journal of Politics and International Relations,* 15: 394–415.

Held, V. (2006), *The Ethics of Care,* Oxford: Oxford University Press.

Heller, J. (1961), *Catch-22,* New York: Simon and Schuster.

Hennessey, R. (2011), *Relationship Skills in Social Work,* London: Sage.

Horne, N. (1999), *Values in Social Work,* 2nd edition, Aldershot: Ashgate.

Hothersall, S. and Maas-Lowitt, M. (eds) (2010), *Need, Risk and Protection in Social Work Practice,* Exeter: Learning Matters.

Hugman, R. (2012), *Culture, Values and Ethics in Social Work: Embracing Diversity,* London: Routledge.

Hugman, R. (2013a), *A-Z of Professional Ethics,* Basingstoke: Palgrave Macmillan.

Hugman, R. (2013b), 'Ethics' in M. Davies (ed.), *The Blackwell Companion to Social Work,* pp. 379–86, Chichester: Wiley-Blackwell.

Hugman, R. and Smith, D. (1995), *Ethical Issues in Social Work,* London: Routledge.

Hunt, G. (ed.). (1998), *Whistleblowing in the Social Services: Public Accountability and Professional Practice.* London: Arnold.

IASW (2007), *IASW Code of Ethics,* Dublin, Irish Association of Social Workers.

IASWG (2006), *Standards for Social Work Practice with Groups,* 2nd edition, International Association of Social Work with Groups.

IFSW/IASSW (2004), *Ethics in Social Work: Statement of Principles,* Berne: International Federation of Social Workers / International Association of Schools of Social Work, accessed at: http://ifsw.org/policies/statement-of-ethical-principles/ on 3 March 2016.

IFSW/IASSW (2014), *Definition of Social Work,* International Federation of Social Workers/International Association of Schools of Social Work.

Italian National Council (2009), *Codice Deontologico dell'Assistente Sociale.*

Janis, I. (1972), *Victims of Groupthink.* Boston, MA: Houghton Mifflin.

Jayaratne, S., Croxton, T. and Mattison, D. (1997), 'Social Work Professional Standards: An exploratory study', *Social Work,* 42(2): 187–96.

Jetter, M. (2014), 'Terrorism and the media', discussion paper No 8497, Bonn, Germany, accessed at: http://ftp.iza.org/dp8497.pdf on 3 March 2016.

Joseph, J. and Fernandes, G. (eds), (2006), *An Enquiry into Ethical Dilemmas in Social Work,* Mumbai: College of Social Work.

Justice Committee (2011), *Eighth Report: The role of the Probation Service,* London: Parliament, accessed at: http://www.publications.parliament.uk/pa/cm201012/cmselect/cmjust/519/51902.htm on 3 March 2016.

Kant, I. (1797/1991), *The Metaphysics of Morals,* translated by Mary J. Gregor, Cambridge: Cambridge University Press.

Kant, I. (1784/1998), *Groundwork of the Metaphysics of Morals,* edited and translated by M. Gregor, Cambridge: Cambridge University Press.

Keeney, A. J., Smart, A. M., Richards, R., Harrison, S., Carrillo, M. and Valentine, D. (2014), 'Human rights and social work codes of ethics: an international analysis', *Journal of Social Welfare and Human Rights* 2(2): 1–16.

Kemshall, H. (2002), *Risk, Social Policy and Welfare,* Buckingham: Open University Press.

Kemshall, H. (2013), 'Risk assessment and risk management' in M. Davies (ed.), *The Blackwell Companion to Social Work,* pp. 333–42, Chichester: Wiley-Blackwell.

Korean Association of Social Workers (undated), *Code of Ethics,* accessed at: cdn.ifsw.org/assets/ifsw_12405-10.pdf on 3 March 2016.

Krinsky, C. (ed.) (2013), *The Ashgate Research Companion to Moral Panics* London: Routledge.

Ledesma, K. and Casavant, V. (2011), 'Enhancing the reach and outcomes of child welfare programs through social media' in T. LaLiberte and E. Snyder (eds), *Child Welfare and Technology* (Spring 2011), University of Minnesota: Centre for Advanced Studies in Child Welfare.

Leopold, A. (1949), *A Sand County Almanac,* Oxford: Oxford University Press.

Locke, J. (1689/1956), *Second Treatise on Civil Government,* Library of Alexandria.

Lonne, B., Harries, M., Featherstone, B. and Gray, M. (2015), *Working Ethically in Child Protection,* London: Routledge.

Lymbery, M. and Butler, S. (eds) (2004), *Social Work Ideals and Practice Realities,* Basingstoke: Palgrave Macmillan.

Mallon, G. and Betts, B. (2005), *Recruiting, Assessing and Supporting Lesbian and Gay Carers and Adopters,* London: BAAF.

Mann, J. (2016), in A. Bellinger and D. Ford (eds), *Practice Placement in Social Work,* pp. 165–80, Bristol: Policy Press.

Mansbach, A. and Bachner, Y. G. (2009), 'Self-reported likelihood of whistleblowing by social work students', *Social Work Education* 28(1): 18–28.

Marquis, R. and Jackson, R. (2000), 'Quality of life and quality of services relationships: experiences of people with disabilities', *Disability and Society,* 15(3): 411–25.

Marsh, P. and Doel, M. (2005), *The Task-Centred Book*, London: Routledge/ Community Care.

Marx, K. (1875), *Critique of the Gotha Programme*, accessed at: https://www. marxists.org/archive/marx/works/download/Marx_Critque_of_the_Gotha_ Programme.pdf on 3 March 2016.

Maslow, A. H. (1943), 'A theory of human motivation', *Psychological Review* 50(4): 370–96, accessed at: http://psychclassics.yorku.ca/Maslow/motivation. htm on 3 March 2016.

Mattison, M. (2000), 'Ethical decision-making: The person in the process', in *Social Work*, 45(3): 201–12.

Mayer and Timms (1970), *The Client Speaks*, London: Routledge & Kegan Paul.

McEwan, I. (2014), *The Children Act*, London: Jonathan Cape.

McKenna, K. Y. A. and Green, A. S. (2002), 'Virtual group dynamics', *Group Dynamics: Theory, Research and Practice*, 6(1), 116–27.

Meagher, G. and Parton, N. (2004), 'Modernising social work and the ethics of care', *Social Work and Society*, 2(1): 10–27, accessed at: http://www.socwork. net/sws/article/view/237/412 on 3 March 2016.

Mental Welfare Commission for Scotland (2015), *Adults with Incapacity Act*.

Mill, J. S. (1863), *Utilitarianism*, London: Parker, Son and Bourn.

Moore, G. E. (1903), *Principia Ethica*, Cambridge: Cambridge University Press.

Munro, E. (2011), *The Munro Review of Child Protection: A child-centred system (Final Report)*, Norwich: The Stationery Office.

Murphy, R. (2011), *The Courageous State: Rethinking Economics, Society and the Role of Government*, Kindle.

Nagel, T. (1979), *Mortal Questions*, Cambridge: Cambridge University Press.

NASW (2008), *Code of Ethics*, National (US) Association of Social Workers.

National Audit Office (2014a), *Government Whistleblowing Policies*, London: UK Parliament.

National Audit Office (2014b), *Assessment Criteria for Whistleblowing Policies*, Supplementary Report, London: UK Parliament.

Nelkin, D. K. (2013), 'Moral luck', in Edward N. Zalta (ed.), *The Stanford Encyclopedia of Philosophy* (Winter 2013 edition), accessed at: http://plato. stanford.edu/archives/win2013/entries/moral-luck/ on 3 March 2016.

Nietzsche, F. (1886/1973), *Beyond Good and Evil*, translated by R. J. Hollingdale, Harmondsworth: Penguin Books.

NISCC (2002), *Codes of Practice for the Degree in Social Work*, Northern Ireland Social Care Council.

NISCC (2009), *Codes of Practice for Social Care Workers and Employers of Social Care Workers*, Northern Ireland Social Care Council.

Nolan Committee on Standards in Public Life (1995), *First Report of the Committee on Standards in Public Life*, (Nolan Principles), p. 14, accessed at https:// www.gov.uk/government/uploads/system/uploads/attachment_data/ file/263360/285002.pdf on 3 March 2016.

Oakwater, H. (2012), *Bubble Wrapped Children: How Social Networking Is Transforming the Face of 21st Century Adoption*, London: MX Publishing.

O'Sullivan, T. (1999), *Decision Making in Social Work,* Basingstoke: Palgrave Macmillan.

Parrott, L. (2006), *Values and Ethics in Social Work Practice*, Exeter: Learning Matters.

Parsloe, P. (ed) (1999), *Risk Assessment in Social Care and Social Work*, London: Jessica Kingsley.

Parsons, R. D. (2001), *The Ethics of Professional Practice,* New York: Pearson.

Parton, N. (2003), Rethinking professional practice: the contributions of social constructionism and the feminist 'ethics of care', *British Journal of Social Work*, 33: 1–16.

Payne, M. (2007), 'Performing as a "wise person" in social work practice', *Practice* 19(2): 85–96.

Payne, M. (2009), 'Practice theory: ideas embodied in a wise person's professional process' in B. Borden, *Reshaping Theory in Contemporary Social Work: Toward a Critical Pluralism in Clinical Practice*, pp. 234–54, New York: Columbia University Press.

Plamenatz, J. (1938), *Consent, Freedom and Political Obligation,* Oxford: Oxford University Press, 2nd edition published 1968.

Pollard, N. (2014), 'Concepts of justice and the non-traditional placement', *Journal of Practice Teaching & Learning*, 13(2–3): 88–108.

Porter, E. (1999), *Feminist Perspectives on Ethics,* London: Longman.

Pullen-Sansfaçon, A. and Cowden, S. (2012), *The Ethical Foundations of Social Work,* New York: Pearson.

Rabinowitch, E. (1972), 'Living dangerously in the age of science', *Bulletin of the Atomic Scientists*, 28(1): 5–8.

Rawls, J. (1958), 'Justice as fairness', *Philosophical Review,* 68: 164–94.

Ray, M., Bernard, M. and Phillips, J. (2009), *Critical Issues in Social Work with Older People,* Basingstoke: Palgrave Macmillan.

Reamer, F. G. (1998), 'The evolution of social work ethics', *Social Work,* 43(6): 488–500.

Reamer, F. G. (1999), 'Boundary issues in social work: managing dual relationships', *Social Work,* 48(1): 121–33.

Reamer, F. G. (2004), 'Ethical decisions and risk management' in M. Austin and K. M. Hopkins (eds), *Supervision as Collaboration in the Human Services: Building a Learning Culture,* pp. 97–109, Thousand Oaks, CA: Sage.

Reamer, F. G. (2006), *Social Work Values and Ethics*, 3rd edition, New York: Columbia University Press.

Relton C., Whelan, B., Strong, M., Thomas, K., Whitford, H., Scott, E. and van Cleemput, P. (2014, 19 November), 'Are financial incentives for breastfeeding feasible in the UK? A mixed methods field study', *The Lancet*, 384, Special Issue, S5.

Rifkin, J. (2009), *The Empathic Civilization: The Race to Global Consciousness in a World in Crisis,* New York: J. P. Tarcher/Penguin.

Rogowski, S. (2010), *Social work: The Rise and Fall of a Profession,* Bristol: The Policy Press.

Rooney, R. (2009), *Strategies for Work with Involuntary Clients*, 2nd edition, New York: Columbia University Press.

Ruch, G., Turney, D. and Ward, A. (eds) (2010), *Relationship-Based Social Work*, London: Jessica Kingsley.

Saarnio, P. (2000), 'Does it matter who treats you?', *European Journal of Social Work*, 3(3): 261–68.

Sartre, J-P. (1946), *Existentialism and Humanism*, Paris: Les Editions Nagel.

SASW (2004), *Code of Professional Ethics*, Singapore Association of Social Workers.

Selwyn, J., Wijedasa, D. and Meakings, S. (2014), *Beyond the Adoption Order: Challenges, Interventions and Adoption Disruption*, Bristol: Department for Education.

Sieminski, S. (2013), 'Social work practice and the challenge of later life' in M. Davies (ed.), *The Blackwell Companion to Social Work*, pp. 267–73, Chichester: Wiley-Blackwell.

Singer, P. (1973), *Democracy and Disobedience*, Oxford: Oxford University Press.

Slovic and Fischhoff (1980), 'How safe is safe enough?' in J. Dowie and P. Lefrere (eds), *Risk and Chance*, pp. 121–47, Milton Keynes: Open University Press.

Smith, R. (2005), *Values and Practice in Children's Services*, Basingstoke: Palgrave Macmillan.

Smith, R. (2010, 15 January), 'Social Work, Risk and Power', *Sociological Research*, accessed at: www.socresonline.org.uk/15/1/4.html on 3 March 2016.

Some, M. P. (1997), *Ritual: Power, Healing and Community*, Penguin Group USA.

SSR (2006), *Ethics in Social Work: An Ethical Code for Social Work Professionals*, Stockholm: Swedish Association of Graduates in Social Sciences, Personnel and Public Administration, Economics and Social Work.

Stanley, N. and Manthorpe, J. (2004), *The Age of the Inquiry: Learning and Blaming in Health and Social Care*, London: Routledge.

Tawney, R. H. (1926), *Religion and the Rise of Capitalism*, Middlesex: Pelican.

TCSW (2012), *Practice Educator Professional Standards for Social Work*. London: The College of Social Work.

Tew, J. (2002), *Social Theory, Power and Practice*, Basingstoke: Palgrave Macmillan.

Tew, J. (2006), 'Understanding power and powerlessness: towards a framework for emancipatory practice in social work', *Journal of Social Work* 6(1), 33–51.

Thompson, N. (2012), *Anti-discriminatory Practice*, 5th edition, Basingstoke: Palgrave Macmillan.

Thompson, N. (2016), *The Authentic Leader*, Basingstoke: Palgrave Macmillan.

Thoreau, H. D. (1866), 'Civil disobedience', in *Resistance to Civil Government*, accessed at: https://sniggle.net/TPL/index5.php?entry=rtcg on 3 March 2016.

Titmuss, R. M. (1970), *The Gift Relationship*, London: reprinted, 1997, by the New Press.

Toseland, A. (1997), 'The impact of validation group therapy on nursing home residents with dementia' in *Journal of Applied Gerontology*, 1(1): 5–50.

Trevithick, P. (2012), *Social Work Skills: A Practice Handbook*, 3rd edition, Milton Keynes: Open University Press.

Turner, M. and Pratkanis, A., (1998), 'Twenty five years of groupthink research', *Organizational Behavior and Human Decision Processes*, 73(2), 105–15.

UK Government (2011), *Prevent Strategy*, London: HMSO, accessed at: https://www.gov.uk/government/uploads/system/uploads/attachment_data/file/97976/prevent-strategy-review.pdf on 3 March 2016.

UNCRC (1989), *Convention on the Rights of the Child*, United Nations, accessed at: http://www.ohchr.org/EN/ProfessionalInterest/Pages/CRC.aspx on 3 March 2016.

Ungar, S. (2001), 'Moral panic versus the risk society: the implications of the changing sites of social anxiety', *British Journal of Sociology*, 52(2): 271–91.

Walker, N. (1996), *Dangerous People*, London: Blackstone Press.

Warburton, N. (2004), *Philosophy: The Basics*, 4th edition, Abingdon: Routledge.

Ward, A. (2007), *Working in Group Care: Social Work and Social Care in Residential and Day Care Settings*, 2nd edition, Bristol: Policy Press.

Warnock, G. J. (1967), *Contemporary Moral Philosophy*, Basingstoke: Palgrave Macmillan.

Warnock, M. (1998), *An Intelligent Person's Guide to Ethics*, London, Duckworth.

Warren, J. (2007), *Service User and Carer Participation in Social Work*, Exeter: Learning Matters.

Webb, S. (2006), *Social Work in a Risk Society*, Basingstoke: Palgrave Macmillan.

Wenger, E. (1998), *Communities of Practice: Learning, Meaning, and Identity*, Cambridge: Cambridge University Press.

Westwood, J. (ed.) (2014), *Social Media in Social Work Education*, Northwich: Critical Publishing.

Whiteford, A. (2016), 'Getting our hands dirty: reconnecting social work education as if the earth matters', in A. Bellinger and D. Ford (eds), *Practice Placement in Social Work*, pp. 103–120, Bristol: Policy Press.

Williams, B. (1981), *Moral Luck*, Cambridge: Cambridge University Press.

Wolff, J. (2011), *Ethics and Public Policy: A Philosophical Inquiry*, London: Routledge.

Yassour-Borochowitz, D. (2004), 'Reflections on the researcher-participant relationship and the ethics of dialogue', *Ethics and Behavior*, 14(2), 175–86.

Zerbe, W. J. (2008), 'Feelings about ethical decisions: The emotions of moral residue', in W. J. Zerbe, C. E. J. Härtel and N. M. Ashkanasy (eds), *Emotions, Ethics and Decision-Making*, pp. 109–129, Bingley: Emerald Group.

# INDEX